Physical Education 5–11

Physical Education 5–11 is about lighting or relighting a fire in all those who have the privilege and the responsibility of teaching children physical education in Primary schools today. It is written at a time of great change: a revised Primary curriculum, an increased drive to raise achievement and potentially a narrowing of curricular scope in favour of literacy and numeracy. It is little wonder that teachers are looking for certainty and answers to questions such as:

- What do I teach in PE?
- What do I need to know about children's development?
- What does good teaching look like in PE?
- How can I assess such a practical subject effectively?

This new and updated edition provides answers to those questions, covers issues in physical education and provides a wealth of practical advice on teaching across the stages of the new 2014 curriculum.

Drawing upon the authors' experiences both as teachers, coaches and lecturers, the book delivers a justification for PE as an essential element in the Primary curriculum, imbues a theory into practice approach that provides readers with clarity, instils confidence and offers a licence to teach all practical aspects of PE effectively and creatively underpinned by knowledge of children's development, their learning and the critical professional issues in PE today.

This book is the essential companion to inform and inspire students and practising teachers in this most dynamic and exciting of subjects!

Jonathan Doherty is a Principal Lecturer at Leeds Trinity University, UK.

Peter Brennan is Lead Primary Physical Education Specialist at the Comberton Academy Trust and is former Director of Specialism at Hinchingbrooke School in Huntingdon, UK.

The *5–11* series combines academic rigor with practical classroom experience in a tried and tested approach which has proved indispensible to both trainee PGCE students and to practicing teachers. Bringing the best and latest research knowledge to core subject areas, this series addresses the key issues surrounding the teaching of these subjects in the primary curriculum. The series aims to stay up to date by reflecting changes in government policy and is closely related to the changing curriculum for the primary core subjects.

Each book contains lesson planning guidance and methods to develop pupils' understanding as well as offering creative and innovative ways to teach subjects in the primary classroom.

Titles in this series include:

Physical Education 5–11, Jonathan Doherty and Peter Brennan

History 5–11, Hilary Cooper

Modern Foreign Languages 5–11, Jane Jones and Simon Coffey

English 5–11, David Waugh and Wendy Jolliffe

Physical Education 5–11
A guide for teachers
Second edition

Jonathan Doherty and
Peter Brennan

Routledge
Taylor & Francis Group

LONDON AND NEW YORK

First published 2014
by Routledge
2 Park Square, Milton Park, Abingdon, Oxon OX14 4RN

and by Routledge
711 Third Avenue, New York, NY 10017

Routledge is an imprint of the Taylor & Francis Group, an informa business

British Library Cataloguing in Publication Data
A catalogue record for this book is available from the British Library

Library of Congress Cataloging in Publication Data
Doherty, Jonathan, 1961–
    Physical education 5–11: a guide for teachers/Jonathan Doherty, Peter Brennan.
    – Second edition.
    pages cm. – (Primary 5–11 series)
    1. Physical education for children – Study and teaching (Early childhood) 2. Child
    development. I. Brennan, Peter. II. Title.
    GV443.D562 2013
    372.86 – dc23
    2013026003

ISBN: 978-0-415-63531-8 (hbk)
ISBN: 978-0-415-63532-5 (pbk)
ISBN: 978-0-203-09382-5 (ebk)

Typeset in Bembo and Helvetica
by Florence Production Ltd, Stoodleigh, Devon, UK

Printed and bound by CPI Group (UK) Ltd, Croydon, CR0 4YY

*This book is dedicated to
the memory of Ally Brennan,
inspirational teacher and trailblazer
for high quality physcal education.*

Contents

Acknowledgements   ix

Introduction   1

Part 1: Foundations of Primary physical education   5

  1 PE: a unique subject   7

  2 Understanding child development   29

  3 Learning to move and moving to learn   42

Part 2: PE in a professional context   59

  4 Issues in PE today   61

  5 Physical education in Key Stage 1   87

  6 Physical education in Key Stage 2   109

Part 3: Planning, teaching, assessment   139

  7 What happens *before* the lesson? Planning and preparation   141

  8 What happens *during* the lesson? Teaching a lesson   163

  9 What happens *during* and *after* the lesson? Assessment, recording
     and reporting   181

 10 Physical education in the future   201

Index   205

Acknowledgements

We would like to express our sincere thanks to colleagues at Routledge/David Fulton and in particular to Helen, James and Amy for their continued support and encouragement throughout the writing of this book. Not least, we would like to thank all the teachers, students and pupils with whom we have worked over the years for their enthusiasm, constant questioning and willingness to keep pushing the boundaries in PE. Finally, a special thanks to our families for their unfailing encouragement and continuing inspiration.

Jonathan Doherty and Peter Brennan

Introduction

This book is written at a time of yet further change in education. Stoll *et al.* (2003) argue that 'the agenda for reform must be redirected towards the essential purpose of education: learning – learning to create, solve problems, think critically, unlearn and relearn, and to care about others and the environment' (p. 18). Schools are changing rapidly with Academies, Free schools and Teaching schools heralding a very different future under the current Coalition Government's vision. Sweeping reforms to the National Curriculum promise that the 'aspirations we set for our children match those in the highest-performing education jurisdictions, and giving teachers greater freedom over how to teach' (DfE, 2013a). New Teachers' Standards and a revised Inspection framework bring sharper accountability and a renewed focus on the quality of teaching and learning in classrooms. Penney's words are a stark reminder of the pace of such change, when she wrote that 'the past decade and a half has been a time of unprecedented externally driven curriculum "change" in education and physical education specifically' (2006, p. 565). The debate on the justification of physical education (PE) in the Primary curriculum is intensified as it fights for its place alongside the core subjects. The successes of the Olympics and Paralympic Games in 2012 fuel the debate on competitive school sport that is central to the new PE curriculum in schools and globally we battle with an obesity epidemic that has its roots even before children start Primary school. Primary schools are to receive £150 million per annum for the academic years 2013/14 and 2014/15, money that is ring-fenced to improve the quality of sport and PE for children. Ofsted will strengthen its coverage of sport and PE within the Inspectors' Handbook and supporting guidance, so that schools know how sport and PE will be assessed in future as part of the school's overall provision offered. Schools will be required to include details about their sporting provision on their school website, alongside their curriculum details, so parents can compare sports provision between schools, both within and beyond the school day. Schools will be able to draw on information on effective practice taken from case studies provided by the very best schools.

The accomplished poet W.B. Yeats once wrote that 'education is not filling a pail but the lighting of a fire'. A principal aspiration in writing this book is to do precisely that: to inspire readers to light the fires of those young people in their classes so that they too will be inspired and enthralled about the unique subject that is physical education. This aspiration tasks us as authors to go beyond informing about curriculum requirements or providing an 'off the shelf' manual of activities. In order to realise this aspiration we need to go much further. We need to excite you as a reader about the depth and the scope of PE and to encourage you to want to understand it as fully as possible. We want to make you knowledgeable about children's development until the end of their Primary school years and we want to share with you stimulating ways to plan for, teach and assess children in PE in the areas of the statutory curriculum. We want to do this in ways that will enable you to look critically and respond creatively and skilfully in teaching the areas of learning in PE.

The book draws heavily upon our earlier book *Physical Education and Development 3–11* (Doherty and Brennan, 2008) but differs in that this book has a focus solely on the Primary age range. It is aimed mostly at teachers who are non-specialists in PE, higher level teaching assistants (HLTAs) and other para-professionals who wish to update their knowledge and pedagogy through the ideas presented in this text as a school resource or as a supplement to Inset courses, and undergraduate and post-graduate students on Primary education courses. The reduction in time given to PE in many teacher education courses has resulted in many students exiting their training with only a general subject knowledge and a modicum of pedagogical skills to deliver the subject. As authors we have found that a number of teachers and students approach PE with a degree of negativity, often based on their own personal experiences at school, and lack confidence in their abilities to teach it effectively to children. Based on our experiences of teaching across the Primary age range and of teaching specialist and non-specialist physical education courses to university students, we hope we are in a position to write a book that meets the needs of such a readership and redresses such negative experiences of PE.

A variety of pedagogical features are included to make the book accessible. These include chapter objectives, boxed examples, tasks for reflection, chapter summaries and further reading that are linked to practical teaching and education research. We believe that this book has three compelling features that make it distinctive from other texts. First, it retains the principles of PE from 3–11 in the earlier book and updates readers on the new National Curriculum for PE (DfE, 2013b) and the revised Early Years Foundation Stage (DfE, 2012) within one book. Second, it combines theoretical frameworks with practical activities and teaching ideas into one book. Third, its style of writing we hope is accessible to readers and provides a worthy overview of physical education and a vision for its future, as well as a 'dip in' resource bank of developmentally appropriate practical ideas to teach all activity areas in PE confidently and proficiently.

The book's structure of ten chapters is divided into three parts. Part 1 offers an overview of the subject and considers developmental aspects in relation to PE and skill acquisition. Chapter 1 begins by considering personal views of and experiences in PE reported by teachers, student teachers and pupils. This leads on to a discussion on defining and characterising physical education for children from the research literature in which the historical and contemporary aims of the subject and its underpinning values and key principles are made explicit. The chapter concludes by addressing the concept of children as physically educated learners to complement the rationale for physical education and in keeping with the philosophy of a whole child approach advocated in the chapter and the book. The contribution that PE makes to whole child development is taken up in Chapter 2, discussing how physical education contributes to children's physical, intellectual, linguistic, social and emotional development in the Primary school years. Chapter 3 discusses how movement is at the heart of PE and suggests practical ways in which movement can be integrated and progressed in PE. With reference to motor learning theories, we show how movement skills progress from simple to complex and from general to specific movements relevant to the 5–11 age range.

Part 2 of the book considers PE in its professional context. Chapter 4 discusses a range of contemporary issues relating to teaching and learning in the subject. This includes: partnerships; critical thinking; health; teaching and learning (with reference to the new Ofsted framework; Professional Standards for Teachers); school sport post Olympics and transition into Key Stage 1 (KS1) from the recently revised EYFS framework.

Chapter 5 and Chapter 6 examine PE in Key Stage 1 and Key Stage 2 (KS2) respectively, with reference to the new National Curriculum (2013) and provide ideas to deliver meaningful learning experiences to pupils in both key stages. The practical activities in the chapters are road-tested with Primary children first-hand, through personal teaching experiences and in professional discussions with colleagues over a number of years.

In Part 3, planning, teaching and assessment are considered and a range of practical strategies are offered to help readers feel confident and competent in preparing, delivering, assessing and reporting children's PE experiences. Chapter 7, *What happens before the lesson? Planning and preparation*, covers the pre-lesson preparation needed and the lexicon of planning for short-, medium- and long-term teaching episodes. The chapter retains the focus on the pupil and links activity areas to pupils' thinking. Examples from an authentic school policy and planning grids are provided, including the STEP framework to guide differentiation, that will assist readers to construct quality schemes and individual teaching episodes for all learners. Chapter 8, *What happens during the lesson? Teaching a lesson*, outlines the characteristics of effective teaching and considers various strategies (such as observation, explaining, demonstrating and the use of questions) and teaching styles in PE to provide a toolkit of instructional ideas. The chapter returns to the movement concepts and skills described in Chapter 3 as organising centres that give cohesion to teaching the curriculum in a sequential and progressive way. Chapter 9, *What happens during and after the lesson? Assessment, recording and reporting*, demystifies the whole area of monitoring and assessing children's achievement in PE. It helps you understand the principles and purposes associated with effective assessment of pupils' achievement and progress in PE, using real examples of qualitative and quantitative data. The importance of observation and the use of technology to support this assessment tool are highlighted, and a section on assessment for learning (AfL) emphasises the links between planning and assessment. Excellent examples of recording and reporting are given in this chapter to enhance your skill in judging pupil attainment in PE and providing reliable evidence for those judgements. Chapter 10 is a vision for PE in the future, summarising the coverage in the book from my articulation of PE, and the unique contribution it makes to the education and lives of all pupils in Part 1, through to the knowledge and skills demanded from those who plan, teach, assess and report progress in Parts 2 and 3. It highlights some of the challenges facing professionals charged with the responsibility of teaching PE to children both now and in the future and concludes by proposing a series of solutions to these challenges.

Jonathan Doherty
and Peter Brennan

References

Department for Education (2012) *Statutory Framework for the Early Years Foundation Stage*. London: DfE.

Department for Education (2013a) *Reform of the National Curriculum in England*. National Curriculum consultation document. London: DfE.

Department for Education (2013b) *Physical Education. Programmes of Study for Key Stages 1–4*. February. London: DfE.

Doherty, J. and Brennan, P. (2008) *Physical Education and Development 3–11. A Guide for Teachers*. Abingdon, Oxon: Routledge.

Penney, D. (2006) 'Curriculum construction and change'. In D. Kirk, D. Macdonald and M. O'Sullivan (eds), *The Handbook of Physical Education*. London: Sage (pp. 565–79).

Stoll, L., Fink, D., and Earl, L. (2003). *It's about Learning (and It's about Time): What's in it for Schools?* London: RoutledgeFalmer.

Foundations of Primary physical education

1

PE: a unique subject

Chapter objectives

By the end of this chapter you should be able to:

■ Justify physical education (PE) based on knowledge of its purpose, scope and contributions and the new definition of it presented.

■ Know the aims of the subject and appreciate how historical aims have influenced contemporary ones.

■ Know and value the key principles that underpin the subject for children 5–11.

■ Understand the concept of children as physically literate and educated learners.

Perceptions of physical education

In writing the first chapter of this book it seems appropriate that we begin by describing how different people perceive physical education, since perceptions of what physical education is, and what it has to offer children, are coloured by our past and present experiences of it. These perceptions have obvious implications for the status of the subject in Primary schools and the value placed on it. For many children, trying to promote PE and sport at the start of Secondary education is too late (Jess et al., 2007). In Primary schools, PE experiences that are memorable for children are largely dependent upon the teachers who deliver it (Stidder and Hayes, 2002). Research findings and an abundance of anecdotal evidence indicate that teachers, student teachers and pupils view PE as a unique and therefore essential area of the Primary school curriculum and support the view that PE is at the heart of the curriculum. Such a view is reflected in the comments from teachers below:

'It's so important nowadays. I worry that children don't move around as much as they used to. School for them is quite sedentary. More should be made of PE in schools.'

'There is too much emphasis on what might be called 'academic subjects' in Primary schools. There are children in my class who are really good at PE and for some this might be the only area in school they can really excel in. It helps their self-esteem so much.'

'I love teaching PE. I'm not very sporty myself but I love teaching it. You can see real improvements. Children get so much out of it.'

'I worry that Primary schools are all about targets. I know Literacy and Numeracy are important but school shouldn't all be about that.'

(Teachers' comments)

These views are quite typical of teachers' perceptions of PE that endorse it as a subject that offers something very special indeed for children and deserves to be at the heart of the school curriculum.

Comments from student teachers who were not PE specialists in a small survey carried out by the authors in both our institutions indicated that their Primary school experiences of PE were very rewarding. The quotes that follow from trainee Primary teachers reflect this and give an indication of the type of activities that formed their physical education experiences:

'I remember the climbing frame. It seemed huge. I used to love going on this!'

'We played a lot of Rounders and Netball in my final year.'

'Country dancing and we had music and movement a lot too. I think it's good to do this. It makes you think about what your body can do.'

'I loved primary – but not secondary.'

(Trainee teacher comments)

Positive again, but a less-than-positive view from one trainee teacher pointed to the restrictions of her PE curriculum in Primary school:

'Your teacher stumbled across Rounders or Gymnastics and that was it – you were stuck. Week in, week out, the same equipment came out of the games cupboard and the same people would smile; others cringe.'

Such a comment signals that it is not PE *per se* that justifies its vital place in the curriculum, but quality PE experiences that excite and challenge children, taught by informed and skilled teachers. The voices of children also present feelings of the worth of PE experiences in school and these are expressed with the clarity and sincerity of youth. Two voices from Primary aged pupils exemplify what PE means to children in Margaret Talbot's address to the World Summit on Physical Education in Berlin (1999), which we retain in this book for the candour of children and the honesty of their voices:

'On Mondays we do ball skills; on Tuesdays we go swimming; on Thursdays we dance; on Fridays we do gymnastics – in gymnastics we do jumping, rolling and thinking.'

'It makes me feel as if I could fly away.'

More recently Primary children commented that:

'PE is different from doing literacy and Numeracy. Schools would be boring if we didn't do PE.'

'When you do skills, you can see yourself getting better. I'm in Year 5 and I'm not getting better at Reading.'

(Children's comments)

These three perspectives on PE, from teachers, trainee teachers and pupils, serve to say something about the essence of PE and the type of activities that begin to define it: its 'physical' nature and also its 'educational' nature. But it is by no means a totally positive picture. PE is at a crossroads. A new curriculum is with us. In schools it is sometimes seen as the poor relation to the core curriculum subjects of English, Maths and Science. According to Green (2008) there are those who would argue that the growth of sport has led to PE losing its coherence, making it difficult to pin down as its terrain develops and its borders becoming more blurred. The emphasis placed on competitive sport in schools in the new PE curriculum adds to this blurring. Some point to its state of decline and marginalisation – as measured by limited curriculum time, it being outsourced to non-qualified teachers, the low status of subject leaders and limited professional development opportunities (Pickup and Price, 2007). There is evidence of its down turn in countries across the world (Doll-Tepper, 2005). Hardman and Marshall (2000), in their world-wide survey, found its provision minimal or even non-existent in a third of the countries surveyed. Since, in most Primary schools, PE is both co-ordinated and taught by non-specialists, concerns about subject knowledge are never far away (Chedzoy, 2000; Green, 2008; Keay and Spence, 2012). Closer to home is the less-than-positive view of PE expressed by a teaching colleague in a Year 3 class some years ago:

'PE is important but parents won't come to you and say, My child can't do a forward roll. They will come and say, My child can't read.'

Yet this book argues for PE's unique place in the curriculum and importantly in the lives of children. Primary PE provides the first experiences of organised physical experiences to children at an impressionable age (Sloan, 2010). It could be argued there is now more continuity in PE. There is, for example, continued concern about the relationship between health promotion and on-going lifelong participation in sport. Physical educationalists are now part of a much larger network of people interested in the relationship between PE and youth sport, and educational achievement and health than before (Green, 2008). As professionals, we need to fully understand what PE is all about to be able to justify it as a learning experience for children and articulate this to a variety of audiences inside and outside education. It is a hope that this book will provide knowledge to help readers working with Primary age children to articulate the uniqueness of the subject and the demands (and delights) of its pedagogy. In this next section we consider the purpose and contribution that PE makes in more detail. Before this, spend fifteen minutes recollecting your own experiences of PE in the Primary years in the task that follows.

TASK: MEMORIES OF PRIMARY PHYSICAL EDUCATION

Recall what physical education meant to you as a pupil in Primary school. Think about the experience and the types of activities you took part in before writing anything down. The following prompts should help you:

- Would you say PE was an enjoyable experience for you? Why was this?
- If the experience or some of the experiences were not so enjoyable, what were the reasons for this?
- What activities can you remember? Did these change as you progressed through Primary school?
- Where did PE generally take place for you in Primary school? Outside, or in the school hall?
- What can you remember about how PE was taught?
- Are these experiences different to the experiences of children in schools nowadays?
- Would you change anything about the experiences you had?
- What does the type of PE provision recollected tell you about your school's priorities for PE?

Defining and characterising physical education for children 5–11

The obvious questions of 'What is the purpose of physical education?' and 'Why is it important?' begin this section as these underpin any discussions on the purpose and value of PE.

On average children experience around five hundred hours of teaching across their Primary school experience, based on two lessons of PE per week for each term in each year. That equates to a considerable amount of learning time and one might expect a clear understanding of the nature and purpose of the subject. This appears to not be the case, with a lack of agreement on the subject's aims and outcomes still too common a picture. Hunter (2006) talks of the subject in Primary schools as being under-researched and under-theorised. Capel (2000) points out that when asked about the nature of PE, many people proceed to offer a list of activities associated with it but decline to provide their own, or indeed an agreed, definition of the subject. You may have noted that many of the quotes in the previous section in this chapter talk of activities such as 'Gymnastics',

'Rounders', 'country dancing', and so on. One reason, she suggests for the propensity to list activities, is that there in fact exists a lack of consensus of a definition of PE with little agreement inside and outside of the teaching profession as to what PE actually has at its core. The absence of such conceptual agreement has been highlighted by many writers in the period leading up to the establishment of the National Curriculum in the 1980s but remains so in the present day (Murdock, 1986; Parry, 1988; Alderson and Crutchley, 1990; Kirk and Tinning, 1990; Penney, 1998) as we undergo yet another National Curriculum. By way of addressing this shortfall, we present a new definition of physical education that reflects our interpretation of the subject today and our aspirations for it for the future:

> 'Physical education, as part of the whole education process, is a field of endeavour that is concerned with lifelong physical, intellectual, social and emotional learning that accrues through experiencing physical activities in a variety of contexts'.

We feel it important that readers of this book are presented with the key determinants of the subject in a clear form, in order to understand the nature of the subject more fully. Evidence of what amounts to a robust rationale for PE, ironically, does exist in the literature and is highly convincing. For more detailed philosophical discussions on the nature of the subject than are possible in this text, readers are encouraged to consult a number of other writers – Arnold, 1997; Carr, 1997; Parry, 1998; Reid, 1997; Green, 2000.

PE's professional organisations voice the subject's potential for learning and in the lives of children (BAALPE et al., 2005). Learning through moving and doing, which is discussed subsequently in this book, provides a direct link to contemporary teaching and learning approaches. Movement is a child's first language and it is through this medium that young children encounter and make sense of the world. PE is a direct and immediate vehicle for learning that starts from the child. As a medium for learning it is unique. Its learning contexts, school halls, playgrounds, classrooms, swimming pools, track and playing fields offer varied challenges for high quality physical learning experiences for all children.

Streamlining an early list of the characteristics of PE from Talbot (1999) encapsulates the breadth of the subject and portrays its core ingredients admirably.

Physical education:

- is an entitlement for all children
- has a focus on the body and its movements
- is associated with the overall development of young people
- uses the physical to make demands and increases in physical capacities such as skills, speed, stamina, mobility and physical responsiveness
- is central to the whole learning process
- passes on knowledge, understanding and respect for the body and its achievements
- involves the learning of physical skills, critical refection, refinement and improvement
- is working towards physical competence and physical literacy
- integrates the physical self with the thinking and social person

- has a shared language and value system that has the capacity for adaptation of practice according to children's needs
- has activities that meet developmental and individual learning needs
- works towards understanding and appreciation of the role of physical development and physical activities in personal development, health maintenance and social lifestyle.

(Adapted from Talbot, 1999, p. 107)

For their academic review of the educational benefits of PE and school sport (PESS) Bailey et al. (2009) adopted a framework made up of physical, social, affective and cognitive domains. They acknowledge the distinctive contribution PESS makes to children's education in the physical domain but add that claims for the physical benefits have changed over time. They inform us that recent research on the importance of establishing movement foundations for participation and performance, and the health drive to engage young people in lifelong learning for lifelong engagement in physical activity, has resulted in gradual changes to PESS programmes. In the social domain, the value of PESS lies in the acquisition and accumulation of various personal, social and socio-moral skills, which, in turn, can act as social capital to enable young people to be successful in a range of social situations. They argue that the claims made for the social benefits of PESS centre on developing young people's abilities to interact positively with others that can, as a consequence, result in wider gains for them, their schools and communities. Although overlapping with the social domain, the affective domain is synonymous with psychological and emotional wellbeing and encompasses a range of assets that include mental health, positive self-regard, coping skills, conflict resolution skills, mastery motivation, autonomy, moral character and confidence (NRCIM 2002). Finally, cognitive benefits test out the well-known phrase that 'a healthy body leads to a healthy mind' and while a number of studies have found cognitive gains (such as concentration and arousal) from engaging in physical activity, a causal relationship is more difficult to determine and the authors call for further research. These authors conclude that an analysis of the evidence suggests that PESS has the potential to make contributions to young people's development in each of the four domains.

Many ways of describing the subject have been put forward in the past by academics and practitioners. Whitehead (2000) distinguishes between physical education and sport. PE is part of the school curriculum and, in England, is governed by the National Curriculum for physical education, which has just undergone a further revision and a new curriculum produced recently (February 2013). Sport, on the other hand, is referred to as a physical activity with a competitive element. It usually has a cost involved and it may be delivered by a professional player or unpaid enthusiast. Activities embrace individual, partner, team, contact and noncontact, motor-driven or perceptually dominated sports (Coalter, 2001). Arnold (1979) referred to PE's firm associations with movement. Parry (1988) saw its status linked it to the promotion of valued cultural norms. Almond proposed it as 'an umbrella term for a wide range of purposeful physical pursuits that can enrich lives and improve the quality of living' (2000, p. 4). A most helpful categorisation was that provided by Kirk (1993) who identified the domains of psychomotor, cognitive, social and affective that comprise the subject. As we argue in this book, PE has a strong physical dimension but is also concerned with the development of the intellect, ways of working with other people and the development of attitudes and character dispositions. In short – whole child development.

Our starting point involves reference to PE in the whole process of education (Bruner, 1972). Physical education is part of this broad process and is concerned with developing children's full potential to enrich their lives and the culture in which they live. Added to this, its content areas must contain activities of intrinsic value. In their analysis of the goals of education, Dewey's idea of study being inappropriate 'unless it is worthwhile in its own immediate having' (1916, p. 109) and Peters' idea of 'worthwhile activities' (1963, p. 144) become immediately relevant. We, as authors of this book in advancing a rationale for PE that includes a new definition of it, champion its uniqueness and support this claim in two important ways. First, by evidencing its distinctiveness in the process of education with characteristics that no other school experience shares. It is the physical development area of learning in the Early Years Foundation Stage (DfE, 2012) and remains a Foundation subject in the new National Curriculum for Key Stages 1 and 2 (DfE, 2013). As part of the wider school curriculum it also contributes to learning across the curriculum and to a variety of community partnerships which extend learning outside of schools. The following are some of the unique and specific contributions that PE makes to the educational process:

- Through its emphasis on the body it contributes to all aspects of children's education (including spiritual, moral, social and cultural understanding).
- It remains the only 'subject' that focuses on the body and physical development (DES, 1991) and learning in/through/about the physical (Kirk, 1997).
- It includes all children regardless of gender, ability, ethnicity.
- It fosters the development of a range of physical skills (Sallis et al., 1997).
- It makes positive contributions to the development of self-esteem (Fox, 2000).
- It educates children about health and fitness.
- Cognitive skills of problem-solving, decision-making, creative thinking, strategising and evaluating are developed (Doherty, 2003).
- It fosters critical thinking (Bell and Penney, 2004).
- It develops personal qualities such as independence, tolerance and empathy.
- It provides real contexts for learning about fairness, competition and sportsmanship. Teachers and leaders are well placed to model such behaviours (Parker and Stiehl, 2005).
- It enables an appreciation of skilful performance by developing artistic and aesthetic understanding within and through movement (PEA UK, 1998).
- It uses movement as integral to the whole process of education and involves 'learning to move' and 'moving to learn' (Sugden and Talbot, 1998).
- It helps improve pupils' attendance, behaviour and attitude in school (QCA, 2001).
- It contributes to and reinforces learning across the curriculum (language, numeracy, ICT, safety, etc.).
- It is positively associated with good psychological health, e.g. reduced stress, reduced anxiety and reduced depression (Hassmen, Koivula and Uutela, 2000).

- It has a unique role to play in raising standards, promoting healthy living, helping pupils manage risk and developing physical literacy and confidence in movement (CCPR, 2001).

Our second claim is that PE makes a unique and sustainable contribution to the lives of children. Again drawing upon a variety of sources, the following statements are made in support of this claim:

- It enables the promotion of personal autonomy and decision-making to make informed choices about lifelong involvement in recreation and sport.
- It encourages healthy lifestyles and prevents certain risk behaviours (Boreham et al., 1997; Freedman et al., 2001).
- It plays an important role in promoting lifelong physical activity (Penney and Jess, 2004).
- It helps children acquire the basic movement foundation needed to access a wide range of physical activities across their lifespan (Jess and Collins 2003).
- It is fundamental to the expression of young people's human rights.
- It helps to develop coping strategies to deal with success and failure.
- It promotes an understanding of risk and the development of survival skills.
- With links to health promotion, it encourages children to respect their own bodies and those of others.
- It promotes a sense of national identity and cultural pride.
- It provides knowledge and skills relevant to vocational opportunities in later life.
- Through outdoor adventure and leadership experiences, it increases connectivity in the curriculum through relevance to life beyond school (Penney and Chandler 2000).
- It provides a sound preparation for children's future lives.

Physical education is a unique subject: both in the curriculum and in the lives of children.

Historical and contemporary aims of PE

There is no doubt that the history of physical education has served to shape many of the aims and objectives of contemporary PE. It has reflected the changing economic, industrial, religious and cultural environments of people and the dominant ideas of particular times and places. In primitive societies, proficiency in physical skills, especially those needed for hunting, raised the social standing of warriors as prowess in throwing the spear and covering huge distances in search of food were deemed essential survival skills. The importance of ceremonies that involved dancing to appease tribal gods and celebrations of wedding alliances or rites of passage portray primitive societies with aims closely linked to survival. These aims would have been achieved through indoctrination into the ways of that culture and by children imitating the behaviours of adults (Van Dalen and Bennett, 1971). Physical education in Greek society varied according to the ethos of its city states. In Sparta, physical training dominated a harsh disciplined society where, as Laker (2000) points out, it was education of the physical in its extreme! In contrast, Athenian culture prized social and moral attitudes alongside physical development and may well have used physical education as a means of educating the citizenry to prepare them for life in an educated culture (ibid.). From Roman society we inherit an emphasis on health where sport was for all the population to participate in and lifelong participation in physical activity was positively encouraged. Similar aims are evident in our programmes today.

Moving from the 'dark times' of Renaissance Europe, to nineteenth-century Britain where the public school system was born, a strong tradition of games playing and 'athleticism' emerged (Mangan, 1981). Indeed some would argue that games playing as the dominant ideology for PE has not left us. The end of that century saw a combination of Swedish Gymnastics in all-girls schools through the influence of Mathias Roth. Military drill was commonplace in the belief that its adoption would lead to health and physical development and good habits of obeying orders. By the beginning of the twentieth century, schools had a responsibility to develop fair play and loyalty to one another, which was seen as a basis for loyalty in later life (McIntosh, 1976). In elementary schools freestanding exercises, playground games, swimming and some field games were introduced in a period characterised by a reduced formality in the curriculum and teaching methods. After the Second World War, movement became a principal aim of school PE. This was supported by the publication in 1952 of the Ministry of Education's *Moving and Growing* and, in 1953, *Planning the Programme* and the influential Rudolph Laban claim that moving was fundamental to all PE, which remains evident in Dance and educational Gymnastics programmes in many Primary schools today.

The Education Reform Act (1988) and the establishment of the first National Curriculum in England and Wales represented a major landmark for education. National Curriculum Physical Education (NCPE) became a compulsory subject in the 5–16 curriculum, securing its place for the first time among other traditionally more 'academic' subjects. This articulated the entitlement for all pupils to receive a curriculum that was both broad and balanced and included PE. The importance of the physical dimension was still very much in the minds of policy makers as an aim for the subject. The purpose of learning in the subject was to develop specific knowledge, skills and understanding and to promote physical development and competence (DES, 1992). Non-statutory guidance highlighted the emphasis on the physical, confirming the emphasis on learning in a mainly physical context. A further aim was to 'teach pupils, through experience, to know about and value the benefits of participation in physical activity while at school and throughout life' (NCC, 1992), signifying the importance of lifelong learning and involvement in PE. In 1995, the Office for Standards in Education (Ofsted) published their survey of PE and sport in schools, which contained the following aims:

> Physical education, as a foundation subject, aims to develop control of the body, to improve physical skills, to give pupils the ability to make decisions and to apply their growing knowledge and understanding about movement and the body in a variety of activities and contexts.
>
> (Ofsted, 1995)

With the further revision of the curriculum in 1995 (DfE, 1995), the alliance between PE and sport, which had been stressed as separate in the 1992 curriculum, gathered momentum. The gauntlet was thrown down by the then Prime Minister John Major, who vowed to 'put sport back at the heart of weekly life in every school' (DNH, 1995, p. ii) and the publication of *Sport: Raising the Game* (DNH, 1995) was a direct and unequivocal statement on school sport from Government never witnessed before. Almost in parallel was an identification of the process that defined PE in this new curriculum. The importance of this was to firmly establish planning, performing and evaluating as the interrelated elements to be addressed in teaching curriculum PE. The emphasis on educational processes, not sporting outcomes, reflected an increased interest in learning, its nature and its place in society (Murdoch, 1997).

In what was a decade of enormous changes for teachers, yet another National Curriculum was established around the same time (DfEE, 1999). In PE, four aspects were established through which pupils could progress within and across the key stages by:

- Acquiring and developing skills
- Selecting and applying skills, strategies, tactics and compositional ideas
- Evaluating and improving performance
- Knowledge and understanding of fitness and health

(DfEE, 1999, p. 6)

These four aspects of PE were developed through the practical activities that formed the programmes of study in the NCPE areas of Gymnastics, Dance, Games, Outdoor and Adventurous Activities, Athletics and Swimming. The strands also had links to other domains: physical (skill development); social (working with others); and affective (promoting positive attitudes to healthy lifestyles by raised self-esteem (Pickup and Price, 2007). These aspects were the contexts and experiences through which the knowledge, skills and understanding that defined the subject were taught. Critics highlighted the mandate to follow programmes of study in multiple areas, believing that they increased teachers' feelings of inadequacy in teaching NCPE and diminished the unity of the learning experience for pupils (Almond, 1997). Others suggested that the areas of activity framework imposed a 'secondary and distinctly specialist frame' upon PE in the Primary sector and encouraged curricular divisions rather than linkages in teaching and learning (Penney and Evans, 1999, p. 22).

The whole child experience, which is a key message for physical education in this book, was very clear in the breadth of *Every Child Matters* (DfES, 2003) through its unique position to promote learning and development in a wider sense and being central to the broader aims of Primary education. Further changes to the landscape followed with the Physical Education, School Sport and Clubs links strategy (PESSCL) and a Government investment of £1.5 billion into UK sport and PE. The strategy, now disassembled, included the pledge to offer opportunities for children to engage in at least two hours minimum PE at school each week and a further cash injection through the Physical Education and Sport Strategy for Young People (PESSYP) (DCSF, 2008a). Significant here was the increase in adults other than teachers (AOTTs), such as sports, Development Officers delivering PE in Primary school to meet the Public Service Agreement targets of the two and subsequent five hours PE offer to children. Against a backdrop of low confidence from many Primary teachers to teach PE, there have been concerns voiced from within the profession about Primary schools' willingness to hand over curriculum delivery of PE to sports coaches (Blair and Capel 2008; Lavin et al., 2008). With planning, preparation and assessment (PPA) time introduced in 2005, many schools chose to cover the timetable by employing non-qualified teachers such as sports coaches for as little as £20 per hour rather than employing qualified teachers (Griggs, 2010). With the current drive towards schools becoming Academies, we have now a situation where headteachers and Governors can employ whoever they wish in schools. Given the emphasis on core subjects in Primary schools, PE will have to fight hard to justify its uniqueness in the school curriculum and have absolute clarity about the aims and purposes of the subject.

A Secondary curriculum was introduced in 2007 that removed the previous practical activity areas and replaced them with 'range of content', emphasising the 'key concepts' of competency, performance, creativity and healthy lifestyles, and 'key processes' of skills, decision-making, physical and mental capacity, evaluation and making informed choices about healthy lifestyles (QCA, 2007). What this failed to do was to align with the new Primary curriculum proposals or with the new framework for children under five. The Early Years Foundation Stage (EYFS) framework (DCSF, 2008b) aimed at laying foundations of learning for children 0–5 years and incorporated early movement and PE experiences through the area of Physical Development (DCSF, 2008b). Yet this is not a constant picture across the UK. Changes in curriculum thinking have taken place that promise an interesting future for schools. In 2011, Wales introduced the Foundation Stage for 3 to 7 year olds to replace the Key Stage 1 National Curriculum programmes of study and retains PE as one of twelve subjects at Key Stage 2. This curriculum claims to be broadly balanced to promote spiritual, moral, cultural, mental and physical development of all pupils and prepare pupils for the opportunities, responsibilities and experiences of adult life (DCELLS, 2008). Scotland's strategy has been to develop a more coherent and flexible curriculum for pupils from 3–18 in *Curriculum for Excellence* (LTS, 2009) and PE is located in the health and wellbeing area. This encourages learners to take responsibility for their own health and wellbeing and has more cross curricular focus than previously so. A revised Primary curriculum in Northern Ireland (CCEA, 2007) has its starting point that meets the needs of individual children. Children's personal development and the explicit development of thinking skills and personal capabilities feature highly in this framework as does promoting knowledge and skills to prepare young people for a rapidly changing world. A clear direction in these curricula is to try to ensure the cross-curricular subject links emphasise a child-centred approach to learning. Aims for PE in the new Programmes of Study (DfE, 2013) are that all pupils:

- develop competence to excel in a broad range of physical activities;
- are physically active for sustained periods of time;
- engage in competitive sports and activities;
- lead healthy, active lives.

You, the reader, are encouraged to form your own opinion on the viability and integrity of the latest PE curriculum in England in 2013, which we discuss later in Chapters 5 and 6 of the book. The next task requires you to rank some of the key aims of contemporary PE in order of their importance to you.

TASK: RANKING AIMS OF CONTEMPORARY PE

Below are listed ten aims of physical education. You are asked to rank them 1–10 (where 1 is the most important and 10 is the least important) in order of their importance to you. This is a 'non versus' exercise, i.e. no one aim is better than another – they just reflect different priorities.

Aim	Ranking
To promote physical literacy	
To educate children about health and fitness	
To contribute to all aspects of children's education	
To foster holistic development	
To lay the basis for lifelong participation in physical activity	
To develop personal qualities such as independence, tolerance, empathy	
To contribute to the development of self-esteem	
To develop a range of physical skills	
To contribute to and reinforce learning across the curriculum	
To meet developmental and individual learning needs	

Key underpinning principles

Earlier in this chapter it was stated that when asked what PE is, the response from many people, including many PE teachers, is often a list of activities that amounts to what is taught in a PE curriculum rather than a definition of the subject (Capel, 2000). The point was made that in order to justify its unique place in the curriculum, PE as a subject area must be more than a list of activities in which pupils participate. For this to be the case, a set of principles that underpin any activities that children are engaged in is needed. Table 1.1 summarises the principles upon which physical education is founded for children in Key Stages 1 and 2. A successful PE curriculum for all children demands but also utilises these important principles. By using them as the starting point for designing a PE curriculum, it avoids a curriculum that is little more than a hodgepodge of activities with no common bonds and is irrelevant to the individual needs of every child. In doing so, it moves from an emphasis on product (e.g. specific skills and drills to be learned and performed) to a desirable process model that all children can enjoy, learn from and discover their full potential. Blurred aims for the subject do not allow this, nor will they provide clarity in describing what a child going through such a programme should be able to do, know and understand. In contrast, agreed aims, and a clear view of what in essence makes

TABLE 1.1 Principles on which physical education depends for children aged 5–11

Key principle	Descriptor
Access	Children need access to a programme of study appropriate to their age/ability.
Opportunity	All children have opportunities to participate in and achieve in different activities.
Inclusiveness	Every child is important. The achievements of all children are valued.
Breadth	A broad curriculum allows children to appreciate what each activity area can offer and the learning experiences in each.
Balance	Allows every child to benefit from the richness of PE. Each area of activity offers its own unique challenge and suits different needs.
Coherence	Planned as a whole experience and not as discrete unconnected units. Mapping each child's experiences and progress through this curriculum is vital.
Integrity	It is not sufficient to engage children in physical activities. What is required for them is purposeful physical education.
Differentiation	Matches tasks to ability, needs and interests. It balances challenge with achievement.
Relevance	Takes into account previous learning, readiness, interests and achievements.

a physically educated person in the subject, will. This is the topic we address in the next section.

A joint statement from professional organisations in the National Summit on PE in 2005 referred to the systematic development of children's physical competence as the aim of PE and its outcome as physical literacy. Whitehead (2001) proposed that the concept of physical literacy is not only about being able to 'do'. The notion of an ability in its physical sense could be conceived as involving little more than muscle strength and joint flexibility. She argues that physical literacy is a broader term and includes aspects concerned with being able to perceive intelligently and respond appropriately. Physical literacy encompasses more than physical movement; it includes, for example, the ability to 'read' the environment and to respond effectively. Physical literacy plays a very significant part in the development of self-realisation, self-confidence and positive self-esteem (ibid). There have been a number of attempts to establish standards in relation to the knowledge, skills and understanding of PE, mastery of which is assumed to correspond to a person being physically educated. Contemporary views associate it with: having an understanding of the history of physical education and the cultural role of sports; having an understanding of health, nutrition and physical fitness; valuing being healthy; and possessing skills to enable participation in everyday life, as well as sport and recreation.

Whitehead (2006, with Murdoch) describes physical literacy as the 'motivation, confidence, physical competence, understanding and knowledge to maintain physical activity at an individually appropriate level, throughout life'. Thus a physically literate individual will:

- move with poise, economy and confidence in a wide variety of physically challenging situations;
- be perceptive in 'reading' all aspects of the physical environment, anticipating movement needs or possibilities and responding appropriately to them, with intelligence and imagination;
- have a well-established sense of self;
- show an ability to identify and articulate the essential qualities that influence the effectiveness of his/her own movement performance;
- have an understanding of the principles of maintaining their health, in relation to exercise, sleep and nutrition.

The process of acquiring physical literacy, Whitehead (2006) argues, stretches across the lifespan. She identifies six stages of development in which the individual is likely to be presented with opportunities and experiences that will contribute to their confidence and competence as well as their knowledge and understanding of movement. For our purposes it is appropriate to consider in more detail the first stages in this process. In the first stage, the pre-school period, the foundations for the development of physical literacy are laid. It is important that at this stage all those with responsibility for the care of the child should seek out, encourage and support opportunities for movement development. The child should be exposed to movement opportunities in a range of different environments – in and around the home, the local environment, child care settings and activity clubs – conducive to developing a broad repertoire of movement experience. Developing physical literacy at this stage is significantly in the hands of the child's extended family.

In the Primary school years, the fundamentals of physical literacy need to be further developed and embedded (see Table 1.2). This is a crucial period when competences are developed and attitudes formed, none so important as motor competence and self-confidence in physical activities. Developing physical literacy at this stage is significantly in the hands of teachers conducting physical education lessons, but also with adults leading activity clubs, sports coaches, parents, grandparents, siblings and peers. Environments that are needed to support this stage of development include the school, the home, local clubs and open access recreational facilities such as parks, cycle ways and woodland trails.

Children as physically educated learners

An alternative approach is to consider what it means to be physically educated. To be educated mathematically would involve competence in areas such as number, shape and space, measure, etc. We also talk about being 'literate' in subjects such as technology,

TABLE 1.2 Developing physical literacy

Acquiring, developing and refining
Goal of PE Knowledge Motivation Understanding Motor competence Movement confidence Dispositions and attitudes
Influence of significant others
Teachers Coaches Teaching assistants Parents and family Peers
Enabling pedagogy
Planning Lesson objectives Inclusion Progression Resources Teaching strategies Feedback
Supporting environments
School hall School grounds Gym Track Swimming pool Playground Parks Home Local facilities and clubs

Adapted from www.physical-literacy.org.uk/plchart26.doc

TASK: WHAT CHARACTERISES A PHYSICALLY EDUCATED CHILD?

- In your opinion what are the characteristics of such a child?
- Are these characteristics constant across the Early Years Foundation Stage and KS1 and KS2?
- Will these characteristics change for Secondary pupils in KS3 and KS4?
- How do these relate to the aims of the subject?
- Is it possible to be physically educated in one or more practical activity areas only (e.g. a games specialist or a swimmer)?
- Do current or proposed modes of assessment allow for such identification?

and the term 'computer literate' is used in common parlance. Is there an equivalent in physical education and if so how is this defined?

There is no professional consensus of what being 'physically educated means exactly. Alderson and Crutchley (1990) concluded that there is a belief that involving children in physical activities somehow achieves educational ends. This appears to fall far short of explaining what it is to be physically educated. Maude (2001) helpfully writes of the contexts in which children can become physically educated, which include:

- Environments, equipment and resources in and outside school designed for the modern child.
- Curriculum, with its breadth and depth of opportunities.
- Time to embed physical education experience and knowledge.
- National and local schemes and partnerships that extend PE opportunities.

In Chapters 5 and 6 we describe these contexts in relation to the new PE National Curriculum.

Of particular importance in developing our understanding of the concept and its practical application to children in schools, was the 'Outcomes Project' of the National Association for Sport and Physical Education (NASPE) (1990) in the USA. They identified five categories to describe a physically educated individual:

1   possession of relevant motor skills;
2   physical fitness;
3   participation in physical activity;
4   knowledge of the benefits of involvement in physical activities;
5   an appreciation of the values of physical activity and its contribution to a healthy lifestyle.

Accompanying these categories is a series of twenty benchmark statements intended to assist teachers in assessing pupil progress towards becoming physically educated. Of interest and pertinent to our discussion here are that nine of these relate to physical outcomes while the remaining eleven relate to nonphysical ones. The complete benchmark statements are:

A physically educated pupil is one who:

Has learned skills necessary to perform a variety of physical activities:

1   Moves using concepts of body awareness, space awareness, effort and relationships
2   Demonstrates competence in a variety of manipulative, locomotor and nonlocomotor skills
3   Demonstrates competence in combinations of manipulative, locomotor and nonlocomotor skills performed individually and with others
4   Demonstrates competence in many different forms of physical activity
5   Demonstrates proficiency in a few forms of physical activity
6   Has learned how to learn new skills

Is physically fit:

7   Assesses, achieves and maintains physical fitness
8   Designs safe, personal fitness programs in accordance with principles of training and conditioning

Does participate regularly in physical activity:

9   Participates in health-enhancing physical activity at least three times a week
10   Selects and regularly participates in lifetime physical activities

Knows the implications of and the benefits from involvement in physical activities:

11   Identifies the benefits, costs and obligations associated with regular participation in physical activity

12 Recognizes the risk and safety factors associated with regular participation in physical activity

13 Applies concepts and principles to the development of motor skills

14 Understands that wellness involves more than being physically fit

15 Knows the rules, strategies and appropriate behaviours for selected physical activities

16 Recognizes that participation in physical activity can lead to multicultural and international understanding

17 Understands that physical activity provides the opportunity for enjoyment, self-expression and communication

Values physical activity and its contribution to a healthful lifestyle:

18 Appreciates the relationships with others that result from participation in physical activity

19 Respects the role that regular physical activity plays in the pursuit of lifelong health and wellbeing

20 Cherishes the feelings that result from regular participation in physical activity

(NASPE, 1990)

Physical education is concerned with what children can do, know and understand. These elements define what PE is all about and are explicit in the NASPE construct. The different domains of PE through which PE is commonly understood in the UK are also clearly present. Statements 1–6 refer to the psychomotor domain (as do statements 7–10 on physical fitness), the cognitive domain is covered by statements 11–17, and the affective domain by the final statements, 18–20. Such a framework does three important things. First, it encapsulates what a physically educated individual is. Second, it reinforces the importance of PE's physical dimension and the complementary role of the cognitive and affective dimensions. Finally, it gathers together aims, characteristics and dimensions of the subject into one coherent rationale for PE that is relevant to children of all ages. For readers who prefer a summary statement of this rather than a set of benchmark statements, the one provided by Stephen Klesius fits very well. He describes the physically educated person as

> being able to select developmentally appropriate physical activities, participate voluntarily and regularly in these activities, and enjoy these activities as evidenced by positive verbalization patterns, and observable efforts to find opportunities to extend the repertoire of skill, increase the level of performance, or intensify the frequency of participation. This person is self-directing and self-actualizing.
>
> (Klesius, 1971, p. 47)

We conclude that becoming physically educated might well be seen as the ultimate goal of any programme of physical education, and in the chapters that follow we endeavour to provide guidance as to the content material to support physically educated learners, teaching approaches and assessment modes to foster this goal in the Primary school.

Chapter summary

Physical education has a unique contribution to make to the Primary school curriculum and to the lives of children. In this chapter a rationale for PE was discussed that embraces its purposes, characteristics and values, and a new definition that reflects the different domains that it incorporates was presented. Although the physical dimension is paramount, both cognitive and affective domains are integral to this definition and understanding of how the subject is conceptualised. Contemporary aims have come about from a varied world history and led to current aims for the subject relevant to children across the Primary years. The concept of children as physically educated learners and that of physical literacy complements the rationale for physical education presented in the chapter and is in keeping with our philosophy of a whole child approach to PE.

Questions for reflection

- Can you describe the essence of PE in terms of knowledge, concepts, skills and attitudes?

- What should learning outcomes for PE attempt to do and is there research evidence to support them?

- Do the aims of PE reflect areas unique to the subject or do they relate to the aims across the Primary school curriculum?

- What does it mean to be a physically educated learner at ages 5, 7, and 11? Does this change as children grow older or does it remain constant?

Further reading

Bailey, R. (2001) *Teaching Physical Education: A Handbook for Primary and Secondary Teachers*. London: Kogan Page.
The first chapter is a most readable and succinct summary of the aims of PE and its statutory requirements.

Bailey, R., Armour K., Kirk, D., Jess, M., Pickup, I., Sandford, R. and the BERA *Physical Education and Sport Pedagogy Special Interest Group*. (2009) The educational benefits claimed for physical education and school sport: an academic review. *Research Papers in Education* Vol. 24, No. 1, March, pp. 1–27.
A critical academic reading but one in which the arguments for the contribution PE makes to young people's development is excellent.

Carney, P. and Winkler, J. (2008) The problem with primary physical education. *Primary Physical Education Matters,* 3(1), pp. 13–15.

DES (1972) *Movement: Physical Education in the Primary Years*. London: HMSO.
Although not current, this book is the bedrock for all subsequent books. The first three chapters are especially relevant here.

Griggs, G. (2012) (ed.) *An Introduction to Primary Physical Education*. London: Routledge.
Part 1 has four chapters that introduce Primary schools in much detail. Very good text.

Laker, A. (2000) *Beyond the Boundaries of Physical Education: Educating Young People for Citizenship and Social Responsibility*. London: Routledge-Falmer.
Chapter 2 on the history of physical education is not bettered anywhere else.

Lawrence, J. (2012) *Teaching Primary Physical Education*. London: Sage.
Recent book. Clear rationale for the subject. Very accessible text.

Morgan, P. and Bourke, S. (2008) Non-specialists teachers' confidence to teach physical education: the nature and influence of personal experiences in physical education. *Physical Education and Sport Pedagogy*, 13(1), pp. 1–29.

Whitehead, M. (2000) Aims as an issue in physical education. In S. Capel and S. Piotrowski (eds) *Issues in Physical Education*. London: Routledge-Falmer, 7–22.

Whitehead, M.E and Murdoch, E. (2006) Physical Literacy and Physical Education – Conceptual Mapping. *Physical Education Matters*, 1(1). Summer.

References

Alderson, J. and Crutchley, D. (1990) 'Physical education and the National Curriculum'. In N. Armstrong (ed.) *New Directions in Physical Education*. Vol. 1. London: Human Kinetics.

Almond, L. (1997) 'The context of physical education'. In L. Almond (ed.) *Physical Education in Schools*. London: Kogan Page.

Almond, L. (2000) 'Physical education and primary schools'. In R.P. Bailey and T.M. Macfayden (eds) *Teaching Physical Education 5–11*. London: Continuum.

Arnold, P.J. (1979) *Meaning in Movement, Sport and Physical Education*. London: Heinemann.

Arnold, P.J. (1997) *Sport, Ethics and Education*. London: Cassell.

BAALPE, CCPR, PEAUK and PE ITT Network (2005) *Declaration from the National Summit on Physical Education*. London: 24 January. p. 4.

Bailey, R.P., Armour, K., Kirk, D., Jess, M., Pickup, I., Sandford, R., and the BERA Physical Education and Sport Pedagogy Special Interest Group (2009) 'The educational benefits claimed for physical education and school sport: An academic review'. *Research Papers in Education*, 24(1): 1–27.

Bell, T. and Penney, D. (2004) 'Developing thinking and problem-solving skills in the context of National Curriculum for physical education in England'. In J. Wright, D. Macdonald and L. Burrows (eds) *Critical Inquiry and Problem-Solving in Physical Education*. London: Routledge.

Blair, R. and Capel, S. (2008) 'The use of coaches to cover planning, preparation and assessment time – some issues'. *Primary Physical Education Matters*, 3(2): ix–x.

Boreham, C.A, Twisk, J., Savage, M.J., Cran, G.W. and Strain, J.J. (1997) 'Physical activity, sports participation and risk factors in adolescents'. *Medicine and Science in Sports and Exercise, 29*: 788–93.

Bruner, J. (1972) *The Relevance of Education*. London: Allen and Unwin.

Capel, S. (2000) 'Re-reflecting on priorities for physical education: Now and in the twenty-first century'. In S. Capel and S. Piotrowski (eds) *Issues in Physical Education*. London: RoutledgeFalmer.

Carr, D. (1997) 'Physical education and value diversity: A response to Andrew Reid'. *European Physical Education Review*, 4(1): 75–91.

Central Council for Physical Recreation (CCPR) (2001) *Charter for Physical Education and School Sport*. London: CCPR.

Chedzoy, S. (2000) 'Students' perceived confidence to teach physical education to children aged 7 to 11 years in England'. *European Journal of Physical Education*, 5: 104–27.

Coalter, F. (2001) *Realising the Potential: The Case for Cultural Services: Sport*. London: Local Government Association.

Council for the Curriculum, Examinations and Assessment (2007) *The Northern Ireland Curriculum Primary*. Belfast: CCEA.

Department for Children, Education, Lifelong Learning and Skills (DCELLS) (2008) *Physical Education in the National Curriculum for Wales*. Cardiff: DCELLS.

Department for Children, Schools and Families (2008a) *Physical Education and Sport Strategy for Young People*. London: HMSO.

Department for Children, Schools and Families (2008b) *The Early Years Foundation Stage*. London: HMSO.

Department for Education and Science (1991) *Physical Education for Ages 5–16*. London: HMSO.

Department for Education and Science (1992) *Physical Education in the National Curriculum*. London: HMSO.

Department for Education and Skills (2003) *Every Child Matters*. London: DfES.

Department for Education and Employment and the Qualifications and Curriculum Authority (DfEE/ QCA) (1999) *The National Curriculum for Physical Education*. London: HMSO.

Department for Education (1995) *Physical Education in the National Curriculum*. London: HMSO.

Department for Education (2012) *Statutory Framework for the Early Years Foundation Stage*. March. London: DfE.

Department for Education (2013) *Reform of the National Curriculum in England*. National Curriculum consultation. London: DfE.

Department of National Heritage (1995) *Sport: Raising the Game*. London: DNH.

Dewey, J. (1916) *Democracy and Education: An Introduction to the Philosophy of Education*. New York: Free Press.

Doherty, J. (2003) 'Extending learning in physical education. A framework for promoting thinking skills across the Key Stages'. *British Journal of Teaching Physical Education*, Autumn, 34(3).

Doll-Tepper, G. (2005) 'The UK in the world of physical education'. *British Journal of Teaching Physical Education* 36(1): 41–3

Fox, K. (2000) 'The effects of exercise on self-perceptions and self-esteem'. In S. Biddle, K. Fox and S. Boutcher (eds) *Physical Activity and Psychological Well-Being*. London: Routledge.

Freedman, D., Kettel Kahn, L., Dietz, W., Srinivasan, S. and Berenson, G. (2001) 'Relationship of childhood obesity to coronary heart disease risk factors in adulthood: The Bogalusa Heart study'. *Pediatrics*, 108: 712–18.

Green, K. (2000) 'Exploring the everyday 'philosophies' of physical teachers from a sociological perspective'. *Sport, Education and Society*, 5: 109–29.

Green, K. (2008) *Understanding Physical Education*. London: Sage.

Griggs, G. (2010) 'For sale – Primary physical education, £20 per hour or nearest offer'. *Education, 3–13*, 38(1): 39–46

Hardman, K. and Marshall, J.J. (2000) *World-Wide Survey of the State and Status of School Physical Education: The Final Report to the International Olympic Committee*. Manchester: University of Manchester.

Hassmen, P., Koivula, N. and Uutela, A. (2000) 'Physical exercise and psychological wellbeing: A population study in Finland'. *Preventative Medicine, 30*(1): 17–25.

Hunter, L. (2006) 'Research into elementary physical education programs'. In D. Kirk, D. Macdonald and M. O'Sullivan (eds), *The Handbook of Physical Education*. London: Sage (pp. 571–586).

Jess, M. and Collins, D. (2003) 'Primary physical education in Scotland: The future in the making'. *European Journal of Physical Education, 8*: 103–118.

Jess, M., Pickup, I. and Hadyn-Davies, D. (2007) 'Physical education in the primary school: a developmental, inclusive and connected future'. *Physical Education Matters, 2*(1): 16–20. In S. Sloan (2010) 'The continuing development of primary sector physical education: Working together to raise quality of provision'. *European Physical Education Review, 16*(3): 267–81.

Keay, J. and Spence, J. (2012) 'Addressing training and development needs in Primary Physical Education'. In G. Griggs (ed.) *An Introduction to Primary Physical Education*. London: Routledge.

Kirk, D. (1993) 'Curriculum work in physical education: Beyond the objectives approach?' *Journal of Teaching in Physical Education, 12*(3): 244–65.

Kirk, D. (1997) 'Schooling bodies for new times: The reform of school physical education in high modernity'. In J-M. Fernandez-Balboa (ed.) *Critical Aspects in Human Movement: Rethinking the Profession in the Postmodern Era*. Albany: SUNY Press.

Kirk, D. and Tinning, R. (1990) *Physical Education, Curriculum and Culture: Critical Issues in Contemporary Crisis*. London: Falmer Press.

Klesius, S.E. (1971) 'Physical education in the seventies: Where do you stand?' *Journal of Health, Physical Education and Recreation 42*: 46–7.

Laker, A. (2000) *Beyond the Boundaries of Physical Education. Educating Young People for Citizenship and Social Responsibility*. London: RoutledgeFalmer.

Lavin, J., Swindlehurst, G. and Foster, V. (2008) 'The use of coaches, adults supporting learning and teaching assistants in the teaching of physical education in the primary school'. *Primary Physical Education Matters, 3*(1): ix–xi.

Learning and Teaching Scotland (LTS) (2009) *Curriculum for Excellence*. Edinburgh: LTS.

McIntosh, P. (1976) 'The curriculum of physical education – an historical perspective'. In J. Kane (ed.), *Curriculum Development in Physical Education*. London: Crosby Lockwood Staples.

Mangan, J.A. (1981) *Athleticism in the Victorian and Edwardian Public School*. Cambridge: Cambridge University Press.

Maude, P. (2001) *Physical Children, Active Teaching*. Buckingham: Open University Press.

Ministry of Education (1952) *Moving and Growing*. London: HMSO.

Ministry of Education (1953) *Planning the Programme*. London: HMSO.

Murdoch, E. (1997) 'The background to, and developments from, the National Curriculum for PE'. In S. Capel (ed.) *Learning to Teach Physical Education in the Secondary School: A Companion to School Experience*. London: Routledge.

Murdock, E. (1986) *Sport in Schools – A Desk Study for DES/DoE*. London: Sports Council.

National Association for Sport and Physical Education (1990) *Definition of the Physically Educated Person: Outcomes of Quality Physical Education Programs*. Reston, VA: NASPE.

National Curriculum Council (1992) *Physical Education: Non-statutory Guidance*. York: NCC.

National Research Council and Institute of Medicine (NRCIM). (2002) *Community Programs to Promote Youth Development*. Washington: National Academy Press.

Office for Standards in Education (Ofsted) (1995) *Physical Education and Sport in Schools – A Survey of Good Practice*. London: HMSO.

Parker, M., and Stiehl, J. (2005) 'Personal and social responsibility'. In J. Lund and D. Tannehill (eds), *Standards-based Physical Education Curriculum Development*. Boston, MA: Jones and Bartlett (pp. 130–53).

Parry, J. (1988) 'The PE curriculum from 5–16'. In P. Wiegand and M. Rayner (eds) *Curriculum Progress*. Brighton: Falmer Press.

Parry, J. (1998) 'Reid on knowledge and justification in Physical Education'. *European Physical Education Review* 4(1): 70–4.

Penney, D. (1998) 'Positioning and defining physical education, sport and health in the curriculum'. *European Physical Education Review* 4(2): 117–26.

Penney, D. and Chandler, T. (2000) 'A curriculum with connections?', *British Journal of Teaching Physical Education, 31*(2):37–40.

Penney, D. and Evans, J. (1999) *Politics, Policy and Practice in Physical Education*. London: Routledge.

Penney, D. and Jess, M. (2004) 'Physical education and physically active lives: A lifelong approach to curriculum development'. *Sport Education and Society*, 9: 269–87.

Peters, R.S. (1963) *The Study of Education*. London: Woburn Press.

Physical Education Association of the United Kingdom (PEA UK) (1998) 'Mission statement'. *British Journal of Physical Education 29*(2): 4–7.

Pickup, I. and Price, L. (2007) *Teaching Physical Education in the Primary School. A Developmental Approach*. London: Continuum.

Qualifications and Curriculum Authority (1999) *Early Learning Goals*. London: QCA.

Qualifications and Curriculum Authority (2001) *PE and School Sports Project*. www.qca.org.uk/ca/subjects/pe/pess.asp (accessed 11 February 2013).

Qualifications and Curriculum Authority (2007) *The National Curriculum for Physical Education at Key Stage 3 and 4*. London: QCA.

Reid, A. (1997) 'Value pluralism and physical education'. *European Physical Education Review, 3*(1): 6–20.

Sallis, J., McKenzie, T., Alcaraz, J., Kolody, B., Faucette, N. and Hovell, M. (1997) 'The effects of a 2 year physical education programme (SPARK) on physical activity and fitness of elementary school children'. *American Journal of Public Health* 87: 1328–34.

Sloan, S. (2010) 'The continuing development of primary sector physical education: Working together to raise quality of provision'. *European Physical Education Review* 2010, 16(3): 267–81.

Stidder G. and Hayes, S. (2002) 'A survey of physical education trainees' experiences on school placements in the South-East of England'. *British Journal of Teaching Physical Education, 33*(2): 28–32.

Sugden, D. and Talbot, M. (1998) *Physical Education for Children with Special Needs in Mainstream Education*. Leeds: Carnegie National Sports Development Centre.

Talbot, M. (1999) *The Case for Physical Education*. Paper presented at the World Summit on Physical Education, Berlin.

Van Dalen, D.B. and Bennett, B.L. (1971) *A World History of Physical Education: Cultural, Philosophical, Comparative*. Englewood Cliffs, NJ: Prentice-Hall, Inc.

Whitehead, M. (2000) 'Aims as an issue in physical education'. In S. Capel and S. Piotrowski (eds) *Issues in Physical Education*. London: RoutledgeFalmer.

Whitehead, M.E. (2001) 'The concept of physical literacy'. *European Journal of Physical Education, 6*(2): 127–138.

Whitehead, M.E. with Murdoch, E. (2006) 'Physical literacy and physical education – conceptual mapping'. *Physical Education Matters, 1*(1), Summer.

2

Understanding child development

Chapter objectives

By the end of this chapter you should be able to:

■ Know key milestones in early and middle childhood development: physical, social, cognitive, linguistic and emotional and recognise how PE contributes to all aspects of development.
■ Understand the importance of early experiences to stimulate brain growth.
■ Know the categories of gross and fine motor skills and how these skills are progressed.
■ Recognise the implications of each of the above areas for physical education.

The growing child is a unique individual whose all-round development occurs rapidly in the early and middle childhood years. Understanding how children develop is important for physical educators for many reasons, but chief among these is that it provides information for the basis of developmentally appropriate practice in PE. To achieve the aims of the subject outlined in the previous chapter, planning, teaching and assessment must be appropriate to the needs of all children. A major impediment to this is a starting point in some PE programmes that assumes adult sports skills and games are appropriate for this age group. Nothing could be further from the truth – children are not mini-adults and practices that treat them as such can only serve as a recipe for frustration, anxiety, boredom and possible injury. Practices that engage children below the age of 11 in adult-type games are governed by adult rules, or that use inappropriate equipment form no part of a quality and a developmentally appropriate programme of physical education. Quality PE comes from lessons that are developmentally and instructionally matched to the needs of the children engaged in them.

■ What do you think constitutes developmentally appropriate practice in PE?
■ What constitutes developmentally inappropriate practice and what does this look like?
■ Can you list some examples of both?

To assist the reader's understanding it may be useful at this point to introduce and explain the terminology associated with development. *Development* is usually categorised into physical, intellectual, linguistic, emotional and social (and remembered through the unfortunate mnemonic of PILES!). *Maturation* is the genetically programmed sequence of change towards a mature state. *Learning* is a change in behaviour due to experience. We cannot see learning taking place in the same way as maturation or development, but we can see its end product. We can see when it has taken place. Take the example in Games where children are learning to shoot a unihoc puck for accuracy to a target goal. Improved performance, 3 out of 5 successful strikes, is evidence that learning has taken place as the skill level has improved.

Let us begin with development. Development is a lifelong process of change that is the product of the interplay between genetic inheritance and the environment. Bronfenbrenner's bio-ecological model (1989) is an excellent way of understanding this connection since it views the developing child within a complex set of relationships with other people and how they affected by the surrounding environment. The model is represented by a set of concentric circles that places the child at the centre. The first set of circles is the microsystem, represented in the model by the interactions the young child has with closest family members: parents and carers. It is the interactions here that have a lasting effect as a child inherits certain characteristics from parents which he/she carries through life. If we go to the next set of circles the range of interactions is extended to neighbours and to pre-school and school settings in what is termed the exosystem. Home school support and opportunities to engage in active recreation are fostered or denied here. The outer layer or macrosystem includes the cultural setting in which the microsystem and exosystem are embedded, and includes the values, resources and customs that affect the growing child on a larger scale. This relationship between the child and the environment takes place like a serve and return just as in a game of tennis. The adult gives and the child receives. As above, the interactions begin with parents and carers and, as the child grows older, include early years practitioners, teachers and sports coaches in a widening circle of influence.

Development is a complicated process of change. Most researchers agree that it is a result of the interaction of both maturation and learning (Gallahue and Ozmun, 1998) and this is certainly obvious in PE. This interaction can also be seen by the difficulties experienced by a child of 5 learning to control a ball in the Early Years Foundation Stage to the proficiency that the same child later in Year 6 demonstrates in dribbling a basketball. Most authorities also emphasise connections between the areas of development. Wright and Sugden's transactional model (1999) links an individual's maturation to the learning and experiences within the environment and to the particular demands of the task itself. This characterises the important role that teachers play in providing activities and contexts that best fit the needs of the individual child and adapting the learning environment to accommodate them. In PE, much attention is given to the physical dimension but it is also vital to consider the other aspects of development in a holistic way.

Experiences matter

The engine that drives all development is the brain and the brain thrives on stimulation. Through maturation the growing brain's specialist functions allow important motor, language, visual and auditory processing to take place. If we consider the physical accomplishments of Primary age children – running, jumping, balancing, swimming and so on – their capacity to use quite sophisticated language, form friendships with different people and how they can express a range of emotions and understand them in others, then we can soon see why the human brain has to be the size it is. At birth, a newborn's brain weighs about 450 grams. As a fully mature adult it will be three times that weight. It grows at an astonishing rate, so much so that by the time a child is 3 years old, the brain is 75 per cent of its adult weight and by age 6 it is 90 per cent (Harris and Butterworth, 2002). Between 2 and 4 years, the brain growth is slow with a growth spurt experienced at 4 years. Between 6 and 8 years, two important growth spurts in brain development occur. The first is linked to improvements in fine motor skills and hand–eye co-ordination. The second, taking place at about age 10, is in the frontal lobes area of the cerebral cortex. This is the area responsible for logic and planning, which are dramatically increased at this time. Additionally this spurt is associated with improvements in memory (Hepworth et al., 2001).

What a child experiences early in their life helps to build brain architecture by laying down important neural pathways. The human brain has a plastic or malleable quality, meaning that it is capable of forming and reforming in accordance with the types of stimulation it receives. Without proper stimulation the synapses and dendrites that form the brain actually wither in a process known as 'pruning'. Readers may be familiar with the phrase, 'use it or lose it'. That is exactly the same with the human brain. It demands stimulation for healthy growth. Many of the basic aspects of brain architecture are laid down well before a child enters school (NSCDC, 2007). Years ago it was argued that 50 per cent of our ability to learn is developed by the age of 4 (Bloom, 1964). This is prime learning and development time when learning pathways are set down. All future learning is built upon this base. Input is critical. In the pre-school years this is provided by parents and family and extends in the Primary years to teachers, coaches and peers. Our genes determine what and when brain circuits are formed (hard wiring) and lay down rules for connecting brain cells in and across circuits. The experiences a child has (soft wiring) shape them. This interplay of genetics and environment is a continuous process.

The brain forms low-level circuits early in life and, in the initial months, what is needed are sensory, social and emotional experiences. The early years are the important years for optimising brain growth in what Diamond and Hopson referred to as 'exuberant connectivity' (1998, p. 63). This is characterised by increases in neural growth. These are the bricks and mortar that promote development and the foundations for all learning (Langston and Doherty, 2012). As a child gets older, more sophisticated experiences are needed to shape higher-level circuits. Growing brains thrive on stimulation and active learning in PE offers an immediate and excellent vehicle for this. To stimulate brain development and lay down this kind of properly functioning circuitry, children's early experiences must be varied and exciting and they must be age-appropriate (Black and Greenough, 1986). This means movement experiences and opportunities to move in different ways, to handle equipment and to acquire and progress physical skills. Physical activities in the home environment for young children are based around play where children can challenge themselves physically and they experience different movement challenges. As children mature, this means walking, cycling, going to the swimming pool and being active often with the family. In later years it is through quality lessons in National Curriculum PE and outside school involvement in sports.

Early development

For many years it was thought that newborn babies come into this world as helpless beings, far from capable of thinking or communicating. Flailing arms and legs were assumed to be randomised insignificant movements. Untrue! We know that development proceeds at an amazing pace in all areas. Those randomised insignificant movements are the first means by which the newborn child communicates with those around. We are just beginning to discover how much has already taken place during the period in the womb. Rather than the 'blank slate' notion put forward by philosophers such as Locke centuries ago, newborns arrive with a repertoire of skills, abilities and dispositions that enable them to survive and to start them off on their individual developmental journey. They are born with a range of reflexes, psychological and behavioural capabilities ready to meet the challenges ahead of them and are eager to find out more about the strange new world that surrounds them and, importantly, how to move.

Sensory development of the senses allow the newborn to experience the world first hand and to survive in it. The newborn's sense of touch is well developed at birth. Touch is an important way for babies to communicate in their new surroundings. They can identify pleasant smells and turn away from unpleasant ones. There is a sensitivity towards the mother's milk which fulfils an important early bonding role as well as a survival one. They have the capacity to experience the four taste sensations – salty, sour, bitter and sweet – but show a preference for sweet taste by licking and smiling. Systems associated with hearing function well at birth but by comparison early visual development is poor. Visual acuity, or the sharpness of vision is limited to objects up to about 20 centimetres away. Visual accommodation, which brings objects into focus is also poor, but improves quickly. The distance of 20 centimetres is important as it equates to the distance the face of an adult cradling a baby is away from the baby's face, a vital component for mother–child bonding. A sixth sense, proprioception gives an awareness of where the body is and what it is doing, is quite well developed and has already provided important information on position, limb and body position and balance in the womb (Doherty and Hughes, 2009).

Development proceeds in an ordered fashion, although at an individual pace. Cephalocaudal development ensures the fastest growth is from the head downwards, through the neck to the shoulders, trunk and lower body. This gives the typical baby appearance of being 'all head', which is in fact not far from being true since when a baby is born, the head makes up 25 per cent of the total body weight. Proximodistal development is growth starting from the centre of the body and moving to the outer extremities like hands and fingers (Santrock, 2007). This is observed in a young child's early mark-making. Large actions of the shoulder are seen long before fine motor forms are developed (Gabbard, 1992). The pre-school years between 2 and 5 reveal further remarkable changes taking place. Note the frustrations of the 2 year old who is yet to play co-operatively with other children, who moves around with some confidence but still requires a lot of concentration to do so, and keenly observes adults and copies what they do as a way of learning. So too the 3 year old gaining hand–eye co-ordination, who feels more confident in social situations and whose intellectual progress can be seen in maths activities and learning to recognise words in print. 4 year olds have friendships that are more stable. Gender stereotypes are established that result in different expectations for boys and girls and they have some understanding of 'right' and 'wrong'. Manipulative skills have increased and they enjoy experimenting with movement in activities like hopping, running and jumping. The 5 year old has a vocabulary of several thousand words, values the friendships of other children, has an increased memory, is physically much taller and heavier and has developed hand–eye co-ordination. All these advances prepare the child for the advent of formal schooling and have implications for physical education.

Early movement experiences are crucial in helping to establish and maintain the desire to be active and to use their bodies both for fun and learning. Babies learn where their body ends by flicking fingers and toes. Control of neck and head improves quickly, as does general body strength, and the perceptual mechanisms to enable hand–eye co-ordination are established. As toddlers, movement explorations allow navigations of a wider area that develop their awareness of space, fully integrate both sides of the body and begin a host of new movement patterns. Between 3 and 5, running, jumping and climbing are sources of real enjoyment for children and their sense of accomplishment and confidence performing these and many other activities is to be easily seen all over their faces!

Development in middle childhood

The explosion of growth and physical ability characteristic of the early childhood phase just described is not sustainable in the next phase of development. In the middle and late childhood years (6–12 years), physical growth slows down as if this is a time to consolidate the development in the earlier years and to prepare the body for the tumult of puberty that is to follow shortly. The trend is rapid acceleration in early childhood, then a slower steady rate in the middle childhood years, which is followed by a sharp increase again into adolescence. Although general physical development follows a predictable path, the growth rate is not constant.

The Primary school years are those where children are steadily gaining in height and body mass and undergoing changes in body proportions. Height and weight increases for boys and girls are broadly similar, with height gains of about 2 inches each year on average and weight gains of 5 to 7 pounds through the middle childhood period. By age 11 typically girls become taller and heavier due to the early onset of their pubertal growth spurt. Individual variations are important here and need to be considered in lesson planning around individual differences and the implication for using equipment and for group formation. By the end of Key Stage 2 we can see height differences of 6 inches and weight differences of 30 to 35 pounds between children in the same year group. Growth in body proportions also varies. By six years of age a child's head is ⅙ of the total body size and is proportionally smaller as the trunk and lower limbs grow.

The cephalocaudal pattern of development, where head growth proceeded growth that was vital to steer early whole body development, decelerates. This results in more stability and is observed in a more upright posture and increased balance when undertaking rolling activities such as in Gymnastics.

Height and weight gains are also accompanied by increased muscle strength (Malina and Bouchard, 1991). The increase in muscle growth for both boys and girls has implications for body management in activities, for example in Gymnastics and Dance. Because of these similarities, boys and girls can, and should, take part in the same physical activities in Primary PE. Girls show some excess fat on their legs and around their upper arms that continues into puberty, while boys are broader across the shoulders and show slightly more muscle development in the upper trunk than girls (Pickup and Price, 2007). Muscles and bones become thicker and longer in middle childhood. Muscle growth increases steadily in childhood and then dramatically in adolescence. For boys the increase is 150 times greater than for girls in relation to muscle size and heart and lung capacity (Rogol et al., 2002). Children's stamina is increased in the Primary years. If you observe a child in the Early Years Foundation years using an outdoor space you will see short bursts of activity followed by periods of rest. This intermittent nature of exercise continues into the Primary years where the periods of sustained exercise are extended and periods of rest decreased. Understanding this has direct implications for planning games and athletic activities that involve running: short periods of exercise or activity with adequate rests in lessons are needed in keeping with the physiological capacities of the growing child.

Perceptual-motor development continues to refinement in the Primary years. Spatial perception, that is being able to identify and act upon objects in space, such as a ball, undergoes further refinement in middle childhood. Brain development allows for better communication between the hemispheres and advances from age 8 onwards (Roberts and Bell, 2000). The ability to make predictions about movement of objects in space, called spatial cognition, continues to develop with marked increases in male development, which may be due to biological factors or indeed play preferences between the sexes. Figure-ground perception, the ability to distinguish an object from its background, increases for children throughout Key Stage 1 and this capacity is important in throwing and catching activities and in many games in Key Stage 2. Being able to track an object, such as a ball in the air, is vital in games and children require much practice to develop this capacity. Development in depth perception, important for example in judging the distance to throw a ball in a mini-rounders game is refined until about 12 years of age. Kinaesthetic memory, or the ability to reproduce movements from memory, shows increased performance after the age of 5. Kinaesthetic acuity, the ability to detect differences in location, distance, force and speed of the body, is almost at adult level by age 8 (Doherty and Bailey, 2003). Children need many experiences of sending and receiving different sizes and weights of objects in the air and along the ground using a variety of equipment to develop this capacity.

Much of what has been written so far in this chapter has concentrated upon physical development. We have stressed the importance of viewing development from a whole child perspective. Other areas of a child's development are also important in relation to physical education (remember the PILES mnemonic). Cognitive development refers to the changes in intellectual abilities and includes such mental processes as attention, decision-making, memory, and critical and creative thinking. According to Piaget the concrete operational stage from 7–11 years represents a major milestone of cognitive development in which different stages of development follow a hierarchical structure of 'simple to complex', and 'concrete to abstract'. He argued that we do not start out as thinkers, but through our developing motor and perceptual capacities, we construct and refine our mental structures (Doherty and Hughes, 2009). A child's ability to conserve, to classify and to order objects in length or weight (seriation) increases as they get older. Spatial reasoning increases. They are not constrained by the limitations of the earlier pre-operational stage and can think flexibly, more logically and in more complex ways. They are now able to process information much more quickly and use an increasing range of memory retrieval cues. In Key Stage 2 PE for example, children can now create sequences in Gymnastics that comprise three to five actions. Constructions of Dance are more complex. They have begun to understand about tactical considerations and strategy in Games and can transfer learning in one activity area to other areas. They can solve physical challenges much more effectively using a variety of mental strategies. They can apply skills in one Games genre to another, having an understanding for example that skills and tactics in one Invasion Game transfer to another. They use creative thinking to design Dance motifs and Gymnastics sequences and think critically to evaluate their or others skill performances, and use analysis to work out winning strategies in Games.

Language development is increased in the Primary years. Many children can use complex conversation structures and communicate clearly with adults and with peers. The average vocabulary of a 10 year old is about 10,000 words. Metalinguistic awareness develops to support an increasing range of language skills. They grasp meanings and appreciate that words have multiple meanings. They use compound and complex sentences and can refine grammatical structures. They adapt to listeners' needs in different communicative situations and evaluate the clarity of others' messages (Berk, 2002). They have enhanced understanding of metaphor and humour and have made huge leaps in their reading and writing abilities. In PE, this transfers to following and giving instructions both orally and in written form. They can use a range of accurate words to describe their movement expressions. They understand specific terminology in relation to the practical activity areas and can record learning and progress using their increased literary capacity. Writing match reports, commenting on a mini game, designing skill cards to improve techniques and peer teaching are all examples of using oral and written language in the context of PE lessons.

Socially, Primary age children base understanding of others' intentions on a wider range of social cues, and their ability to interpret and influence others' emotional reactions improves. They have become less dependent on adults to provide a moral compass. They consider issues of right and wrong carefully and combine their previous experiences and positive behaviours into rules for good conduct (Berk, 2002). Perspective-taking is greatly improved in middle childhood, in part based on a basic cognitive understanding of reciprocity and perspective-taking (Bee, 2007). Strategies for self-regulating emotions improve their ability to deal with their own feelings and with conflicts with peers. Friendships based on mutual trust are formed and interactions with other people are on the whole more pro-social. They can share, take turns and offer help to others.

TABLE 2.1 Developmental milestones in the Primary years 5–11

Development in relation to age	Physical	Intellectual	Linguistic	Emotional	Social
2	Runs with confidence. Can build a tower of six blocks. Pushes trike. No steering. May do and undo own buttons.	Enjoys role play and imaginative play. Can point to major body parts. Recognises self in photographs.	Asks many questions. Listens to answers. Chats continuously at play. Obeys simple requests.	Is prone to temper tantrums. Still requires adult reassurance. In need of constant love and attention.	Plays near but not with others. Is unable to share toys. Likes outside environments but unaware of dangers.
3	Walks upstairs unassisted. Uses spoon and fork. Pedals and steers trike. More competent in locomotion.	Asks questions constantly. Short-term memory has increased. Can relate past and present.	Talks in sentences of four or five words. Carries out simple oral instructions. Asks meanings of words.	Fewer tantrums. Is more confident in new situations. Still emotionally vulnerable.	Enjoys helping adults. Can be part of a small group. Keen to please adults.
4	Builds a tower of ten blocks. Can use scissors. Accomplished trike rider. Shows agility in locomotion. Can throw and catch a ball.	Able to compare two objects. Well developed imaginative play. Enjoys practical work.	Able to draw houses and people. Mostly uses correct grammar. Often has difficulties with w, f, th.	Inclined to be cheeky. Developing a sense of humour. Takes some responsibility for personal hygiene.	Likes the company of other children. May boast and boss others. Has learned to share.
5	Skilled in climbing on apparatus. Responds well to music. Good pencil control. Kicks and throws with some accuracy.	Drawings become more recognisable. Distinguishes between truth and lies. Enjoys games with rules. Clear sense of humour.	Speaks correctly. Able to write own name. Recognises some printed words. Knows over 2000 words.	Shows care towards others. Understands the need to have rules. Overall balanced.	Chooses own friends. Separates well at nursery or playgroup. Can co-operate with others.

They understand that the relationships they have with other people present particular demands that have consequences for their social and emotional functioning. In this phase children are becoming much more independent and responsible. While the family remains the key agent of socialisation and directly shapes attitudes and values of social class, education, religious beliefs and significantly influence personality, the influence of peers, and to an extent teachers and coaches, increases markedly from age 7 onwards. In PE, they are now able to work co-operatively in groups and in competitive situations in Key Stage 2. They work in groups of different sizes and with different people. They can share equipment and realise the importance of working in a team and of having different roles, including being a leader. In competitive situations they are developing better understanding of fairness, of the need to have rules and show sportsmanship-like conduct.

Many of the key milestones in development to age 11 are summarised in Table 2.1.

Progression in motor skills

Allied to the development changes described comes a steady increase in children's co-ordination, body strength and physical ability in the Primary school years. Improvements in flexibility and power enable faster, farther and more accurate body movements in a variety of PE activities. Improvements in speed, agility and balance are immediately obvious. Reaction time improves with the average 11 year old able to react twice as quickly as a 5 year old (Band *et al.*, 2000). This skill is vital, for example, in striking an oncoming ball with a bat and requires a combination of cognitive skills: stimulus recognition, decision-making, planning and executing a motor response (there is more on this in the next chapter). These years up until the onset of puberty have been described as the 'skill hungry years' (Maude, 1996) and for very good reason. Neurological development allows for greater control of motor skills. Earlier skills are revisited and improved. Previously acquired motor skills are integrated into more complex dynamic systems of actions. By the end of KS2, children will be able to link complex movement patterns in readiness for specific sports skills in Secondary school. Experience also has a vital role to play and it is during these years that children should be given as many opportunities in school PE, and in leisure pursuits or organised sports outside school, to participate in a wide range of physical activities.

Motor development includes both gross and fine motor skills and both types are present from birth. *Gross motor skills* involve the large muscles of the body in actions such as running, hopping and jumping and are in general developed earlier than *fine motor skills* such as picking up and holding objects and writing and drawing. Watch a 5 year old using scissors to cut a piece of paper. It is a whole body action. The entire arm is used, the back and trunk are held at an angle. The head is tilted to one side and usually the tongue is out to help with concentration. The same 5 year old is quite adept at running, jumping and hopping, but has yet to master these and other skills and include variations of pace, direction and levels. By age 9 or 10 the same child is now quite skilled at these and many more basic actions. Gross motor skills improve steadily across middle child-hood and many children readily engage in activities that involve large muscles, such as throwing and catching. A 6 year old can competently climb, jump, run and hop. By ages 7 and 8, balance has improved significantly allowing better stability in Dance and

Gymnastics. Everyday fine motor skills needed in fastening buttons and zips, tying shoe laces, and even brushing teeth become much more co-ordinated from 7–11. Drawings become much more detailed and organised. 8 and 9 year olds can hold pencils with fingertip control, and write neatly. Hand–eye co-ordination is improving rapidly. Ossification, the process of bone hardening shows steady development throughout early and middle childhood but the development of the bones in the hand and wrists occurs earlier for girls than boys. As a consequence girls' fine motor control is advanced and noticeable in activities such as drawing and handwriting. They can throw a ball in PE with increased accuracy using wrist and finger release. The performance of motor skills is very similar for boys and girls with few gender differences, with the exceptions that increased muscle strength in boys assists in the execution of throwing and striking, and girls, whose flexibility and limb co-ordination is marginally better than boys, perform well in Dance and balance activities in Gymnastics.

The development of motor skills, from the reflexes and reactions of the newborn baby to the increasingly refined and specialist movement patterns used in sport and PE activities in Key Stage 2 and beyond, is progressive. Figure 2.1 shows a way of conceptualising motor skill development to the end of Primary school.

At the base of the diagram are the first actions in the womb and those the child makes as a newborn baby. Newborns possess a repertoire of early physical skills such as head turning, grasping, performing 'swimming' type actions with arms and legs and even recognisable stepping. Because of neurological immaturity, complete control of voluntary action is not yet possible and so many other actions are reflexive responses. Extending their arms outward when the head is moved forward (Moro reflex), gripping tightly on to an object (Plantar grasp) and the Symmetrical and Asymmetrical Tonic Neck reflexes, allowing flexion and extension of limbs in response to head turning, are exhibited along with other reflexes. As the brain develops, most of these reflexes are replaced by voluntary

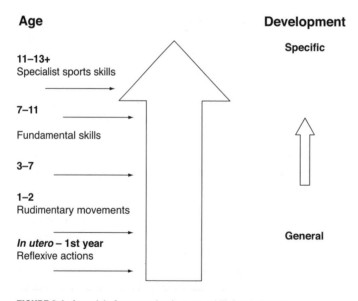

FIGURE 2.1 A model of progression in motor skill development

actions of turning, rolling and twisting movements and the child gains more postural control. By the second year this has advanced considerably, leading to the child being able to sit upright, stand, balance and walk, shown in Figure 2.1 as rudimentary movements.

On entering Primary school, children have achieved a great deal of important motor milestones and from this stage onwards display skills that are at the very heart of physical education – such as skipping, running, dodging, throwing, bouncing, etc. This is a gradual increase and occurs at different times for individual children. In the early stage of running, witness the fat-footed action with little knee-bend, legs swinging out, minimal involvement from the arms, and time off the ground being very limited. By the mid to late Primary years, the skill (as a consequence of maturation and experience) has developed considerably. At this stage we can observe the length of the stride increasing, enabling greater speed, greater flexion of the knee, more involvement from the arms and greater overall extension of the whole body. Even to the untrained eye, the child at this more advanced level has much greater proficiency in this skill.

Chapter summary

PE establishes itself as a wonderful vehicle to promote all-round development. Rudimentary physical skills of sitting, standing and walking remain major achievements in the early years and are replaced by later skills such as jumping, running, skipping, balancing, etc. By seeing development holistically, teachers avoid identifying PE as a solely physical medium and in turn are much more empowered to deliver richer and more meaningful movement experiences for all children. The fundamental skills form the basis of the physical education programme in Key Stages 1 and 2 across all practical areas of activity. Knowing about the progression of motor skills in the middle childhood years and helping children to progress these skills is therefore a prime concern for physical educators.

Questions for reflection

- Do you think it is important that all physical educators have knowledge of child development?
- Is it necessary to know about other aspects of development or have knowledge of physical development only?
- What priority is given currently to children learning motor skills as they progress through the Primary school curriculum?

Further reading

Doherty, J. and Bailey, R. (2003) *Supporting Physical Development and Physical Education in the Early Years*. Buckingham: Open University Press.

Doherty, J. and Hughes, M. (2009) *Child Development. Theory and Practice 0–11*. Essex: Pearson Education.

Gallahue, D.L. and Ozmun, J. (1998) *Understanding Motor Development -Infants, Children, Adolescents, Adults.* Dubuque, Iowa: McGraw-Hill.
A classic text in motor development but one that makes good links to PE. Theoretical, but a really good text.

Haywood, K.M. and Getchell, N. (2001) *Life Span Motor Development.* Champaign, IL: Human Kinetics.

Malina, R.M., Bouchard, C. and Bar-Or, O. (2004) *Growth, Maturation and Physical Activity.* Champaign, IL: Human Kinetics.

Maude, P. (2001) *Physical Children, Active Teaching.* Investigating Physical Literacy. Buckingham: Open University Press.
Chapter 1 discusses early physical and motor development well.

Pickup, I. and Price, L. (2007) *Teaching Physical Education in the Primary School. A Developmental Approach.* London: Continuum.
Chapters 2–4 are excellent.

Sharp, B. (1992*) Acquiring Skill in Sport.* Eastbourne, UK: Sports Dynamics.
For those who wish to find out more about skill and performance. It is not a curriculum book but is an accessible read full of useful information.

Thomas, J.R., Lee, A.M. and Thomas, K.T. (1988) *Physical Education for Children.* Champaign, Illinois: Human Kinetics.
Part 1 has general chapters on development and skill which are very readable.

References

Band, G.P., van der Molen, M.W., Overtoom, C.C.E. and Verbaten, M.N. (2000) 'The ability to activate and inhibit speeded responses: Separate developmental trends'. *Journal of Experimental Child Psychology*, 75: 63–90.

Bee, H. (2007) *The Developing Child.* 11th edition. London: Allyn & Bacon.

Berk, L. (2002) *Infants and Children. Prenatal through Middle Childhood.* 4th edition. London: Allyn & Bacon.

Black, J. E. and Greenough, W. T. (1986) 'Induction of pattern in neural structure by experience: Implications for cognitive development'. In M.E. Lamb, A.L. Brown and B. Rogott (eds.), *Advances in Developmental Psychology*, Vol. 4. Hillsdale, NJ: Erlbaum (pp. 1–50).

Bloom, B.S., Mesia, B.B. and Krathwohl, D.R. (1964) *Taxonomy of Educational Objectives.* (two vols: *The Affective Domain* and *The Cognitive Domain*). New York: David McKay.

Bronfenbrenner, U. (1989) 'Ecological systems theory'. In R. Vasta (ed.), *Annals of Child Development.* Vol. 6,. Boston, MA: JAI Press (pp. 187–249).

Diamond, M. and Hopson, J. (1998) *Magic Trees of the Mind.* New York: Dutton.

Doherty, J. and Bailey, R. (2003) *Supporting Physical Development and Physical Education in the Early Years.* Buckingham: Open University Press.

Doherty, J. and Hughes, M. (2009) *Child Development. Theory and Practice 0–11.* Essex: Pearson Education.

Gabbard, C.P. (1992) *Lifelong Motor Development.* Dubuque, IA: WCB McGraw-Hill.

Gallahue, D.L. and Ozmun, J.C. (1998) *Understanding Motor Development: Infants, Children, Adolescents, Adults.* 4th edition. Boson, MA: McGraw-Hill.

Harris, M. and Butterworth, G. (2002) *Developmental Psychology: A Student's Handbook.* Hove: Psychology Press.

Hepworth, S.L., Rovet, J.F. and Taylor, M.J. (2001) 'Neurophysiological correlates of verbal and nonverbal short-term memory in children: Repetition of words and faces'. *Psychophysiology, 38*: 594–600.

Langston, A. and Doherty, J. (2012) *Thinking, Reflecting and Doing. The Revised EYFS in Practice.* London: Featherstone.

Malina, R.M. and Bouchard, C. (1991) *Growth, Maturation and Physical Activity.* Champaign, IL: Human Kinetics.

Maude, P. (1996) 'How do I do this better? From movement development into early years physical education'. In D. Whitebread (ed.) *Teaching and Learning in the Early Years.* London: RoutledgeFalmer.

NSCDC (2007) *The Timing and Quality of Early Experiences Combine to Shape Brain Architecture: Working Paper #5.* December. Center on the Developing Child at Harvard University: NSCDC.

Pickup, I. and Price, L. (2007) *Teaching Physical Education in the Primary School. A Developmental Approach.* London: Continuum.

Roberts, J.E. and Bell, M.A. (2000) 'Sex differences on a mental rotation task: variations in EEG hemispheric activation between children and college students'. *Developmental Neuropsychology, 17*: 199–224.

Rogol, A.D., Roemmich, J.N. and Clark, P.A. (2002) 'Growth at puberty'. *Journal of Adolescent Health, 31*: 192–200.

Santrock, J. (2007) *Child Development.* Boston: McGraw-Hill.

Wright, H. and Sugden, D. (1999) *Physical Education for All.* London: David Fulton.

3

Learning to move and moving to learn

Chapter objectives

By the end of this chapter you should be able to:

- Appreciate the place of movement as a bedrock of the PE curriculum.
- Understand how movement skill is defined.
- Know of the main theories that underpin skilled performance.
- Recognise what to look for when observing children moving and how to record this and next steps for learning.

Children's movement capabilities

Movement is an integral part of the human condition. We only have to look around us to see movement in everything we do. In our primitive past it was expressed in everyday living and the rituals and traditions of different cultures. We have inherited this legacy today: our daily domestic and professional lives play host to a myriad of movements, many of which we take for granted. Movement in life is very much a tool for life. It has been described as 'a product of being alive' (DES, 1972, p. 3). Simply, the more efficiently one moves, the more meaningful one's life becomes. There is a wonderful versatility too about the ways in which we move. In PE and sport, witness the elegance and grace of the dancer, the control of the gymnast or the explosive power of the athlete in motion.

Movement is a natural part of childhood. Babies communicate their needs and feelings through movement. The pre-school child's movements are driven by a desire to find out more and enquire. Maturation of the brain and nervous systems, alongside increases in body strength, encourage exploration of what the body can do and an eagerness to test it out. Children of this age enjoy the thrill of running, jumping and climbing. Progression into the Primary years sees the same almost limitless energy and enquiring disposition where there is further delight in the accomplishments of how the body is capable of moving. Vital experiments into body balance, heights to jump on to and from, and speeds and directions to run in are constantly being investigated and new limits set. In this desire for knowledge, movement remains a child's principal medium of self-discovery and learning.

Movement and its development are key concerns for physical educators. Movement has been linked to the promotion of health and increased self-esteem and is directly linked to learning. Piaget defined thinking as internalised action (1977). It integrates and anchors new information and experiences into our neural networks and is vital to every action through which we express learning, understanding and ourselves. Movement anchors our thinking. Every time we move in an organised way, brain activation and integration takes place and the door to learning opens (Hannaford, 1995).

A key role for educators is to help children move more efficiently and to increase the quality of their movements. Movement is at the heart of PE in the Primary years and intrinsic to all activities in Key Stages 1 and 2. Each area of activity has a different stress and taxes the body's capacity to move in different ways. (Further discussion and practical guidance on the kinds of movement experiences for Primary children are given in Chapters 5 and 6.)

Movement education is an important aspect of PE programmes in Primary schools. It exploits the science of movement and is designed to help young children become more aware of their bodies and how to move more efficiently (Bucher, 1979). The characteristics of movement education are that it:

- is child centred;
- involves problem-solving;
- is less formal than traditional PE;
- involves equipment;
- facilitates the learning of motor skills;
- seeks to produce a feeling of satisfaction in movement;
- encourages an analysis of movement.

Arnold (1988) proposed four reasons why movement merits a place in the curriculum. First, it articulates movement as a field of study that has academic interest and is worthy of study in its own right. Second, it fulfils an instrumental role if it can be demonstrated that other educational or desirable ends are served. The third reason is that it is an intrinsic and valued part of culture that should be transmitted on to future generations, and finally, it is the only area of the curriculum directly concerned with the experiences of moving which form an integral part of what it is to be a person. These dimensions of movement provide an excellent basis for curriculum development and are the basis for our discussion here.

Education *about* movement

This first aspect refers to enquiry into movement itself and poses questions about learning to move and theories of motor learning that underscore this enquiry. It is also concerned with how the body is organised to support movement, ways of moving and how to classify and analyse movement. There is a knowledge connection here, predominantly of the type Hirst (1974) labelled 'propositional knowledge', or 'knowing that'. Reid (1998) suggests that this form of knowledge functions as technical knowledge. How this form of knowledge relates to movements of young children is through their knowledge of rules, procedures and concepts within their PE experiences. It is the type of knowledge that is embedded in the natural play of young children and also in later structured PE experiences such as Gymnastics. Consider the following three scenarios that demonstrate children's theoretical knowledge in PE.

Propositional knowledge is acquired mostly through information that is provided by the teacher, but also through working in a cross-curricular way. The popular topic of 'Movement', and emphasis on the ways in which animals, humans and machines move, presents valuable sources of theoretical knowledge about movement as more scientific work on forces and levers through Science taught in Key Stage 1. Observation and the type of knowledge gleaned through observation are important so that children can make reasoned judgements about the movements they observe. These can be their own, the movements of their peers or expert performances of top athletes watched on DVD.

In order that children develop their knowledge and understanding about movement, it is necessary that they know the range and character of the different activity areas in PE. A curriculum that is broad and balanced provides all pupils with the best opportunities

---

CHILDREN DEMONSTRATING LEARNING *ABOUT* MOVEMENT

Knowledge of concepts

Maria in a Year 3 Gymnastics lesson is learning to balance on three points. She needs to have some knowledge about bases, stability and centre of gravity to balance effectively.

Knowledge of procedures

Carla in Year 4 knows the importance of cooling down after exercise to prepare her body gradually after the strenuous exercise of the Athletics lesson she has just enjoyed. She knows that cool downs are movements that gradually decrease exercise intensity that allow her heart rate to drop and breathing to return to normal and help circulate blood around her body, so gentle jogging and walking is required for several minutes. She also knows that stretching muscles will help maintain flexibility and reduce stiffness and so some whole body stretches are included in her cool down.

Knowledge of rules

Hadid in Year 5 is playing an opposed sending and receiving game based on netball. He is aware that he cannot travel with the ball so he uses this knowledge of the game and its strategies to put himself in a position to receive a pass from his team-mates and to move to a position on court that gives him the best chance of scoring.

to experience the demands and challenges of different practical activity areas. Bailey makes the point that a narrow interpretation of a competitive team-games curriculum alienates a large number of pupils and robs them of valuable learning experiences. He states that 'an adequate education about movement, therefore, introduces the full range of movement experiences, and offers each pupil the opportunity to excel' (2001, p. 8).

Education *through* movement

This refers to the use of physical activities as a means to achieve educational aims that may not be intrinsic to those activities. They relate to the broader aims of education in two ways. They can illustrate a point that has arisen, for example in another curriculum area, or they can refer to a question that has arisen, for example from earlier work or work elsewhere. The illustrative function, suggests Arnold, is best understood in terms of a question such as, How can I (as the teacher) help my class learn by actively using movement? The referent function he suggests might be understood in a question from pupils such as, Why is it necessary to have rules in games?

These two questions might well arise during the course of normal classroom situations or through PE lessons as is illustrated below.

This aspect highlights how movement can contribute to learning in other areas of the curriculum by working in a cross-curricular way. Hopper and colleagues suggest that the potential for this type of learning is nowhere more evident than in interpreting movements into the spoken word. They suggest that language offers 'a treasure chest of descriptive, directional and action words for children to explore and experience' (2000, p. 91). With older children, the use of score sheets, reading from work cards, writing instructions for games and marking movement performances of others provide many rich opportunities to enhance learning elsewhere in the curriculum.

CHILDREN DEMONSTRATING LEARNING *THROUGH* MOVEMENT

- Year 1 pupils Yasmin and Gethin practise letter formations *p* and *d* by tracing out letters in the air which will assist in writing activities.

- Ben and Matt in Year 2 measure the length of their classroom by pacing it out. Their teacher will follow this up with a discussion on standard units of measurement later.

- In a PE lesson with Year 3, the class are using a warm-up game called North, South, East and West that involves them running and touching different areas of the hall. This helps their understanding of compass points.

- As part of a Year 5 Games lesson, the teacher takes some time to talk about fair play after witnessing some unsporting behaviour from two pupils.

Education *in* movement

Education in movement is the most fundamental dimension of the physical education curriculum (Doherty and Bailey, 2003). This is because learning occurs through active participation in movement activities. A different type of knowledge is required here, which is expressed in practical ways. This is practical knowledge or 'knowing how'.

For Arnold (1988) this is essentially concerned with mastering skills and being able to participate in activities successfully with understanding. He writes that its distinctive features are that it involves practice and not just theory; action, not just thought or belief and intentionally doing something, rather than providing information about it or speculating about it (ibid).

PE is part of the wider process of education, and by offering children opportunities for movement and physical activity, we introduce them to a physical dimension that brings its own intrinsic worth and enjoyment. Children of all ages love to move and demonstrate their physical skills and therefore to deny them this important part of their education is to deny them something that is fundamental to the whole human experience.

Education in movement involves participation that provides a unique opportunity to enjoy it 'from the inside'. A broadly based PE curriculum from 5 to 11 can provide children with experiences that are valuable and worthwhile in their own right. Here are some examples from such a curriculum that offers a range of movement experiences.

Clearly there are overlaps between the three components of movement. This is inevitable and their interrelationship should be promoted if children are to achieve their full potential in PE. A planned physical education curriculum from 5 to 11 with multiple learning outcomes is required. If based upon key principles, with movement as its cornerstone, it will help young children become more aware of their bodies and move more effectively. In the next section we consider the concepts that form such a movement education.

CHILDREN DEMONSTRATING LEARNING *IN* MOVEMENT

- Matti and Harry in Year 1 are enjoying exploring the outside area around their school nursery.

- Jack in Year 3 has learning difficulties. He looks forward to when his class go swimming as he loves to feel the water on his skin and move freely around the shallow end.

- Mrs Taylor has brought a visitor into her Year 5 class who will teach the children a traditional Asian hand dance.

- This term Bev and Jon in Year 6 have been improving their striking and fielding skills and have been excited to take part in a 'kwik cricket' game against another local school.

Adopting a movement approach

In his comparison of the alphabet as a function of formal language with the concepts pertaining to movement, Buschner (1994) coined the phrase 'movement alphabet'. Where the traditional alphabet has twenty-six letters, the movement alphabet contains twelve movement concepts and eighteen movement skills that also require mastery. Drawing upon early work of Melograno (1979), he links movement concepts and movement skills (considered later in this chapter) as organising centres that give cohesion to the curriculum in a sequential and progressive way. Buschner argues that these should be placed at the centre of the PE curriculum to allow for applications into Sports, Dance, Exercise and Gymnastics later in a sequence of developmentally appropriate learning. This mirrors the progression from early years and Primary through to more complex and applied movements in the secondary phase. References elsewhere in the literature to movement concepts and skills under other labels are also to be found (Kirchner, 1992; Nichols, 1986; Thomas *et al.*, 1988). Let us now turn to look at movement concepts.

We might wish to consider Graham *et al.*'s useful description of movement concepts as the adverbs that modify the skills in such an alphabet (1993). Distinguishing between the two, movement concepts describe how a skill is performed. A practical example of this should aid clarification. If we take a movement skill such as running, this can be altered in many ways. I can run fast, slow, backwards, sidewards, or alongside another person. I can run on toes, on heels, with high knees or with exaggerated steps. I can mix speeds or directions as I wish. I can change the skill in these ways and many others just as I can with any other movement skill. A framework comprising four features is commonly used to describe movement. The influence of Rudolph Laban's work in this country in the 1930s can be seen in much of the work today in school educational Gymnastics and Dance. The four factors below are all observable in bodily movement in structured PE lessons.

Body awareness

Young children have little awareness of what their bodies are doing as they move. Activities like naming body parts and forming shapes help them become more aware of their bodies and what their bodies can do. 'Make your body as wide as an ocean' or 'Can you make your body as tall as a tree?' are good early movement challenges for children. Key Stage 1 pupils can explore this further through symmetrical shapes in Gymnastics and in Key Stage 2 find out about symmetrical and asymmetrical shapes and their properties dynamically as they roll, jump and run.

There are various non-locomotor movements including body flexion, extension and rotation, which are commonly described as bending, stretching and twisting and which appear in various forms in PE that help develop understanding of body awareness more fully. Others in this category include actions such as spinning, stepping or travelling and those of different body parts that either lead movement or support it.

Space awareness

Since all movements take up space, children should be aware of their bodies in space (self-space). As they move around and engage in different activities and in different situations, the need to understand the space around them becomes more marked (general space). One reason why Primary children should not play full-sided games is because their awareness of general space is not developed sufficiently to know where to move on the pitch or court. With experience this will happen but Games lessons with large numbers on large areas of play should be avoided with Primary pupils. Movements can also involve the six directions of upwards, downwards, left, right, backwards and forwards. They can be at three different levels: high (the space above shoulder height), middle, and low (below the knees). Pathways are either straight, curved or zig-zag. Finally, movements may be made near to the body or far from it, such as catching a ball with the arms beside the body or extended away from it.

Effort

This aspect considers how the body moves. Its abstract nature can make it a concept that is often forgotten in Gymnastics or Dance lessons but its inclusion is vital. If we were to observe elite athletes in action this quality would be immediately apparent in their movements. Can we say the same about a class of movers in Primary school? Three elements define this concept. The first is time, which if fast suggests quickness, suddenness and explosiveness. Ballistic movements such as starting off in a sprint or throwing in athletics typify fast movements. In contrast, the movements of a 5 year old walking across a beam in Gymnastics are characterised by slowness and sustained effort. The force component has two opposites: strong and light. Both may be witnessed in Dance lessons where children are encouraged to move like a giant (strong) or like snowflakes (light). Flow is also commonly represented in Dance lessons. It can be bound where movement responses are robot-like (jerky and restricted) or free and show fluidity, continuity and smoothness.

Relationships

This concept is associated with whom or with what the body moves. With younger children, since their interest is primarily about themselves, lessons to identify their own body parts are essential. With older children they should be encouraged to note the position of their limbs in executing movements. In Games, attention might be drawn to the position of the arms in performing a tennis serve action or the position of the supporting foot in preparation for kicking a ball.

Relationships to objects include balls, hoops, mats, Gymnastics equipment or line markings on the ground. Relationships to others are often seen in Key Stage 2 Gymnastics lessons working on a theme of 'Partners'. This provides children with ample opportunities to explore concepts such as meeting and parting, following and leading, or mirroring and matching. The four concepts of movement can be described in diagram form as in Figure 3.1.

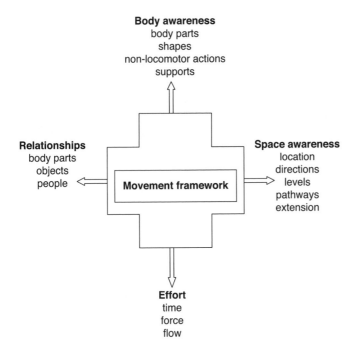

FIGURE 3.1 A qualitative movement framework based on Laban

The development of movement

In the book's opening chapter we highlighted that the child who is physically educated displays competency in a variety of movement skills and in this chapter we outline some of the processes involved in acquiring and developing movement skills.

Although the term *skill* has been variously defined by many writers, several common features can be identified. McMorris, in his book *Acquisition and Performance of Sports Skills* (2004), presents four features that are common in most discussions on how skill is represented. First, skill is learned. The execution of all skills involves complex learning processes. It occurs either implicitly, for example in many of the skills in early childhood such as crawling, or explicitly and involves some formal instruction, such as how to execute the drive shot in cricket. It is not inherited but performance is dependent upon practice and experience. The second feature is that skill is consistent. A one-off shot into a netball ring is not characteristic of skilled performance if the majority of other attempts have been unsuccessful. Such consistency will inevitably involve economy of effort. Skilled movements look the same each time. They are efficient in terms of the performer's time and expenditure outlay. Third, it is specific. Chipping a football for height and kicking a football for distance are examples of two particular skills that are required in the game of soccer for different purposes, over and above merely kicking the ball. Finally, skill is goal-oriented. In other words there is an outcome or end result. Learning to accelerate at the start of a sprint race is important in order to improve running time. It has a clear purpose and direction. The goal can only be achieved by learning to carry out the action.

TASK: CATEGORISING MOVEMENT SKILLS

One way to categorise movement skills is according to their most important characteristics (Schmidt and Wrisberg, 2000). Taking a task perspective, physical skills can be categorised as being closed (performed in an environment that does not change) or open (where the environment is constantly changing). Another system classifies skills according to their organisation. Discrete skills are those with a distinct beginning and end. In contrast, continuous skills have neither and are usually repetitive in nature. Use this information to give examples from physical education for these ways of categorising movement skills.

Closed skills
e.g. performing a forward roll

Open skills
e.g. playing a game of basketball

Discrete skills
e.g. catching a ball

Continuous skills
e.g. swimming

It may be useful at this point to briefly introduce another term closely related to skill but which is distinctly different. The term *ability* is more general than skill and refers to the innate actions that underlie skilled performance. Unlike a skill which is a learned response, abilities are genetically endowed and are only marginally improved through practice because of genetic limitations. You can thank or blame your parents for this. The ability to aim at a target, to react quickly to a stimulus and to maintain a steady hand are all examples of innate human abilities that will show little improvement regardless of the amount of time spent practising! Skills and abilities do interact though. The skill of throwing a ball, for example, requires the thrower to possess a number of different abilities – balance, hand–eye co-ordination, kinaesthetic awareness, arm speed – for successful execution. It is also important to note that children (and adults) may perform the same skill differently because they possess different abilities and that these abilities can change over time. Given that everyone has different abilities, it raises the question of the appropriateness of teaching everyone to perform skills according to a standard 'textbook technique'. Diversity is the stuff of life!

Children learning movement skills

In early infancy, children use movement skills to learn about themselves and their physical and social environment. Reaching out to grasp a bright toy prompts the co-ordinating systems responsible for the reaching–grasping action to function. Further investigation of the object provides information about its shape, weight, size and texture that fuels the growing brain. It is through movement and the exploration of the environment that infants and carers develop signals, which lead to communication and later speech in what Maude refers to as the 'language-movement triangle' (2001, p. 49). She sees early movement as the springboard for language learning and the basis for PE. Relevant vocabulary such as 'over', 'through', 'along', 'below' and 'beside' etc., help children understand the spatial and body-related aspects of how they move. Curriculum areas such as Dance offer particularly good contexts to understand the language of movement and express it. Words like ' shrivel', 'creep', 'slither', 'glide' and 'tremble' will give many opportunities for movement development.

The middle childhood years are a time to learn new skills and refine existing ones. Success in gross and fine motor skills reflects increasing maturity and personality traits such as persistence and self-confidence. Being competent in motor skills increase acceptance from peers and enhances personal esteem (Rathus, 2006). For those children whose abilities are not as advanced as other children and who find PE a time of anxiety, educators have to be sensitive to individual needs. They need to understand how to break down movement skills to optimise learning and give plenty of praise and encouragement. Writers Pickup and Price (2007) caution against the pitfalls of a 'technical' approach to developing movement skills and stress that the way in which teaching episodes are framed is critical. They talk of the myth of a technical rather than a skill approach. In physical education there is not only one way to kick a ball, or execute a roll to develop movement skill. Engaging children in problem-solving, adopting alternative approaches, working with others to solve physical challenges and planning links to wider educational objectives is the approach taken not only with Primary age children but with elite performers.

In order to understand how children acquire movement skills, it is necessary to make reference to the theories of motor learning. Research into motor learning and performance can be traced back to the early part of the last century where association (stimulus-response) and cognitive approaches competed for acceptance as the solution to how physical skills are acquired and developed. The period from the 1950s onwards heralded changes in thinking and many new advances in this area. Today there are still many unanswered questions and no single theory has been able to provide the solution. Questions, such as How are new movements performed? What cognitive processes are involved in controlling fast and slow movements? What role does the environment play in movement skill learning? remain hotly debated. What is certain is that the combined wisdom of these different approaches has increased our knowledge of this area considerably. Key points from the four theories of movement learning are presented now but rather than view these as four separate and competing 'manifestos', readers are encouraged to consult the recommended further reading at the end of the chapter for more detailed information.

Two main motor learning perspectives exist and the main theories are briefly discussed. First, the information processing perspective (Welford, 1968). This is best understood as the input and output of a computer. Information from the environment (e.g. the ball is in the air, it is travelling fast, it is beginning to drop, there is a defender between myself and the ball) comes into the brain, which processes this information throughout processes of perception organisation and decision-making that leads ultimately to a movement output. The system is heavily reliant upon both internal feedback from the body and external feedback from the often changing external environment and is stored in the brain in motor programmes, similar to files stored on a PC. Fitts and Posner's three stage model (1967) identified the *cognitive stage* as the first stage of learning in which the learner makes most errors, and the errors are large. Take catching a ball as an example. The learner may be in the wrong position, he or she may well not be looking at the incoming ball and hands and body position may not be aligned to catch it successfully. The result is a dropped catch. With practice learning the skill enters the second or *associated* phase. Here there is most consistency and fewer errors. Movements are learned and relearned. In the final or *autonomous* phase, the skill is now learned. This allows the performer to concentrate on other aspects, which in a game situation means understanding the field of play, or 'reading the game' for example, and means not having to focus cognitive energy on the execution of individual techniques.

Adams' closed-loop theory (1971) has two similar stages of skill learning. The first or *verbal-motor* stage is similar to the first stage in Fitts and Posner's model but has more body involvement. We can think of this as 'muscle memory'. Previous memories of performing the skill successfully are stored in a memory trace, which allows unsuccessful movement errors to be corrected. This leads to the second and final stage called the *motor stage* where the movements are automatic and do not require much conscious thinking to perform successfully, for example catching a ball at different speeds and trajectories while performing different footwork, selling a dummy to a defender or paying closer attention to the changing field of play. In this theory, skill arises from matching the memory trace with feedback built over practice of the skill. Schmidt's schema theory (1975) disagreed that movements are controlled by a memory trace. This theory supports the idea that every movement is different since our brains cannot contain a memory for every single movement action or component action. This model emphasises the role of experience, feedback and error correction. Memory stores contain schemas (sets of generalised rules), rather than specific movement traces and it is through successful practice that these schemas become part of our brain 'software'. To illustrate this in practice, let us use the example of a Year 2 pupil aiming a quoit into a hoop on the ground. In the early attempts the throw will be too long or too short. The child is learning to associate the movement with distance and accuracy. With practice and feedback provided internally (i.e. the child sees the throw is too long or too short) or externally by the teacher, the schema becomes strengthened and the skill successful. The motor response schema takes responsibility for the set of rules governing the action in this particular set of circumstances.

Offering quite a different perspective to movement skill learning is the ecological perspective. Dynamic systems theory (Thelen and Smith, 1994) rejects that skill is developed in a series of stages. In this more modern theory action and skill combine together and movement is self-organising. That is to say, joints, muscles and nerves work together to create movement. The theory argues that movement is functionally specific, such as being able to kick a ball, rather than general as with the information-processing approach. It takes the view that motor co-ordination takes place through changes in the environment and the demands of a specific task but the process is not centrally organised. This emphasises the role played by the environment and proposes that development is inseparable from the context in which a person develops. The 'rules' are different for each person and learning occurs by trial and error and self-discovery, rather than through explicit instruction. If we look at the running technique of the great sprinters you will see immediately they are slightly different. Body angles, height of knee lift, length of stride and leg extension, and arm positioning are individually different. All this is a persuasive argument for this theory and against central processing. Does it apply to Primary

TASK: YOUR PERSPECTIVE ON MOVEMENT SKILL ACQUISITION

No one perspective explains movement skill performance entirely. Which perspective do you believe best explains it? Review the last section. Which of these is most convincing?

age children? Yes, it does. Look at three children running in the playground. You will see individual differences in their techniques as each child organises their running action slightly differently. If the environment were changed, i.e. the ground was slippery or the challenge was to run at speed around cones, the task demands would require different movement responses. This is also how new motor patterns emerge: as older ones become less efficient, new patterns emerge that are not planned in detail beforehand but are refined by the specific demands of the task and the situation (Doherty and Hughes, 2009).

Earlier in this chapter the concept of a movement alphabet was introduced and movement concepts were likened to adverbs. The second component of this alphabet are movement skills, which may be thought of as similar to verbs. Both movement concepts and movement skills are essential in a quality programme of physical education: movement skills define what actions children perform in PE lessons and movement concepts characterise how these may be performed. Using running as an example to illustrate this point, a child may run (skill) but may do so in a variety of ways, e.g. forwards and alongside a partner (concept). By itself, the skill of running is bland but, by colouring it with one or more movement concepts, it becomes interesting, varied and more challenging for the performer.

What are the typical movement skills that Primary school children display in PE? Children need to master three prime categories of movement for survival and effective interaction with the world around them (Gallahue, 1993). In their first two years of life they need to strive towards an upright sitting and standing posture (stability), be able to move with efficiency (locomotion) and have meaningful contact with objects with hands and feet (manipulation). These rudimentary movements are part of a continuum of movement that progresses from the Early Years Foundation Stage through Key Stages 1 and 2.

Stability

This is the building block of all future movement. It involves children establishing and maintaining their bodies' relationship to gravity. From the outset it has direct association with posture and how they support their bodies as the centre of gravity is changed. A fine example of this is in gymnastic movements that extend from the base of support in static balances such as stork balances, arabesques and handstands to dynamic balances such as cartwheels, where the centre of gravity shifts as limbs move away. Stability is also needed for axial movements that involve the body bending and twisting in a stationary position. As children's movement skill repertoire increases, these axial movements are intrinsic to actions in diving, swimming and tumbling activities.

Locomotion

This aspect is concerned with the body moving through space. The body is projected in space by changing its position in relation to fixed points. Typically, children in the Early Years Foundation Stage have achieved some degree of competence in a skill such as running, but require opportunities for practice and improvement for progress in the skill alone or so that it can be linked with other skills, such as bouncing a ball. Curriculum requirements at Key Stage 2 for Games demand some level of competency in many of the locomotor skills and a lack of proficiency will impede enjoyment and progress in activities such as soccer, netball, hockey, basketball, etc.

Manipulation

Skills here provide meaningful contact with objects in the immediate world. Manipulation itself is characterised by the relationship to the object in terms of applying force to it or receiving force from it. Hands and feet therefore become the most frequent manipulators. Propulsion is involved in sending an object, such as a ball or beanbag, with different degrees of force, and absorption is involved in cushioning the impact of an object in receiving it. There need to be plentiful opportunities in Key Stage 1 for children to engage in throwing and catching activities in PE lessons with a variety of balls and other objects of different sizes, shapes and weights to develop competency in manipulation. As they become familiar with using different equipment they can explore how sending and receiving with these is accommodated differently and requires different techniques and apply this new knowledge in the context of different games in Key Stage 2.

Examples of skills within each of the three movement categories are shown in Table 3.1.

Movement skills and their development are intrinsic to the whole PE experience. Factors including developmental readiness, clear and informed instruction, teacher feedback, adequate practice time and motivation contribute to skill learning and improvement. The acquisition of fundamental motor skill will not happen unassisted. In the Primary school years it is vital for children to develop an ability to perform basic skills efficiently and to be able to adapt them to suit a variety of movement activities (Jess et al., 2004). The literature also suggests that proficiency in movement development occurs sequentially (Wickstrom, 1983; Graham et al., 1993; Bailey, 2000). David Gallahue (1982) proposes two concepts upon which improvement in movement skill learning depends:

1   Movement skills progress from simple to complex.
2   Skills proceed gradually from the general to specific.

In considering the first of these, it is obvious that children need to master basic movement skills such as balancing, hopping, skipping, throwing and catching before more complicated and activity-specific skills such as passing, dribbling, shooting at a goal in games and various specific Gymnastics actions are tackled. With regard to the second point, it also follows that when early skills such as walking and running are acquired, children need time and proper instruction to enable them to refine and perform these

TABLE 3.1 Categories of movement skills

Stability skills	Locomotion skills	Manipulation skills
Bending	Walking	Handling
Stretching	Running	Ball rolling
Twisting	Chasing	Kicking
Turning	Vertical jumping	Throwing
Reaching	Distance jumping	Catching
Swaying	Hopping	Trapping
Pushing	Galloping	Striking
Pulling	Sliding	Punting
Swinging	Leaping	Dribbling
Dodging	Skipping	Volleying
Rolling	Bouncing	Stopping
Balancing	Climbing	

and other physical skills with increased control and fluency (Haywood and Getchell, 1993). This progression in Gallahue's model establishes a hierarchy that mirrors progression in children's movement skills to the end of Key Stage 2. Its five stages are presented below and are returned to later in the book, under guidance on teaching skills. For the present the stages are:

1   *Exploration* – a pre-control stage where children try to understand the pattern or skill and form a general framework of it.
2   *Discovery* – an early stage involving learning through indirect means such as watching others rather than formal instruction.

TASK: OBSERVATIONS OF PUPIL MOVEMENT

Take one skill from any of the three movement categories (stability, locomotion and manipulation). Observe two children performing the same movement skill at different levels of proficiency (they may or may not be the same age). Child A is learning the skill. Child B has achieved some proficiency in the same skill. Record what you see for both children.

The following prompts should help your observations:

■   What was your overall impression of how this skill was performed?

■   Describe the leg action.

■   Describe the arm action.

■   How would you describe the overall body shape?

■   How well was the skill being performed?

■   Next steps. As a physical educator, what suggestions would you make for both children to improve?

3   *Combination* – involves experimentation with isolated movements in various ways.
4   *Selection* – smoothes out the whole of several skill-related tasks through lead-up games and informal challenges.
5   *Refinement* – selected movements are refined and often performed formally in competition. Skills are automatic by this stage.

(Gallahue, 1982, p. 45)

Chapter summary

This chapter asserted the importance of movement for children. We argued that movement is a cornerstone of PE as well as very much a part of the whole human condition. There followed a discussion on the role of movement and education with examples from the three categories of *stability*, *manipulation* and *locomotion* given. Factors allied to movement skills were presented and theories in motor learning were introduced. The chapter concluded by showing how movement skill is progressed from birth to the age of 11, highlighting that improvement in movement skill progresses from simple to complex and from general to specific movements.

Questions for reflection

■   In this chapter, movement was presented as a cornerstone of physical education experiences. Is this reflected in all age phases of PE? Is it equally reflected?

■   What priority is given to children's learning of motor skills as they progress through the Primary school PE curriculum?

■   What opportunities are there in your school environment to develop children's movement skills?

Further reading

Buschner, C. (1994) *Teaching Children Movement Concepts and Skills*. Champaign: Illinois: Human Kinetics.
Chapters 1 and 3 give a very sound rationale for embedding movement into the PE curriculum.

Jess, M. (2004) *Basic Moves*. Edinburgh: University of Edinburgh.

Magill, R.A. (1993) *Motor Learning: Concepts and Applications*. IW: Brown and Benchmark

Maude, P. (2001) *Physical Children, Active Teaching. Investigating Physical Literacy*. Buckingham: Open University Press.
Chapter 4, Movement observation and assessment is very good.

PEAUK (2003) *Observing Children Moving*. Reading: TackleSport.
CD-Rom illustrating movement in children 3–7.

Pickup, I. and Price, L. (2007) *Teaching Physical Education in the Primary School*. London: Continuum.
Chapter 4 is very good on linking physical skills and movement themes.

Schmidt, R.A and Wrisberg, C. (2000) *Motor Learning and Performance*. Champaign, Illinois: Human Kinetics.
A technical book that goes into movement skill and performance in depth. Some prior knowledge of theories of motor learning might be needed. Adopts an information-processing approach to motor skill learning.

References

Adams, J.A. (1971) A closed-loop theory of motor learning'. *Journal of Motor Behaviour 3*: 111–50.

Arnold, P.J. (1988) *Education, Movement and the Curriculum*. London: Falmer Press.

Bailey. R. (2000) 'Movement development and the primary school child'. In R. Bailey and T. Macfadyen, *Teaching Physical Education 5–11*. London: Continuum.

Bailey, R. (2001) *Teaching Physical Education: A Handbook for Primary and Secondary Teachers*. London: Kogan Page.

Bucher, C.A. (1979) *Physical Education for Children: Movement Foundations and Experiences*. Basingstoke: Macmillan.

Buschner, C.A. (1994) *Teaching Children Movement Concepts and Skills*. Champaign, IL: Human Kinetics.

Department for Education and Science (1972) *Movement: Physical Education in the Primary Years*. London: HMSO.

Doherty, J.W. and Bailey, R. (2003) *Supporting Physical Development and Physical Education in the Early Years*. Buckingham: Open University Press.

Doherty, J. and Hughes, M. (2009) *Child Development. Theory and Practice 0–11*. Essex: Pearson Education.

Fitts, P.M. and Posner, M.I. (1967) *Human Performance*. Belmont, CA: Brooks/Cole.

Gallahue, D.L. (1982) *Developmental Movement Experiences for Children*. New York: Wiley.

Gallahue, D.L. (1993) *Developmental Physical Education for Today's Children*. Madison, WI: Brown and Benchmark.

Graham, G., Holt-Hale, S. and Parker, M. (1993) *Children Moving: A Reflective Approach to Teaching Physical Education*. London: Mayfield Publishing Company.

Hannaford, C. (1995) *Smart Moves. Why Learning is Not All in Your Head*. Arlington, VI: Great Ocean Publishers.

Haywood, K.M. and Getchell, N. (1993) *Life Span Motor Development*. (3rd edition). Champaign, IL: Human Kinetics.

Hirst, P.H. (1974) *Knowledge and the Curriculum*. Routledge and Kegan Paul.

Hopper, B., Grey, J. and Maude P. (2000) *Teaching Physical Education in the Primary School*. London: RoutledgeFalmer.

Jess, M., Dewar, K. and Fraser, G. (2004) Basic moves: developing a foundation for lifelong physical activity. *British Journal of Teaching Physical Education*, Summer, 24–7.

Kirchner, G. (1992) *Physical Education for Elementary School Children*. Dubuque, IA: Brown.

Maude, P. (2001) *Physical Children, Active Teaching. Investigating Physical Literacy*. Buckingham: Open University Press.

McMorris, T. (2004) *Acquisition and Performance of Sports Skills*. Chichester: John Wiley and Sons Ltd.

Melograno, V. (1979) *Designing Curriculum and Learning: A Physical Coeducation Approach*. Dubuque, IA: Brown.

Nichols, B. (1986) *Moving and Learning: The Elementary School Experience*. St Louis: CV Mosby.

Piaget, J. (1977) *Knowledge and Development. The Role of Action in the Development of Thinking*. Geneva: Springer US.

Pickup, I. and Price, L. (2007) *Teaching Physical Education in the Primary School. A Developmental Approach*. London: Continuum.

Rathus, S.A. (2006) *Childhood and Adolescence. Voyages in Discovery*. 2nd Edition. London: Thomson Wadsworth.

Reid, A. (1998) 'The value of education'. *Journal of Philosophy of Education, 32*(33): 319–31.

Schmidt, R.A. (1975) 'A schema theory of discrete motor skill learning'. *Psychological Review, 82*: 225–60.

Schmidt, R.A. and Wrisberg, C.A. (2000) *Motor Learning and Performance*. Champaign, IL: Human Kinetics.

Thelen, E. and Smith, L.B. (1994) *A Dynamic Systems Approach to the Development of Cognition and Action*. Cambridge, MA: MIT Press.

Thomas, J., Lee, A. and Thomas, K. (1988) *Physical Education for Children: Concepts and Practices*. Champaign, IL: Human Kinetics.

Welford, A.T. (1968) *Fundamentals of Skill*. London: Methuen.

Wickstrom, R.L. (1983) *Fundamental Motor Patterns*. Philadelphia: Lea & Febiger.

PE in a professional context

CHAPTER

4

Issues in PE today

Chapter objectives

By the end of this chapter you should be able to:

- Identify key issues with regard to contemporary physical education.
- Understand how these wider issues relate to teaching and learning in school-based PE.
- Appreciate how these broader issues raise questions about the future of PE in schools today.
- Identify any professional development needs that this discussion on contemporary issues might identify for you or your colleagues.

This chapter is aimed at providing as wide a perspective on PE as possible by introducing some of the key and current issues relevant to the teaching and learning of the subject in schools. We believe that it is important and healthy for practitioners to reflect on and debate core issues that impact upon the way we think about, plan and deliver PE in our schools. There are many issues that might have been included in this chapter but the following topics are selected on the basis that they raise important questions about the place of PE in school, both currently and in future.

- High-quality physical education for all children.
- School sport and sport partnerships.
- Critical thinking in PE.
- Continuity of learning: EYFS into National Curriculum.
- Health and physical activity.

High-quality physical education for all children

The Purpose of Study section in National Curriculum PE for Key Stages 1–4 says:

> A high-quality physical education curriculum inspires all pupils to succeed and excel in competitive sport and other physically-demanding activities. It should provide opportunities for pupils to become physically confident in a way which supports their health and fitness. Opportunities to compete in sport and other activities build character and help to embed values such as fairness and respect.
>
> (DfE, 2013, p. 3)

The key word is 'high-quality'. Surely that should be easy to describe and even easier to understand what it means in practice? Not so. Baroness Sue Campbell, Head of UK Sport recently cautioned that Primary school headteachers are failing to provide high-quality PE and sports skills and are happy to see children 'running around, making lots of noise warns' (Vaughan and Maddern, 2013). The first step towards meeting the challenge of providing high-quality physical education (HQPE) is agreeing what the phrase means in practice. Ten outcomes for high-quality physical education were identified to aid teachers, parents and school authorities to assess the quality of the PE experience offered to pupils:

- Learners show commitment to physical education and school sport
- Learners have the confidence to get involved
- Learners willingly participate in a range of activities
- Learners show desire to improve and achieve
- Learners enjoy physical education and school sport
- Learners know and understand what they are trying to achieve
- Learners understand that physical education and school sport are part of a healthy, active lifestyle
- Learners have the skills and control they need
- Learners think about what they are doing and make appropriate decisions
- Learners have stamina, suppleness and strength

(DfES/DCMS, 2004)

While the achievement of these outcomes will help to determine whether provision in any PE context has been of high quality, practitioners may need further guidance along the way. For this reason, accompanying each outcome is a series of performance indicators and suggestions to help teachers, headteachers and other providers to compare their provision against. Table 4.1 identifies some of the key issues that both schools and sports organisations should be working towards in order to deliver this for all pupils.

The unique benefits of physical education to enrich the lives of children formed our discussion in the first chapter of this book. The challenge now is very much upon understanding what PE experiences are 'high-quality' (Casbon et al., 2003). Its essence should be about skills and understanding, a desire and commitment to continue to improve and achieve in a range of PE, sport and health-enhancing activities in line with their abilities (DfES, 2004). So how do we as a profession go about this task? It seems that

TABLE 4.1 Key issues in the delivery of high-quality PE

1. Creating the vision

Head teachers	Sports club leaders/administrators
■ recognise what PE and school sport can achieve for each pupil and the whole school;	■ recognise what their sport can achieve for each young member and the whole club;
■ set high expectations of what individual pupils/participants and the whole school/club can achieve in and through PE and school sport;	■ set high expectations of what each young member and the whole club can achieve in and through their sport;
■ explain the value of PE and school sport to learning, health and well-being in a way that pupils, teachers, parents and governors can understand.	■ explain the value of their sport to learning, health and well-being in a way that young members, coaches, parents and the local community can understand.

2. Inspiring young people to learn and achieve

Teachers	Sports coaches
■ show commitment and enthusiasm and provide positive role models;	■ show commitment and enthusiasm and provide positive role models;
■ show confidence in their pupils' ability to make progress and achieve;	■ show confidence in their young members' ability to make progress and achieve;
■ listen to their pupils and value what they say and do;	■ listen to their young members and value what they say and do;
■ raise their pupils' aspirations and increase their determination to make progress and succeed;	■ raise their young members' aspirations and increase their determination to make progress and succeed;
■ have pride in and celebrate their pupils' successes;	■ have pride in and celebrate their young members' successes;
■ let pupils' parents/carers know what they have learnt and achieved in PE and school sport;	■ let young members' parents/carers know what they have achieved;
■ improve their own subject expertise.	■ improve their own knowledge of how to work with young people of different ages.

3. Helping young people to learn and achieve

Teachers	Sports coaches
■ have a clear plan that sets out steps towards meeting the school's vision and expectations for PE and school sport;	■ have a planned programme of activities that sets out steps towards meeting the club's vision and expectations for the sport;
■ share with pupils what they expect them to achieve in a way that they can understand;	■ share with young members what they expect them to achieve in a way that they can understand

TABLE 4.1 *continued*

■ take into account what pupils have already learnt within and beyond school;	■ take into account what young members have already learnt within and beyond the club;
■ identify the next steps in progression and communicate them to pupils and their parents/carers;	■ identify the next steps in progression and communicate them to young members and their parents/carers;
■ give each pupil relevant learning activities and authentic contexts that interest, excite and motivate them;	■ give each young member relevant learning activities that interest, excite and motivate them;
■ provide opportunities for pupils to analyse, assess and evaluate their own and others' work;	■ give young members opportunities to analyse, assess and evaluate their own progress and achievement;
■ give pupils time to think, reflect and make decisions for themselves;	■ give young members time to think, reflect and make decisions for themselves;
■ allow pupils time to wrestle with problems, while giving well-timed advice and support to advance learning and avoid frustration;	■ allow young members time to wrestle with problems, while giving well-timed advice and support to advance learning and avoid frustration;
■ ensure that they use time, staff, equipment and resources in ways that keep pupils interested and learning.	■ ensure that they use time, staff, equipment and resources in ways that keep young members interested and learning.

(Source: Adapted from DfES/DCMS (2004) *High Quality PE and Sport for Young People* available at http://www.qca.org.uk/pess/pdf/high.quality. guide.pdf)

returning to what constitutes quality teaching and learning is the place to start. Teaching PE is discussed further in Part 3 of this book, so we will concentrate this discussion on learning for the present.

Learning might appear as a simple phenomenon but on closer inspection it is highly complex. The many definitions of it alongside the theories that attempt to explain it reflect its complexity. In its simplest form, learning leads to changes that result in new skills or new knowledge. It is 'a process of interaction between what is known and what is to be learnt' (Wray, 2006). Historically, the behaviourist approach (e.g. Watson and Skinner) argued that learners passively absorbed knowledge through repetition and positive reinforcement using 'skill and drill' methods to provide the repetition necessary to reinforce a response from learners, which showed that learning had taken place. This approach may have found favour again with the current Coalition Government but is widely refuted by educators. The idea that pupils need to be instructed in skills and techniques is a misconception that we strongly refute in this book and argue has no place in any programme of quality PE in schools. In contrast, the constructionist approach (e.g. Piaget) was concerned with internal processes, rather than observable behaviours, and offers a better alternative. Learning is a process of active discovery where children are encouraged to discover meaning themselves and use exploration and trial and error methods to find out. The role of the teacher is to facilitate discovery by setting up the environment and providing resources so new knowledge is added to existing knowledge. This applies to any environment in which PE takes place – school hall, playground, pool, sports field. Bruner (1972) viewed learning as an active process in which learners select information, construct hypotheses and make decisions based on mental models which provide meaning and allow the individual to go beyond the information known (Waller and Swann, 2005). An approach that is very fitting for physical education.

Other theorists adopting a social constructivist approach place emphasis on the importance of social interaction and collaboration with others and argue that learning takes place in a social context (e.g. Vygotsky). When collaboration with others takes place, learners construct knowledge to a higher level than the individual is capable of alone. By working alongside more knowledgeable peers they achieve a greater level of understanding. Teaching utilises collaborative learning methods such as group work, team tasks and pupils engaged in small-sided game activities that reflect good practice across the practical activity areas in PE. Modern theorists (e.g. Lave and Wenger, 1991) believe learning is about social participation and PE is rich with opportunities for group involvement in all the activity areas. Learning is also a metacognitive process. Metacognition can be thought of as viewing one's own thinking and refers to the mechanisms that learners use to regulate their attempts to solve a problem. This includes:

- checking the outcome of what has already been attempted;
- planning the next moves in response to a problem;
- monitoring the effectiveness of the attempted actions;
- testing, revising and evaluating strategies for learning. (Wray, 2006)

Personalised learning has entered the educational vocabulary in recent years. In 2004 David Miliband, in his speech to North of England Education Conference, used the phrase in talking about high expectations of every child through high-quality teaching based on a sound knowledge and understanding of each child's needs. He saw it as 'shaping teaching around the way different youngsters learn; it means taking the care to nurture the unique talents of every pupil'. The Gilbert Report (DfES, 2006) considered personalising learning and teaching as taking a highly structured and responsive approach to each child's and young person's learning, so that all are able to progress, achieve and participate. It means strengthening the link between learning and teaching by engaging pupils – and their parents – as partners in learning. The report recommended that all schools by 2020 should have incorporated learning to learn principles in their school.

In the acclaimed book *Visible Learning* (2011), author John Hattie informs that when teaching and learning are visible there is greater likelihood of increased student achievement. This requires a teacher who is an evaluator and an activator, who knows a range of learning strategies to build deep knowledge and conceptual understanding. His conclusions are as relevant to physical education as they are to all subject areas:

- Teachers are among the most powerful influences in learning.
- Teachers need to be directive, influential, caring and actively and passionately engaged in the process of teaching and learning.
- Teachers need to be aware of what each student is thinking and what they know, and be able to construct meaning and meaningful experiences in the light of this knowledge.

- Teachers need to know the learning intentions and the criteria for student success, know how well they are attaining these criteria and where to go to next.
- Teachers need to move from single ideas to multiple ideas and relate and extend these such that learners construct and reconstruct knowledge and ideas.
- School leaders and teachers need to create schools and environments where error is welcomed as a learning opportunity and in which discarding incorrect knowledge and understanding is welcomed.

(Adapted from Hattie, 2012)

The new framework for school inspections (Ofsted, 2012) is very clearly refocused upon pupil learning. The four judgments made in the new school inspection schedule are:

- achievement of pupils at the school;
- quality of teaching in the school;
- behaviour and safety of pupils at the school;
- quality of leadership in and management of the school.

There are important references to learning in the 2012 schedule and in PE specific guidance material.

Achievement. Inspectors must consider 'how well pupils learn, the quality of their work in a range of subjects and the progress they have made since joining the school' (p. 6). Grade descriptors for *Outstanding* require that 'they (pupils) learn exceptionally well and as a result acquire knowledge quickly and in depth and are developing their understanding . . .'.

PE subject specific guidance states, 'pupils acquire new subject knowledge and skills and gain an in-depth understanding of a range of different activities exceptionally well. They learn, practise and apply skills in a range of different contexts so that progress is at least good in each key stage. Pupils independently explore and experiment with techniques, tactics and compositional ideas in different types of physical activity to produce outstanding outcomes. They show significant levels of originality, imagination or creativity in their understanding and skills within the subject'.

Quality of teaching. Inspectors must consider 'how well pupils understand how to improve their learning as a result of frequent, detailed and accurate feedback from teachers following assessment of their learning' and 'the extent to which teachers' questioning and use of discussion promote learning'. Also important is 'the extent to which teachers use their expertise, including their subject knowledge, to develop pupils' knowledge, skills and understanding across a range of subjects and areas of learning', and 'the quality of teaching and other support provided for pupils with arrange of aptitudes and needs, including disabled pupils and those who have special educational needs, so that their learning improves (p. 11).

Grade descriptors for *Outstanding* require that 'much of the teaching in all key stages and most subjects is outstanding and never less than consistently good. As a result, almost all pupils are making rapid and sustained progress . . .' Consequently, pupils learn exceptionally well across the curriculum. (p. 12). PE subject specific guidance states . . . (teachers) use a very wide range of innovative and imaginative resources and teaching strategies to stimulate all pupils' active participation in their learning and secure outstanding progress across all aspects of the subject. Teachers ensure that pupils of all abilities learn new skills, find out how to use them in different ways, and link them to accurately repeat actions, sequences or team tactics.

Behaviour and safety. Inspectors must consider pupils' attitudes to learning and conduct in lessons and around the school and 'how well teachers manage the behaviour and expectations of pupils to ensure that all pupils have an equal and fair chance to thrive and learn in an atmosphere of respect and dignity' (p. 14).

Grade descriptors for *Outstanding* require that 'pupils make an exceptional contribution to a safe, positive learning environment. [. . .] Pupils show very high levels of engagement, courtesy, collaboration and co-operation in and out of lessons' (p. 16).

Leadership and management. Inspectors must consider whether the school's leadership improves teaching and learning, including the management of pupils' behaviour (p. 18).

Grade descriptors for *Outstanding* require that 'the school's curriculum provides highly positive, memorable experiences and rich opportunities for high quality learning' (p. 18). This section has important implications for senior leaders and also PE curriculum leaders in schools.

TASK: USING OFSTED GRADE DESCRIPTORS OF HQPE EXPERIENCES

Read Ofsted's PE subject specific grade descriptors for PE. Use these not as a checklist but as a 'best fit' and consider how these relate to HQPE experiences in your school.

School sport and sport partnerships

Sport has become a part of twenty-first-century life in the UK as never before. Team GB's successes in both the Olympic and Paralympics Games in 2012 have left a legacy that reverberates into our political, social and economic life, leisure and into education. As a nation we have due cause for celebration. The *Mail Online* (2012) reported that the impact of London's staging of the Olympic and Paralympic Games led to record numbers of men and women playing sport every week. The Active People Survey results covering the year to October 2012 showed that 15.5 million people aged 16 and over play sport each week, a rise of 750,000 compared to 2011 and an increase of 1.57 million from when London won the right to host the Games in 2005. The effect of the successes of these Games, where stars such as Jessica Ennis, Mo Farah, David Weir and Sarah Storey captured the public's imagination, can be seen in increased participation levels after the Games, with cycling, sailing and volleyball gaining a boost in numbers. More disabled people are taking part in sport at least once a week. (*Mail Online*, 6 December 2012).

More funding has been made available to community projects such as Street Games, receiving £20 million. The youth participation strategy, Creating a Sporting Habit for Life, is expected to create a further 1,000 local sports clubs over the next 4 years, and expected to reach 100,000 teenagers who might otherwise turn to crime. In the euphoria generated by the London Games we are urged to seize this one in a lifetime opportunity to tackle social problems, or at least look at them from a new perspective. But is the unifying power of sport exaggerated? Can deeper social and political issues affecting the nation be solved on the sports field?

The Government is clear that competitive sport brings out the best in everyone, from future Olympians to the child who wants to keep fit and have fun through learning new sports and games. Competitive school sport for children is at the heart of the Olympics legacy. The Prime Minister believes that Government has a role to play in capitalising on the inspiration of the Olympics to foster a culture of more competitive sports in our schools. He wants a whole school sporting ethos that gives pupils the skills to enjoy and take part in sport inside and outside of school and extends to local leagues, community and sports clubs. Since 2010, the Coalition has encouraged competitive sport, especially through the creation of the Schools Games, designed to build upon and further the legacy of the 2012 Olympics by promoting intra- and inter-school competition. The Prime Minister is expected to announce a multi-million pound cash boost of around £150 million in order to secure this Olympic legacy, with a large proportion of the money going to Primary schools that are viewed as being under-resourced and ill-equipped to teach PE properly.

Again, all well and good but something of a U-turn. The DfE had just recently removed the duty on schools to report whether they had met the two-hours-a-week school sports target, issuing a statement that it was more of an unenforceable aspiration. The PE and Sport Survey (Quick et al., 2010) found 55 per cent of pupils participated in at least three hours of high quality PE and out of hours school sport during the 2009/10 academic year. This means there has been an encouraging increase of 5 per cent on the previous year's survey. Participation levels are highest in Years 4–6, and also reasonably high in Years 1–3.

Despite the move to stop monitoring whether schools were meeting the target, the Secretary of State was clear that he expected schools to carry on spending as much time on sport as before, maintaining as a minimum the current levels of PE and sport each week for every pupil.

There were no plans to re-commission the Youth Sports Trust after 2011, despite the excellent work in Primary schools through the TOPs programmes, professional development programmes based on quality teaching and learning in physical education in Primary schools in England.. Education Minister Michael Gove ended the £162 million PE and Sports Strategy of the previous administration to give schools time and freedom to focus on providing competitive sport. The Coalition Government wish to encourage more competitive sport in schools, as a vibrant part of the life and ethos of all schools. Yet sport and PE are not the same and must not be seen as such. In sport there is a focus on competition and performance. It has precise outcomes. Sport, though using many of the same activities as PE, is usually taken to mean competitive sport and often high-level competition – the province of a coach with a narrower remit than a teacher who pursues a multiplicity of objectives (Williams, 1989). Physical education in schools is about the broader outcomes discussed in the opening chapter of this book that have the potential to benefit all pupils – not just a talented minority. PE has a different purpose to sport and uses different teaching methods. Look at the DfE website and you will see the very clear direction for school sport that is to de-centralise power and incentivise competitive sport. The words of the new PE curriculum are testimony to this direction where in the Purpose of Study it talks of pupils succeeding and excelling in competitive sport (DfE, 2013, p. 3). This is likely to put extra pressure on Primary and Secondary teachers to win trophies and achieve sporting success to enhance school reputations. It may also divert energy away from the pressures and accountabilities over performance in core subjects in Primary schools.

We believe that the solution is to learn from the successes of School Sport Partnerships (SSPs) and build new partnerships with sports clubs, community groups and other local organisations to stimulate participation and competition in PE and sports. The now discontinued Physical Education, School Sport and Club Links (PESSCL) strategy was begun in October 2002 to enhance the take-up of sporting opportunities for 5 to 16 year olds and to improve the standards of teaching, coaching and learning in physical education and school sport. It had many successes and was later replaced by the Physical Education and Sports Strategy for Young People, which was launched in January 2008. There are many lessons to be learned from the different partnership arrangements and school-community links with clubs, governing bodies, sport associations and local authorities. It is now timely to take this forward.

In the publication *School Sport Partnerships. A survey of good practice* (Ofsted, 2011), inspectors reported a number of common characteristics in the schools visited, which can be identified as key to generating success and bringing about improvements in sport and physical activity. Where there were strong partnerships between schools, local authorities, leisure services, sports organisations and local clubs, these partners formulated a shared vision of high quality PE and sports opportunities. They led by example, worked strategically with headteachers and school staff to promote collaboration and liaised with a wide range of organisations, agencies and volunteers. They brokered arrangements between schools and other organisations to pool resources, source grant monies and invest funds in local projects and events. Importantly they built relations with young people likely to disengage from school or whose lifestyles placed them at risk helping them to re-engage in PE and sport. Their knowledge and skills drove up improvements in school sport and PE and their work had noticeable positive effects on pupil confidence, self-esteem and attitudes towards learning into other subjects. Effective partnerships generated local sustainability by encouraging parents, carers and teaching assistants to gain qualifications and lead lunchtime and after-school clubs and created a local forum for teachers and assistants to plan and access a range of professional development and training. SSPs played an important role in the professional development of teachers providing a regular forum for PE teachers.

One such example of partnership working reported was in Chorley where the SSP and the local authority worked together to improve the quality of teaching and learning in PE in Primary schools by implementing a common scheme of work for PE. This involved joint planning and co-ordinated training for staff to help improve Primary teachers' understanding of PE and added greater consistency and coherence to the provision in Key Stages 1 and 2. A scheme of work was produced, which included procedures for assessing pupils' progress and sharing this information with secondary school staff to aid pupils' transition from Year 6 to Year 7. The vignette below captures this collaboration and impact.

School Sport Co-ordinators and coaches worked alongside teachers to assess the skills, fitness and aptitude of pupils in Year 6. Pupils were given a score for each core task to indicate whether they were working towards, meeting, or exceeding expected levels. This provided Primary teachers with an overview of how well individual pupils were achieving. School Sport Co-ordinators and teachers discussed their assessments to check their accuracy. The information was shared with Secondary school teachers before pupils arrived in Year 7. It was used as a baseline to determine ability groups for PE and informed the Key Stage 3 curriculum so that plans were matched with pupils' starting points. In this way, learning built upon what pupils already knew and could do rather than repeating work done in Key Stage 2.

Critical thinking in PE

Encouraging children to think and improve the quality of their thinking has been a central aim of education since the days of Plato. In the twentieth century, the belief among many educational theorists was that thinking and indeed intelligence were fixed, and therefore strategies to improve children's capacity to think and learn were not pursued by those responsible for the design or implementation of curricula. This was to change towards information–processing and constructivist views on learning as described earlier. Such a view perceives learners as actively seeking out meaning, constructing knowledge of the world through interactions with their environment through organisation of their mental structures. The thinking process is comprised of sets of discreet skills organised hier-archically. These are linked to knowledge and are combined in different ways to yield what we know as thinking operations or processes (Swartz and Perkins, 1990).

A focus upon thinking skills is desirable primarily because it supports active cognitive processing and the result is better learning from pupils. It enables them to search out meaning and to deal systematically yet flexibly with problems and new situations and to communicate this understanding. Current emphasis on raising standards in school and in preparing young people for lifelong learning recognise the importance of deepening pupils' thinking. This is also timely as we as educators strive to unpack the latest version of a new National Curriculum.

Terms like *know, presume, believe, comprehend, guess, ponder, consider, cogitate* and *theorise* are just a few examples of the diversity within the English language and each of these words could be easily replaced by the word 'think'. To give thinking its *critical* quality, there has to be some sort of hierarchy in these skills to make thinking assume 'critical' level

Despite most attention in critical thinking being focused on traditional classroom settings and subjects, there has been renewed attention paid to the possibility of fostering and reinforcing critical thinking in PE. According to McBride (1995), physical education offers an ideal environment for fostering this aspect of thinking skills.

In applying the taxonomy practically to PE, it may be helpful to consider a series of *trigger words* that can be used for each of the six categories. Suggestions are as follows:

Knowledge	Comprehension	Application	Analysis	Synthesis	Evaluation
Tell	Discuss	Apply	Point out	Adapt	Assess
Describe	Explain	Produce	Arrange	Plan	Choose
List	Compare	Complete	Categorise	Invent	Prove
Identify	Contrast	Change	Separate	Develop	Conclude
Name	Interpret	Discover	Classify	Devise	Test
Show	Outline	Use	Select	Generate	Measure
Label	Estimate	Solve	Infer	Combine	Decide
Recall	Predict	Construct	Connect	Make up	Support
Record	Review	Transfer	Examine	Initiate	Appraise
Reproduce	Summarise	Demonstrate	Distinguish	Compose	Judge

Findings by Ennis (1991) revealed that some teachers positively seek to encourage cognitive thinking in a movement context with Primary age pupils. Cleland (1994) found that when young children used critical thinking strategies performance in movement patterns was significantly improved. Other literature lends support to the contribution of critical thinking in PE. Any model of critical thinking will require students to think about what they are learning and to compare and explain their ideas to arrive at a deeper understanding of new information. Buscher (1990) talked about thinking and moving as co-equal partners. Tishman and Perkins (1995) most certainly agreed when they identified thinking processes of reasoning, reflecting, strategising, and planning as part of critical thinking critically in PE. Greenockle and Purvis (1995) advocated that PE provides an excellent vehicle for addressing issues of physical fitness and health behaviours where students are encouraged to reason about their own fitness and health, examine models of good/poor practice and employ decision-making skills in the process.

Components of thinking, skills and dispositions linked to rules and strategies for use are intertwined to produce effective thinking and movement (Clancy, 2006). She identifies four main categories in relation to PE:

1   Acquiring Knowledge – necessary to store, organise and recall memories, to solve movement challenges and understand movement concepts and fitness principles.

2   Creative Thinking – concerned with generating new ideas, such as producing new movement combinations in Gymnastics and Dance. It involves risk taking, seeing things from different perspectives and being adventurous (Swartz and Perkins, 1990).

3   Critical thinking – answers the question 'Why?' This involves suspending judgement, reasoning, using evidence to make judgements and evaluations.

4   Metacognition – this is literally thinking about thinking. In an example where a pupil is asked to identify how he or she arrived at a creative movement by talking through what the thinking involved to come to this.

Examples of these specific skills presented by Clancy (2006) in relation to movement and PE are shown in Table 4.2.

TABLE 4.2 Thinking skills in relation to movement and PE

Thinking processes

Acquiring knowledge	Creative thinking	Critical thinking	Metacognition

Practical Examples

Acquiring knowledge	Creative thinking	Critical thinking	Metacognition
Remembering 'Who can remember what we learned today?'	**Divergent reasoning** 'How many different ways can you pass the ball?'	**Conditional reasoning** 'For us to produce this movement pattern, what has to happen?'	**Identifying** 'What thinking skill are we using here?'
Classifying 'Decide which exercises are appropriate for a warm up'	**Being original** 'Can you develop a new way to skip?'	**Viewing from different perspectives** 'How would you do this move if you were a hip-hop dancer?'	**Deciding** 'What thinking processes will you need to use to complete this problem?'
Ordering 'Be sure your dance has a beginning, middle and end'	**Elaborating** 'Now add two changes of level'	**Identifying personal bias** 'Why do you like the first movement activities more than the second?'	**Paying attention** 'What are the steps we need to follow to develop this exercise sequence?'
Comparing and contrasting 'How is this movement different or the same?'	**Composing** 'Put these individual gymnastic movements together in a new way'		**Reflection on one's thinking** 'How did the thinking process you used work in designing this dance?'
Generalising 'All of the games this week have what in common?'		**Evaluating** 'How did your team perform?'	
Analysing 'What moves are part of a lay-up?'			
Applying 'Use this move in a game situation'			

Thinking skills related to P.E may be exemplified in the following ways:

1 *Information-processing skills*
Skills here involve sorting, classifying, sequencing and decision-making. In different areas of activity pupils will encode information from the environment and process it to implement a particular course of action. In a Games lesson with a Year 1 class for example, the children might be asked to move across the working space safely carrying a ball in a variety of different ways. In this task pupils will have to decide which skills to employ to carry the ball as well as continually process information concerning changes in the environment so as to move across the space safely and effectively.

2 *Reasoning skills*
These skills are associated with justifying reasons, judging, giving opinions and deducing based on the information available. A small group of Year 5 pupils might be asked to

compose a dance using a given stimulus and later explain their reasons for constructing it as they did. Reasoning skills are required by the pupils in this context in understanding the nature of the task set, considering how best to tackle it, constructing the motif and reporting their decisions.

3   Enquiry skills

Pupils asking questions, defining problems, predicting outcomes and planning how to research further information form the basis of these skills. Pupils in Year 6 might be given the research task of finding out information on joints and muscles using different search engines on the internet as part of a project. The group need knowledge of what possible search engines to use, understanding of how these are used and how to collate the information once it has been accessed.

4   Creative-thinking skills

These skills enable pupils to initiate ideas, suggest alternatives and look for other possible outcomes using their imagination and innovation. In Gymnastics, a Year 6 class might be required individually to devise a short sequence of movements involving a jump, a roll and a balance on apparatus showing two changes of body shape. To perform this task the pupils are able to demonstrate their creativity in their selection of each specific skill, the addition of the shape dynamic to the sequence and the linking actions to be performed between each skill.

5   Evaluation skills

These are the skills of observing, copying, judging what is observed, matching perform-ance against criteria and reporting on these evaluations. In a swimming class with Year 4, pupils could be asked to observe a teacher demonstration of the breast-stroke arm action, perform it themselves and comment upon a partner's execution of it. After watching the teacher perform the stroke pattern pupils must copy it matching the correct technique as closely as possible. They must then observe a partner executing the technique and comment upon how this was performed and suggest how this might be improved. Apart from the technicalities of the action itself observation, analysis and oral skills are being developed here.

Existing literature reporting on critical thinking within physical education is scarce and yet the potential for exploring it is largely untapped. It prompts many important questions such as:

- How can children learn to employ critical thinking strategies in their PE lessons?
- What skills do they need to possess and how do they enjoy lessons in which critical thinking plays a significant part?
- How can teachers include critical thinking in PE in an already over full curriculum?

Continuity of learning: EYFS into National Curriculum

The term 'transition' has many meanings and is not readily captured in a single definition. One possible definition might be that a transition is a key event taking place at a specific period or turning point in the life course. Transitions can be thought of in terms of vertical and horizontal 'passages' (Kagan and Neuman, 1998) where 'vertical' is associated with an upwards shift such as moving from the EYFS into Year 1 or from Year 6 into Year 7 at Secondary age. Horizontal transitions are less clear and refer to children's routine movements on a daily basis, such as their journey to and from home to school.

Research has tended to think of transitions as a 'one-point' event such as the first day at school, but since the late 1990s, research now sees transitions as a multi-layered and multi-year process, involving multiple continuities and discontinuities of experience (Petriwsky et al., 2005). They are generally associated with changes in physical and social space, cultural beliefs, and practices.

Children's progress from the EYFS into Primary school is best when both 'phases' have a shared understanding of pedagogy and adopt a consistency of approach, responding to children's developing needs and abilities with appropriate challenge and support. There should be understanding that the EYFS and the National Curriculum are mechanisms for supporting children's progressive learning, and there is a clear linkage between them. Curriculum continuity must be ensured so that individual progression in learning is maximised and all staff are supported to develop their skills in day-to-day and periodic assessment, so that informed professional judgements about children's progress can be shared and built on.

In 2012 after a comprehensive review the EYFS was revised (DfE, 2012) with a division in its framework between the Prime Areas of learning and the applied or Specific Areas of learning. It is differentiated between child development and subject knowledge, where the Prime Areas concentrate on child development and the Specific Areas constructed around the knowledge, skills and understanding associated with school subjects linking into the programmes of study in the National Curriculum for Key Stage 1 (Langston and Doherty, 2012).

Four guiding principles shape practice in the early years:

1   every child is a unique child, who is constantly learning and can be resilient, capable, confident and self-assured;
2   children learn to be strong and independent through positive relationships;
3   children learn and develop well in enabling environments, in which their experiences respond to their individual needs and there is a strong partnership between practitioners and parents and/or carers;
4   children develop and learn in different ways and at different rates. The framework covers the education and care of all children in early years provision, including children with special educational needs and disabilities.

Physical development is one of the three Prime Areas of learning within the revised EYFS framework and provides opportunities for young children to be active and interactive and to develop their co-ordination, control and movement. Children must also be helped to understand the importance of physical activity, and to make healthy choices in relation to food. It is set out under two aspects.

1   *Moving and Handling* – this is about children showing control and co-ordination in large and small movements. It recognises that children move confidently in a range of ways, safely negotiating space. They handle equipment and tools effectively, including pencils for writing.

2   *Health and Self-Care* – children must know the importance for good health of physical exercise, and a healthy diet, and talk about ways to keep healthy and safe. They manage their own basic hygiene and personal needs successfully, including dressing and going to the toilet independently.

The fact that physical development is recognised as a Prime area in the revised EYFS is welcomed. It cements its status that it is fundamental to children's learning and development. It is also a vital component for school readiness. PE in the early years is concerned with improving co-ordination, control, manipulation, movement skills and being active. It also recognises that increases can be expected in confidence levels, self-esteem and in developing a sense of wellbeing. In the EYFS children learn primarily through play and often it is difficult for an observer to distinguish between the two. The nature of play changes as children mature. Children under 2 play alone and scarcely interact with others, whereas children from 3 to 5 engage in associative play where there is some interaction, usually in mixed-sex groups. This leads to cooperative play with shared goals, normally in single-sex groups, as they enter Primary school (Miller *et al.*, 2005). It may be helpful to categorise play in two forms: free play or structured play. In free play, children set their own agenda and pace as well as controlling it themselves. For example, a 4 year old on a trike may choose to roam quite freely inside a safe area and has control over speed, direction or distance. Structured play, in contrast, is play directed by the practitioner who structures the learning environment for the child and is clear about the engagement of the child in this process. An example of this type of play is a 5 year old throwing a beanbag at a target cone. Here, it is the practitioner who controls the object to be thrown, the target, the distance to be thrown, the number of throws and so forth, and directs the child's learning. Both are valid and both have their place in an early years curriculum.

Connecting physical play to the development of physical skills, Maude has this to say, 'play provision should take account of play limitations as well as capabilities, the power of play in facilitating motor skill acquisition and in providing endless opportunities for practice, repetition and refinement of physical skills' (2001, p. 29). Play that promotes physical development can be seen in a child's spontaneous urge to try out physical activities for enjoyment and a sense of mastery in the gross motor skills of running, jumping and climbing and in the fine motor skills of building blocks, mark making and posting shapes in boxes (Anning, 1991). Such play can occur in both indoor and outdoor environments. Since children need sustained periods of time to develop their movement skills, frequent use of the outdoor area is needed and preferably on a daily basis. In resourcing outdoor physical play, the following might well appear:

■   a space large enough for children to run around freely that promotes vigorous heart fitness;

■ large apparatus that offers challenging climbing opportunities –tyres, tunnels, a climbing frame, planks, etc.;

■ a space for wheeled toys –prams, trikes, trucks, trolleys;

■ small apparatus such as beanbags, quoits and hoops to develop co-ordination and balance;

■ different surfaces such as grass, tarmac, bark;

■ quiet areas for refection with blankets or mats;

■ places to hide such as natural areas or even large cardboard boxes;

■ a wild area to explore freely;

■ a garden area.

TASK: AUDITING OUTDOOR PLAY EQUIPMENT

Analyse the provision for outdoor play in your own setting. Compile an inventory of equipment currently in use. What other equipment might be required to supplement the current provision? Make a list.

Outdoor physical play has a great deal to offer children. It contributes to all areas of children's development and to all areas of the early years curriculum. With careful planning, links can be made between indoor and outdoor learning so that children view it as not just a time to 'let off steam'. Creative practitioners can make stimulating environments that are rich with opportunities to promote physical skills and enjoyable, purposeful activity. Table 4.3 lists some practical suggestions that emphasise learning through outdoor play.

With the revised EYFS there is continued recognition that its principles and practice have much to offer later years of school. Approaches to learning and teaching in the early years are directly relevant to Key Stage 1 and 2 and many teachers welcome the interface between the two. In physical education, however, this interface has highlighted a number of differences in teaching and learning, which has resulted in some confusion as to what physical education children should be receiving. Some of the differences in approaches to teaching and learning in PE between the EYFS and Key Stage 1 are neatly summarised by Lavin (2003) and are presented in Table 4.4. (Readers should note that this refers to the previous Foundation Stage curriculum but the same principles still apply.)

Lavin's findings are worrying. As a profession we do need to agree on how our subject is defined and communicate that message to others both inside and outside the profession. An immediate stumbling block is in the interpretation of the framework that shows obvious differences in what and how the subject should be taught. The questions for refection at the end of the section ask you to consider this with regard to lack of consistency between PE in the early years curriculum and PE in the National Curriculum.

The revised EYFS identifies physical development as a key area of learning and development. By combining and encouraging children to be active and healthy, the building blocks of future physical education are laid. This broad base provides a vital

TABLE 4.3 Maximising physical development through outdoor play

Type of outdoor activity	Examples to use in practice
Class games	■ What time is it Mr Wolf? ■ The farmer's in his den ■ Grandma's footsteps ■ Hide and seek ■ Ring-a-ring o' roses
Large apparatus	■ using swings ■ using slides ■ playing on see-saws ■ free play on climbing frames ■ moving through tunnels
Small apparatus	■ handling beanbags, balls, quoits and hoops ■ bouncing large balls ■ throwing and catching, kicking ■ rolling a small ball or beanbag to a target ■ balance boards ■ using skipping ropes
Parachute games	■ passing it around the group ■ passing it around at different levels ■ making waves ■ changing places with a friend inside the canopy ■ bouncing a teddy on top of the chute ■ moving the chute while reciting nursery rhymes
Wheeled toys	■ steering bikes along straight lines on the ground ■ pedalling trikes or go-carts around curves ■ exploring the use of wheelbarrows, trolleys, prams, push-me pull-me vehicles and buggies on the flat and up/down slopes ■ loading materials on to trailers ■ setting up traffic systems that include roundabouts, traffic lights and road signs
Trails and courses	■ take the children on a walk around the local park ■ simple activity circuits to include running, jumping, balancing skills ■ playground markings, e.g. compass points, snakes and ladders, stepping stones, etc.

continued

TABLE 4.3 *continued*

Type of outdoor activity	Examples to use in practice
	■ treasure hunts ■ obstacle courses with tunnels, slides, tyres
Other equipment	■ using space hoppers ■ practising with stilts ■ building with large crates of different sizes and different materials ■ moving on pogo sticks ■ exploring a tree house or disused boat ■ supervised play in a paddling pool

TABLE 4.4 Teaching and learning in PE in the Foundation Stage and Key Stage 1

Foundation Stage Physical Development			National Curriculum PE Key Stage 1		
Play-centred	Exploration	Experimentation	Skill focus	Teacher-directed	Subject-based
Wide range of equipment	Creativity	Autonomy	Developing, selecting and applying skills	Limited equipment/ apparatus	Co-operative working
Manipulation	Co-ordination	Confidence	Exercise and health notions	Compositional ideas	Evaluate and improve performance
Increasing control	Respond to rhythm, safety, music, story	Understanding	Watching and listening	Express feelings through movement	Remember and repeat simple skills and actions

Source: Lavin (2003)

foundation for the more structured requirements of PE in the transition into Key Stage 1 and 2 through Dance, Gymnastics and Games activities. The challenge for the profession is to aim for seamlessness and consistency in transition, so that good practice identified in the early years is taken forward into later years and modified and enhanced to meet the changing learning and development needs of Primary children in PE.

Health and physical activity

The childhood years are recognised as important ones for the prevention of obesity since physical activity patterns, eating habits and lifestyle behaviours are largely formed during this period. Despite the benefits of being physically active to development, general health and fitness, the scale of the problem of overweight adults and children is alarming. Overweight and obesity may well represent the most widespread threat to health and wellbeing in this country. A total of 23 per cent of adults are obese (i.e. have body mass index (BMI) of over 30); 61.3 per cent are either overweight or obese (with a BMI of over 25). The trend has been upward over the past decades, although it appears to have now levelled off in children and there are signs of levelling off among younger adults. However, the absolute level of obesity is very high. England, and the rest of the UK, ranks as one of the most obese nations in Europe and there are few signs yet of a sustained decline (NHS, 2011). Obesity remains high on the international political agendas and continues to influence policy.

Having an overweight population matters to individuals and families, to society and the economy. Diabetes, cancer, heart disease, hypertension, osteoarthritis, osteoporosis, anxiety and depression are all associated disorders linked to excess weight. It can reduce people's prospects in life, affect individuals' ability to work, self-esteem and their underlying mental health. Excess weight costs the NHS more than £5 billion each year. It has a serious impact on economic development (NHS, 2011). The problem is not restricted to adults. Far from it. Data from the Health Survey of England's annual survey (NHS, 2010) provides an alarming picture for children:

- Around three in ten boys and girls were classed as either overweight or obese (31 per cent).
- 17 per cent of boys and 15 per cent of girls (aged 2 to 15) were classed as obese, a steady increase from 1995.
- Around one in ten pupils in Reception class were classed as obese (9.4 per cent) and 1 in 5 pupils in Year 6 (19.0 per cent).

Children who are obese in the pre-school years tend to be obese during adolescence and adulthood (CDCP, 2009). Physical inactivity is an endemic social problem. Only 39 per cent of men and 29 per cent of women in the UK meet minimum physical activity recommendations. Children who engage in physical activity during childhood and adolescence are likely to become physically active adults (Schneider and Lounsbery, 2008). Recent UK-wide guidelines from the Chief Medical Officer (DoH, 2011) provide clear recommendations on appropriate levels of physical activity across the life course to achieve a range of health benefits. These guidelines recognise that, as a nation, we are too inactive and spend excessive periods of time being sedentary, and challenge us to change our activity habits.

Early years (under 5s)

1   Physical activity should be encouraged from birth, particularly through floor-based play and water-based activities in safe environments.

2   Children of pre-school age who are capable of walking unaided should be physically active daily for at least 180 minutes (3 hours), spread throughout the day.

3   All under 5s should minimise the amount of time spent being sedentary (being restrained or sitting) for extended periods (except time spent sleeping).

Children and young people (5–18 years)

1   All children and young people should engage in moderate to vigorous intensity physical activity for at least 60 minutes and up to several hours every day.

2   Vigorous intensity activities, including those that strengthen muscle and bone, should be incorporated at least three days a week.

3   All children and young people should minimise the amount of time spent being sedentary (sitting) for extended periods.

Physical activity has had many definitions. The World Health Organisation defined it for children 5 years and above as including 'play, games, sports, transportation, recreation, physical education or planned exercise, in the context of the family, school and community activities (WHO, 2010, p. 17).

Children should participate in physical activities that are appropriate for their age and stage of development. For them exercise patterns are sporadic (Waring, et al., 2007). It is stop-start and as such measuring levels of activity in children is problematic. The Department of Health guidance tells us that patterns of activity in children commonly involve a mixture of running, jumping, climbing, hopping and skipping activities. These brief periods of activity can also develop object-control (catching, throwing, striking, kicking) and stability (balancing) movement skills, as well as contributing to bone and muscle strengthening recommendations. These patterns are characterised by high intensity activity interspersed with short periods of moderate and light activity or standing. These activities of varying intensity can cumulatively contribute towards the recommended 60 minutes a day if they are at least 10 minutes in duration. This is an important point: physical activity can be interspersed throughout the day. Being active can and should occur every day and in different contexts. This ranges from active travel to school, outdoor play in the park, indoor play in dedicated play centres, physical education, school play-time, participation in sports and Dance clubs, swimming or cycling, outdoor activities (for example, girl guides or scout groups) or martial arts clubs. School break times and lunch times are being underutilised in the context of promoting physical activity (Sleap et al.(2000). Ridgers and Stratton (2005) among others have suggested ideas such as maximising the use of school grounds; introducing creative playground markings; allocating particular areas of the playground to different groups and activities; using lunchtime supervisors to teach children active games; and making small equipment available on a regular basis to help.

Parental influences are also important through the opportunities that are provided for children and families to be active together. Physical activity can be structured or unstructured. Unstructured activity is informal (or free play) and involves activities with little input or direction from parents or carers. (Children under 5 are often extremely active in their play). Structured activity might include elements of formality or facilitation by adults. The Department of Health guidance provides an example of this which is included below.

Peter (aged 7 years)

Peter is the youngest child in a sporty family. They live in a bustling town with good local amenities. His father and mother are active members of the local football club, where his brother, James, excels at under-14 level. His 11-year-old sister, Jane, is also an active member of the local dance school and represents her school at netball and athletics. On weekdays, he does at least 60 minutes of moderate to vigorous physical activity. He walks to school with his older sister. On arrival, he often joins in with playground games such as tag, as well as bone strengthening activities such as hopscotch. He has PE twice a week, where he develops his strength during gymnastics and his aerobic fitness during games. He also plays football during playtime on most days. During lessons, his teacher uses active learning approaches to reduce the amount of time Peter and his classmates spend sitting. After school on a Wednesday, he walks to dance school with his sister and best friend, John, where he develops his movement and rhythm skills through fun dance activities. His mother normally picks them up by car from dance school during the winter months but occasionally walks the mile home with them during the spring and summer. Peter has swimming lessons on Saturday mornings and plays tag-rugby on Sundays. During his free time, he enjoys playing video games, but his mother limits this to short periods. On Sundays, the family normally walk to visit their grandmother, who lives a mile away and Peter, his father and brother play football in the park opposite his grandmother's house, whatever the weather.

It is widely accepted that attempting to encourage young people to be physically active as part of a strategy to tackle obesity is far from straightforward. Accepting responsibility for the popularity of physical activity among young people is one thing but accountability falls collectively on a number of groups, including parents, manufacturers, retailers, advertisers, policy legislators at all levels and pupils themselves. Policymakers concerned with prevention of obesity seem to be intuitively drawn to physical education as an important intervention (Pate, 2011). What is the role of schools and of the PE profession in tackling the reported obesity 'epidemic'?

Professional development can provide opportunities to support schools in tackling obesity and other lifestyle issues by helping them access up to date knowledge about evidence-based interventions in schools and local communities. Part of the Teaching Schools programme is the role that these schools can play a part in supporting pupils' health and wellbeing. Many Primary schools choose to be healthy schools and take a whole-school approach to physical activity, nutrition, wellbeing and health education. The School Games will create the opportunity for every school and every pupil to participate in competitive sport. The Ofsted survey *Healthy schools, healthy children?* (2006) found that many schools are already making a valuable contribution to pupils' health and wellbeing. Reporting on physical education, inspectors found that almost every school visited promoted the importance of physical activity well. A central aim of the most successful schools was to encourage pupils to understand the part physical activity played in a healthy life. A strong ethos encouraged and promoted participation and fun. At least a third of the schools had achieved Activemark accreditation or similar, to recognise and reward commitment to providing good physical activity and promoting its benefits. The best provision in Primary schools was in schools with qualified specialist PE co-ordinators who led the subject and promoted physical activity in PE programmes.

Schools which promoted physical activity well, particularly Primary schools, encouraged it in lessons and out-of-hours clubs, but also as an integral part of the school day.

Playtimes were active. Pupils enjoyed the exercise and were encouraged to take responsibility for organising their own small games. Schools realised that engaging pupils in physical activity reduced behaviour problems during breaks and, often, in subsequent lessons. Schools with good provision usually had a whole-school emphasis on healthy living that included encouraging pupils, especially those in Primary schools, to walk or cycle to school. Primary school teachers involved in these schemes felt that the partnerships with the local sports colleges had helped to increase the confidence, knowledge and skills of staff in teaching PE. Links with local coaches had extended the range of activities and out-of-hours provision. In the survey schools, such links resulted in the introduction of Rugby, Gymnastics, Dance, Indoor Athletics, and 'Kwik Cricket'. Sports coaches acted as good role models for pupils. Pupils engaged positively with them during lessons and were keen to stay for the after-school clubs, which they also led.

The following vignette was captured as part of this survey and illustrates good practice in a health-promoting school.

The new Programmes of Study for PE have two aims relating directly to physical activity to ensure all pupils are 1) physically active for sustained periods of time and 2) lead healthy, active lives.

The ideas above are sound ways for schools to engage pupils in being more active. Waring et al. (2007) believes there is now an ideal opportunity to focus on Primary schools as a key target group for the future. They believe it is imperative that children are introduced to and allowed to explore developmentally appropriate learning experiences around an active lifestyle. They also see the PE lesson as pivotal to this. Citing Fairclough and Stratton (2006), the PE lesson is a regular window of opportunity for young children to be involved in physical activity at moderate and vigorous intensities. There is a number of challenges for physical educators to take forward. Subject knowledge is essential to deliver challenging lessons that enhance physical activity levels. Instructional strategies that do not focus so heavily on skill acquisition. Strategies to engage all pupils. Lesson plans that allow pupils to master skills that they could then apply in more challenging contexts and lessons that encourage all pupils to be active outside competitive sport, which is so clearly emphasised in the new PE National Curriculum.

If it is not the role of physical education to inspire young people and equip them to take up activity, then what is its role? As Armour (2006) points out, the challenge associated with being accountable is that we are forced to confront the consequences of our actions.

INCREASING PHYSICAL ACTIVITY IN A PRIMARY SCHOOL

The school entered the 'Golden Boot' award, a competition which aims to increase the numbers of pupils walking or cycling to school. A prize is awarded to the class in each school that scores the highest number of points. Most points are awarded for walking and cycling while pupils arriving in a car receive a negative score.

The school also introduced a skipping workshop. First, demonstrations were given at assembly and pupils had a chance to copy the steps. An after-school club was attended by 100 pupils from across the school. Rhymes were taught to accompany the skipping games. Morning break and lunchtimes were characterised by pupils singing and skipping.

In PE this means facing up to the harsh reality that continuing with a traditional programme and traditional pedagogy in the face of a changing world is not sustainable. In a climate in which young people expect to exercise choice, exhibit sophisticated tastes and have a huge array of interests competing for their limited leisure time, a traditional PE programme is rendered meaningless for the vast majority of young people. Accepting the challenge of accountability ultimately means that PE will in the medium- to long-term have to change what it claims, what it does, or both. To ensure that we make the right decisions, the challenge for the short term is to nurture a culture of evidence-based practice within PE and embed systems for collecting evidence of the impact of the PE programme on pupils' lives.

Chapter summary

PE in schools is at a cross roads. The issues discussed in this chapter are some of many that lie ahead for teachers in schools. At the heart is a renewed focus on teaching and learning in the subject. It is time to reconsider exactly what high-quality physical education experiences are for pupils and how these extend throughout the Primary years. The PESSCL strategy is no longer, but we must embrace new partnerships and continue to build links with other schools and organisations. School sport is re-emphasised in the new curriculum for PE but it must not dominate it. Providing movement challenges in each practical activity area that require pupils to think, make decisions and to justify their reasons are essential. A recently revised EYFS framework highlights physical development as a Prime Area of learning. The challenge as ever is to unify this curricular framework with National Curriculum so learning is seamless and continuous. With obesity levels rising in children in almost every country, eyes again turn to teachers to address and for school PE to resolve.

Questions for reflection

- Is physical activity increased by pupils' participation in physical education classes?
- Does physical education provide short-term health benefits?
- Does physical education provide long-term health benefits?
- What professional development might you need so that your teaching of PE provides health promoting benefits for all pupils?
- How do the issues raised in this chapter relate to your own teaching of PE?
- These are some contemporary issues. What 'new' issues do you foresee arising in the future?
- Are there CPD needs for you or colleagues in school that become evident on reading and reflecting on this chapter?

Further reading

Armour, K.M. and Duncombe, R. (2004) Teachers' continuing professional development in primary physical education: Lessons from present and past to inform the future. *Physical Education and Sport Pedagogy*, 9(1), pp. 3–22.

Green, K. (2008) *Understanding Physical Education*. London: Sage.

Jess, M. (1012) The future of primary physical education: A 3–14 developmental and connected curriculum. In G. Griggs (ed.) *An Introduction to Primary Physical Education*. London; Routledge.

Harris, J. and Penney, D. (2002) Research in physical education: Priority areas for investigation. *British Journal of Teaching Physical Education*, 33(2), pp. 6–10.

Hayden-Davies, D., Jess, M. and Pickup, I. (2007) The challenges and potential within primary physical education, *Physical Education Matters,* 2(1), pp. 12–15.

Kay, W. (2005) 'A rose by any other name, but physical education and sport are not the same'. *The Bulletin of Physical Education,* 41(1), pp. 15–22.

Kirk, D. (2010) *Physical Education Futures*. London: Routledge.

Lawrence, J. (2012) *Teaching Primary Physical Education*. London: Sage.

Marsden, E. and Weston, C. (2007) Locating quality physical education in early years pedagogy. *Sport, Education and Society,* 12, pp. 383–98.

Ofsted (2005) *Physical Education in Primary Schools*. London: HMSO.

Ofsted (2009) *Physical Education in Schools 2005/8: Working Towards 2012 and Beyond*. London: HMSO.

References

Anning, A. (1991) *The First Years at School*. Milton Keynes: Open University Press

Armour, K. (2006) 'On being accountable: A challenge to physical education teachers and PE-CPD providers'. *New P.E. and Sports Dimension 2.*

Bruner, J. (1972) *The Relevance of Education*. London: Allen and Unwin.

Buschner, C.A. (1990) 'Can we help children move and think critically?' In W.S. Stinson (ed.) *Moving and Learning for the Young Child*. Reston, VA: AAHPERD.

Casbon, C., Walters, L. and Penney, D. (2003) 'Physical education and school sport: a quality debate'. *British Journal of Teaching Physical Education, 34*(3): 6–10.

Centers for Disease, Control and Prevention. (2009) *Obesity Prevalence among Low-income, Pre-school-aged children* (Mobility and Mortality Weekly Report). www.cdc.gov/mmwr/preview/mmwrhtml/mm5828a1.htm (accessed 2 March 2013).

Clancy, M.E. (2006) *Active bodies, Active Brains. Building Thinking Skills through Physical Activity*. Champaign, IL: Human Kinetics.

Cleland, F. (1994) 'Young childrens' divergent movement ability – Study II'. *Journal of Teaching in Physical Education, 13*(3): 228–41.

Department of Health (2011) *Start Active, Stay Active: A Report on Physical Activity for Health from the Four Home Countries' Chief Medical Officers*. London: DoH.

Department for Education (2013) *Physical Education. Programmes of Study for Key Stages 1–4*. February. London: DfE.

DfE (2012) *Statutory Framework for the Early Years Foundation Stage*. March. London: DfE

DfES/DCMS (2004) *High Quality PE and Sport for Young People. A Guide to Recognising and Achieving High Quality PE and Sport in Schools and Clubs*. Available at www.qca.org.uk/pess/pdf/high.quality. guide.pdf (accessed January 2013).

Ennis, C. (1991) 'Discrete thinking skills in two teachers' physical education classes'. *Elementary School Journal*, 91: 473–87.

Fairclough, S. and Stratton, G. (2006) 'Effects of physical education intervention to improve student activity levels'. *Physical Education and Sport Pedagogy*, 11(1): 29–44.

Greenockle, K.M. and Purvis, G.J. (1995) 'Redesigning a secondary school wellness unit using the critical thinking model'. *Journal of Physical Education, Recreation and Dance*. August. pp. 49–52.

Hattie, J. (2011) *Visible Learning for Teachers. Maximizing Impact on Learning*. London: Routledge.

Kagan, S.L. and Neuman, M.J. (1998) 'Lessons from three decades of transition research'. *The Elementary School Journal*, 98(4): 365–379.

Langston, A. and Doherty, J. (2012) *Thinking, Reflecting and Doing. The Revised EYFS in Practice*. London: Featherstone.

Lavin, J. (2003) 'Physical development into physical education: Is it fair play?' In H. Cooper and C. Sixsmith (eds) *Teaching across the Early Years 3–7*. London: RoutledgeFalmer.

Lave, J and Wenger, E. (1991) *Situated Learning: Legitimate Peripheral Participation*. Cambridge: Cambridge University Press.

McBride, R.E. (1995) 'Critical thinking – An idea whose time has come'. *Journal of Physical Education, Recreation and Dance*, 66(6): 22–3.

Mail Online (2012) 'Ennis and Wiggins help inspire a generation as participation in sport rises after London Games' (6 December). Available online at www.dailymail.co.uk/sport/othersports/article-2244007/London-Olympics-sees-surge-men-women-playing-sport-weekly-basis.html (accessed 15 August).

Maude, P. (2001) *Physical Children, Active Teaching. Investigating physical literacy*. Buckingham: Open University Press.

Miller, L., Cable, C. and Devereux, J. (2005) *Developing Early Years Practice*. London: David Fulton.

NHS Information Centre (2010) *Health Survey for England – 2010: Trend Tables*. Available at: www.ic.nhs.uk/pubs/hse10trends (accessed January 2013).

NHS (2011) *Healthy lives, Healthy People. A Call to Action on Obesity in England*. London: DoH.

Ofsted (2006) *Healthy Schools, Healthy Children? The Contribution of Education to Pupils' Health and Wellbeing*. HMI 2563. Manchester: Ofsted.

Ofsted (2011) *School Sport Partnerships. A Survey of Good Practice*. Manchester: Ofsted.

Ofsted (2012) *The Framework for School Inspection. The Framework for Inspecting Schools in England under Section 5 of the Education Act 2005*. Manchester: Ofsted.

Pate, R.R., O'Neill, J.R. and McIver, K.L (2011) 'Physical activity and health: Does physical education matter?' *Quest*, 63(1): 19–35.

Petriwskyj, A., Thorpe, K. andTaylor, C. (2005) 'Trends in construction of transition to school in three Western regions 1990–2004'. *International Journal of Early Years Education* 13(1): 55–69.

Quick, S., Simon, A. and Thornton, A. (2010) *PE and Sport Survey 2009/10*. Ref: DFE-RR032. London: DfE.

Ridgers, N.D. and Stratton, G. (2005) 'Physical activity during school recess: The Liverpool sporting playgrounds project', *Pediatric Exercise Science* 17: 281–90.

Sleap, M., Warburton, P. and Waring, M. (2000) 'Couch potato kids: Lazy layabouts – The role of primary schools in relation to physical activity among children in primary schools'. In A. Williams (ed.) *Primary School Physical Education: Research into Practice*. London: David Fulton Publishers (pp. 31–50).

Schneider, H. and Lounsbery, M. (2008) 'Setting the stage for lifetime physical activity in early childhood'. *Journal of Physical Education, Recreation and Dance,* 79(6): 19–23.

Swartz, R.J. and Perkins, D.N. (1990) *Teaching Thinking: Issues and Approaches*. Pacific Grove, CA: Midwest.

Tishman, S. and Perkins, D. (1995) 'Critical thinking and physical education'. *Journal of Physical Education, Recreation and Dance*. August. pp. 24–30.

Vaughan, R. and Maddern, K. (2013) 'PE is not just a game, UK sport chief says'. *Times Education Supplement,* 8 February 2013.

Waller, T. and Swann, R. (2005) 'Children's learning'. In T. Waller (ed.) *An Introduction to Early Childhood. A Multidisciplinary Approach*. London: Sage.

Waring, M., Warburton, P. and Coy, M. (2007) 'Observation of children's physical activity levels in primary school: Is the school an ideal setting for meeting government activity targets?' *European Physical Education Review* 2007, *13*(1): 25–40

Williams, A. (1989) *Issues in PE for the Primary Years*. Basingstoke: Falmer Press.

World Health Organisation (2010) *Global Recommendations on Physical Activity for Health*. WHO: Geneva.

Wray, D. (2006) 'Looking at learning'. In J. Arthur, T. Grainger and D. Wray, *Learning to Teach in the Primary school*. London: Routledge.

5

Physical education in Key Stage 1

Chapter objectives

By the end of this chapter you should be able to:

- Understand the breadth and scope of PE at Key Stage 1.
- Develop your knowledge of delivering successful learning in Dance, Games and Gymnastics activities.
- Build on information to teach swimming and water-based activities to pupils in the key stage.
- Include the information relating to fitness and health into practical teaching.

Building upon their experiences of moving and being active in the Early Years Foundation Stage, pupils' formal physical education in the National Curriculum begins as they enter Key Stage 1. At this early stage in the PE curriculum the main concern should be to ensure that all pupils enjoy the experience of being physically active. In each of the key stages pupils are expected to know, apply and understand the matters, skills and processes relevant to the Programmes of Study for the key stage. Teachers should exploit pupils' natural enthusiasm for movement and their curiosity about the world in assisting them to become confident, competent and co-ordinated movers. Pupils make best progress when they have regular, high quality and successful activity experiences. These should be planned to ensure that all pupils are suitably challenged and participate in a range of tasks, which should include doing, observing and discussion.

PE in the National Curriculum at Key Stage 1

In this key stage pupils should participate in a range of Dance, Games and Gymnastics activities and Swimming where feasible. Teachers should plan for a progressive and purposeful programme of experiences that stretch pupils physically and intellectually, taking account of their developmental needs. Pupils should develop core movement, become increasingly competent and confident and access a broad range of opportunities to extend their agility, balance and co-ordination, individually and with others. They should be able to engage in competitive (both against self and against others) and co-operative physical activities, in a range of increasingly challenging situations.

Pupils should be taught to:

- master basic movements such as running, jumping, throwing, catching, as well as developing balance, agility and co-ordination, and begin to apply these in a range of activities;
- participate in team games, developing simple tactics for attacking and defending;
- perform dances using simple movement patterns.

Just as all good teachers adjust the level of challenge according to the needs of the pupils in the classroom, in PE all pupils should be set tasks that are appropriately challenging. Teachers should therefore familiarise themselves with simple strategies for differentiating their teaching accordingly. Using the STEP framework is one such strategy. The acronym STEP (space, task, equipment, people) can be a useful reminder to help teachers differentiate activities to help all pupils successfully participate. An example of applying STEP to practical activity in Gymnastics is shown in Table 5.1.

Dance activities

Through dance, teachers can develop pupils' nonverbal communication skills, aesthetic appreciation and artistic expression through movement. Pupils use movement imaginatively, responding to stimuli including music, and performing basic skills such as travelling, being still, making a shape, jumping, turning and gesturing, that show changes in the rhythm, speed, level and direction of their movements. Through experiencing a range of dances from different times and places, by the end of the key stage, pupils should be equipped to create and perform simple dances with confidence. To meet this goal, the teacher needs to have a clear understanding of the dance process. During Key Stage 1, pupils will acquire and develop dance skills through experimenting with a wide range of actions. They will acquire and develop knowledge of basic dance structure and composition through remembering and performing teacher-led dances. As their repertoire of movement skills grows, they will be able to select and apply movements and simple compositional ideas to make changes to dances and eventually create their own dance phrases and simple dances. Through observing dances performed by their classmates they will develop an understanding of high quality movement and begin to recognise what makes a good dance. In so doing, they will develop an appreciation of movement and the effort required to make a dance performance special. The key to good dance composition is the selection of a theme that is meaningful to and excites the imagination of the class. Having identified a topical theme, the quality of the stimuli selected and the discussion that they elicit provides the foundation upon which the dance can be constructed. Introducing one or two stimuli at the start of each lesson to spark ideas and encourage the sharing of thoughts about movement possibilities initiates the composition process.

TABLE 5.1 Applying STEP to practical activities

Practise and repeat a sequence that includes two jumps, a turn and a balance		
STEP	Easier	Harder
Space	In own space	Sharing the space around the room
Task	Copying a set pattern	Invent your own routine
Equipment	On the floor only	Using a mat and a bench
People	Working on own	Working alongside or with a partner/group

---

TASK: DANCE THEMES AND DANCE STIMULI

Select a theme and identify as many different stimuli for it as you can.

KSI theme ideas	Stimuli
■ Nursery rhymes	Visual – pictures, video, colours,
■ Toys	shapes
■ Holidays	Auditory – music, poetry, sound
■ Minibeasts	effects, percussion
■ Pirates	Tactile – textiles, textures, props
■ Dinosaurs	Kinaesthetic – motif, steps
■ Bob the Builder/Fireman Sam	Ideas – stories, characters, emotions

---

TEACHING TIP

In the early stages use flash cards with words and/or pictures to help pupils respond to a stimulus. Spread the flash cards out on the floor and ask the pupils to choose the words/pictures that help to describe the stimulus. Later, as pupils discuss a stimulus in small groups, ask them to write their key words on mini whiteboards to share with other groups. Over a period of several lessons, collect and display the dance vocabulary in the hall to act as a reminder for pupils as they work.

To begin with, pupils need to be helped to develop an enhanced awareness of various body parts and how they can move separately and in combination to express a theme or idea (see Table 5.2).

Using combinations of the above, pupils can begin to move in more controlled, imaginative and thoughtful ways. By developing a wall of images and words (Douglas, 1999) pupils can be challenged to try to move in ever more expressive ways (see Table 5.3).

TABLE 5.2 Enhancing awareness of body parts

Body part	Practise
Head, neck and face	Nodding (up and down), shaking (side to side), ear to shoulder, circling/spiralling action with forehead, move eyebrows, eyelids, cheeks and lips.
Trunk	Bending (forwards, backwards, side to side), twisting, 'snaking' or 'popping' (wave-like action passing through trunk).
Arms	Try each of the following with arms working together or in opposition – swinging, circling, swimming, shaking, 'popping', flapping.
Hands and fingers	Squeeze together, stretch apart, rub, wring, shake and clap hands. Point, drum, walk and crawl with fingers.
Legs	Bend, straighten, kick, cross and shake legs whilst standing, sitting or lying.
Feet and toes	Circle toes and heels. Point and pull toes. Wriggle each toe. Stand on toes, heels, insides, outsides and balls of feet. Practise stepping from heel to toe.

TABLE 5.3 Expressive ways of moving

Prowl	Picture of cat	Leap	Picture of flea	Jump
Picture of lion	Pounce	Picture of tortoise	Crawl	Picture of eagle
Slide	Picture of wader bird	Creep	Picture of rabbit	Bound
Picture of snake	Stride	Picture of giraffe	Scurry	Picture of squirrel
Slither	Picture of snail	Gallop	Picture of elephant	Sway

Once pupils get to know their bodies they can extend these movements further by experimenting with the elements shown in Table 5.4.

To create a dance phrase pupils need to select appropriate actions and order them using simple choreographic ideas. A dance phrase can be easily constructed by selecting a response to each of four key questions:

- WHAT is the body doing?
- HOW is the body moving?
- WHERE is the body being moved?
- WHO (or what) is involved in the movement?

Table 5.5 shows some examples.

A good dance theme is one that draws upon pupils' experience and fires their imagination. Try using some of the suggestions listed in Table 5.6.

TABLE 5.4 Elements of movement

Size	Direction	Level	Pathway
Large, small	Forward, backward, sideways, towards, away from	High, low, medium	Straight, diagonal, L-shaped, zig-zag, curved

TABLE 5.5 Illustration of the four key questions

What	How	Where	Who
Skipping	lightly	around	a hoop
Creeping	slowly	in and out of	the group
Turning	sharply	away from	a partner
Sinking	gently	towards	a marker

TEACHING TIP

'What's in the bag?' Once pupils have developed a repertoire of movement experiences, create a 'what, how, where, and who bag' with a selection of terms in each. Ask four pupils to select one word from each bag and arrange these on a board for the class to see. Pupils should try to move according to the instructions. This can be developed into a guessing game where a group of pupils have to guess the words on the cards from the movements alone.

Learning to appreciate movement begins in Key Stage 1 with learning to sit attentively and quietly during a performance. Practising this skill in the hall while other pupils perform their dances can be quite a challenge. Structuring pupils' observations of one another is the key to making progress in the skills of observing and evaluating performance.

Following these simple guidelines will improve pupils' chances of becoming a better audience:

- Make sure observers are sitting comfortably and have a clear view.
- Reduce distractions by setting performers against a plain backdrop.
- Sit the audience in a circle in the middle of the room facing outward while dancers dance around the outside.
- Encourage observers to watch only one dancer or pair of dancers (dancing nearest to them).
- Ask the observer to look for particular changes (e.g., in level or direction).
- Question the audience after the performance.
- Show appreciation to the performer by smiling or clapping when they have finished.

TABLE 5.6 Suggested dance themes

Theme	Movement ideas	Stimulus ideas
Nursery rhymes	*Incey Wincey Spider* – crawling, creeping and climbing spiders, tumbling and falling.	
	Hickory Dickory Dock – scurrying mice, short sharp changes of direction, jerking, rhythmic clockwork actions.	
Animals	Pets – bounding dogs with wagging tails, swimming and shaking dry. Slinky cats, quietly creeping, curling and sleeping. Hamsters busy, collecting, nibbling, trundling.	
	Wild animals – prowling, slumbering big cats, chasing, roaring. Gliding, snapping, snaking crocodiles. Swinging, scratching, climbing, falling, playful monkeys.	
	On the farm – chickens pecking, flapping, scratching and nesting; lambs suckling, jumping and chasing; pigs wallowing in mud and feeding from the trough; horses pull carts, gallop, jump and rear up.	
Stories	*Jack and the Beanstalk* – growing, climbing, creeping, giant heavy strides, swinging the axe. Other examples such as *Hansel and Gretel* and *The Gingerbread Man*	

Try using these questions to focus the observer's attention:

- Does the dance have a clear beginning, middle and ending?
- Does the dancer control their movements well?
- Can you see the pathways used?

Games activities

Games activities provide multiple opportunities for pupils to work cooperatively and competitively, to develop a sense of fair play and to learn to appreciate the qualities of being 'a good sport'. When taught well, regular games play promotes normal, healthy growth and can foster positive social, emotional and moral development. Learning to play games requires the development of both co-ordination skills and thinking skills. Pupils should be introduced to simple, competitive striking and fielding games; net/wall games;

and invasion games that they and others have made, using simple tactics for attacking and defending.

Table 5.7 describes the key features of these game families.

TABLE 5.7 Classifications of games at Key Stage 1

Game category	Key features
Striking and fielding	Players take turns to either strike or field. When striking the aim is to score as many points as possible. When fielding the aim is to limit the score of the striking team.
Net/wall games	Players from opposing teams are separated by a barrier and take it in turns to try to score points against their opponents. Points are scored when players fail to keep the object in play.
Invasion	Players share the playing area and compete to gain and then retain possession of the object. They try to invade their opponents' territory to score points.

These three categories by no means represent all game forms but collectively draw upon certain fundamental skills that underpin all games play. These are the skills of sending, receiving and travelling, and in those games that permit it, travelling with the object (see Table 5.8). We agree with Bunker et al.'s (1994) suggestion that, in the early stages of games skill development, participation in target games offers pupils the opportunity to develop an understanding of game play in an unopposed context. In target games, pupils have the opportunity to rehearse the core skills of travelling and sending before learning the more complex skill of receiving.

TABLE 5.8 Fundamental skills of games

Sending	Throwing, rolling, kicking, striking, batting, padding
Receiving	Catching, fielding, trapping, blocking
Travelling	Stepping, jumping, running, sliding, turning
Travelling with	Dribbling a ball with feet or a stick

Establishing a framework for teaching and learning core games skills is made easier when the individual actions, and their interdependence, are well understood. Individual skills can be rehearsed and performed in isolation and, through games play, in simple combinations.

Rather than spending too much time rehearsing these core actions through drills, we recommend that, where possible, skill development should be embedded within fun games. It is important to recognise, however, that some games are inherently more complex and demanding than others. Developing Bunker et al.'s (1994) framework for

TABLE 5.9 A framework for the phased introduction of games at Key Stage 1

Game type	FS	KS 1		KS 2
	R	1	2	3
Target	▓▓▓	▓▓▓	▓▓	─
Striking and fielding		▓▓	▓▓	─
Net/wall			▓▓	▓▓
Invasion				
Games making	▓▓▓	▓▓▓	▓▓	▓▓

▓▓ Proportion of curricum time

Source: Adapted from Bunker *et al.* (1994)

the introduction of games in the Primary school, we suggest that, at Key Stage 1, pupils be provided with opportunities to play individual and paired versions of target games, net/wall games and striking and fielding games.

It is important to remember that pupils will need regular practice if they are to improve. In addition to trying these activities during lesson time, pupils should be encouraged to practise the skills during active playtime and at home (see Table 5.9).

The review question at the foot of the table focuses on evaluating and improving performance.

Early travelling games such as tag provide a good introduction to the principles of game play and allow pupils the opportunity to develop travelling skills (running, dodging, avoiding, accelerating, decelerating and turning) and awareness of space (see Table 5.11).

Target games provide a good opportunity to rehearse core skills and challenge pupils to improve their accuracy and consistency. They also introduce pupils to 'turn taking', which is an important feature of both striking and fielding and net/wall games (see Table 5.12).

In the example of a striking and fielding game described next, the focus is on developing an understanding of attacking a space. In this game, pupils will discover that by sending the ball accurately to a space, and far from their partner, they will have more time to score points.

TABLE 5.10 Developing game skills through practice activities

Activity	Adaptations	Technical tips	Signs of success
Balloon bashing – keep a balloon up in the air for a minute. Hit it up and turn around before hitting it again. After three hits, catch the balloon with two hands.	Less air in the balloon/ use a beach ball. Increase the time to keep it up. Use different parts of your body to keep it up. Catch at head height, waist height, knee height.	Keep eyes on the balloon. Move feet to get underneath the balloon. Wait for balloon to arrive.	Pupils become more relaxed and appear to have more time between hits. Pupils hit up with palm of hand. Pupils complete more complex between-hit challenges.
Sliding and skimming – slide or skim a beanbag or quoit along the floor towards a target.	Target further away/ smaller.	Bend knees to get close to the floor. Finish with hand pointing towards target.	Increasing accuracy and consistency over different distances. Pupils can explain how to do it.
Rolling – roll a quoit or ball to a target. 'Under the Bridge' In threes, one player stands with legs wide apart to form a bridge. The other two players count how many times they can roll the ball under the bridge without it touching the sides.	Target further away/ smaller.	Bend knees to get close to the floor. Finish with hand pointing towards target.	Increasing accuracy and consistency over different distances. Pupils can explain how to play the game.
Throwing – throw a beanbag to a target.	Target further away/ smaller	Palm facing upwards. Opposite foot forwards. Finish with hand pointing towards target.	Increasing accuracy and consistency over different distances. Pupils can explain how to do it.
Kicking – kick ball to a target.		Use instep. Place non-kicking foot to the side of the ball. Follow through to the target with kicking leg.	
Bouncing – count how many times you can bounce a ball in a hoop using two hands to send and receive.	Bounce using alternate hands/one hand only. Bounce from side to side. Bounce ball whilst walking around the room.	Push ball down to the ground with fingers.	
Review questions	Can you describe how to catch/throw/roll/kick/bounce?		

TABLE 5.11 Tag games

Activity	Adaptations (applying STEP)	Technical tips	Signs of success
'Count tag' Nominated chasers score points by touching runners trying to escape.	S – Reduce/increase working space. T – Chasers have longer/shorter time limit to score points. E – Introduce hoops as a safe zone for runners. P – Increase/decrease number of chasers/ reduce number of runners – tagged runners become chasers.	Run on the balls of your feet. Push harder with one foot to help change direction. Make small steps and bend your knees when turning.	High-scoring chasers. Pupils run lightly on feet showing change of pace and direction. Chasers and runners remember the rules.
'Bag tag' In groups of eight, two chasers use a beanbag to tag runners. Chasers pass the beanbag between them.			
Review questions	Do you know why you were caught? What can you do to avoid being caught as quickly next time? What makes a good chasing team? Can you describe how you feel before, during and after a chasing game?		

TABLE 5.12 Target games

Activity	Adaptations (applying STEP)	Technical tips	Signs of success
Beanbag skittles – players knock over/move skittles by sliding bean bag/kicking a ball to a target. **Throw golf** – players count how many throws to land your beanbag in the 'hole' (target hoops) spread around the playground/field.	S – Target further away/smaller. T – Try with your other hand. E – Substitute beanbag for a quoit/slightly deflated ball/large foam ball. P – play on own/in pairs.	Look at target. Step towards target with opposing foot. Swing arm in a smooth motion.	Increasing accuracy and consistency over different distances.
Review questions	Can you explain why you sometimes miss the target? Why is it harder to hit a target that is a long way away?		

TABLE 5.13 Kicking rounders

Activity	Adaptations (applying STEP)	Technical tips	Signs of success
Kicking rounders Played in pairs. Players take turns to be the 'kicker' and/or the 'fielder'. 'Kicker' kicks stationary ball and runs between cones. Each cone touched counts 1 point. 'Fielder' collects and puts ball in hoop as quickly as possible. Kicker has three turns to score as many points as possible, then players swap roles. Equip: Ball, 2 x cones and hoop	S – increase/decrease distance to cone. T – ball can be thrown instead of kicked. E – play with different types of ball. P – play with two fielders.	For more distance take two steps into the kick/throw. Hand/foot should finish pointing where you want it to go. Move straight away after kicking/throwing the ball. Fielder, wait on your toes ready to move quickly.	Increasing distance kicked. Introduction of basic disguise. Fielder anticipates/predicts which way the ball will go.
Review questions	When kicking/throwing/hitting, where should you send the ball to score as many points as possible? When fielding, how can you keep the kicker's score low?		

In early net/wall games (see Table 5.14) pupils begin by playing co-operatively to score as many points with their partner as they can. When they have had plenty of practice and established a personal best score, they will enjoy competing against their partner, who then becomes an opponent. The shift from beating your record or best score to beating your opponent is an important transition in games and one that increases the motivation to play once the skills necessary to play have been acquired.

TABLE 5.14 Beanbag ball bash

Activity	Adaptations (apply STEP)	Technical tips	Signs of success
Beanbag ball bash In pairs, stand opposite your partner, behind a set line, with a large foam ball placed in the space between you. Take it in turns to throw three beanbags at the ball to try to move it over your partner's line. Reset game after a line has been crossed and a point scored.	S – Play on a short wide court or a long narrow court. T – Take alternate throws. E – increase/decrease number of beanbags. P - Play 'doubles' with two players behind each line.	*See earlier tips on throwing.* Move along your line to keep ball directly in front of you before throwing. Try to hit the middle of the ball.	Effective throwing – ball rarely missed. Longer 'rallies' – ball is moved backwards and forwards before a point is scored.
Review questions	Can you make your partner go the wrong way? What do you need to improve to play this game better?		

Gymnastics activities

While most people would accept that a physical education would not be complete without some form of Gymnastics experience, the nature and scope of Gymnastics in schools is contested and subject to much debate. From personal experience of working with students and teachers in schools we find ourselves in agreement with Reynold's (2000) view that, 'for many teachers, confusion may persist over what actually constitutes the makeup of the various approaches to gymnastics' (p. 156).

Our focus, however, is the quality of the experience rather than the application of a label to the form of experience offered to pupils. In gymnastic activities, pupils strive to improve gross motor control through engaging in activity experiences on the floor and with apparatus. This context provides children with an opportunity to create, control and link movements in increasingly complex patterns and in which the central challenge remains the replication of high quality movement.

Gymnastics is distinct from other activity areas in that pupils are required to think about how to create, perform and replicate actions, agilities and sequences as accurately as possible. We now turn our attention to gymnastics activities in Key Stage 1.

Building on pupils' experiences of movement in the Early Years Foundation Stage, at Key Stage 1 teachers should continue to provide pupils with a variety of gymnastic challenges to develop basic skills on the floor and using apparatus. They should also choose and link skills and actions in short movement phrases and create and perform short, linked sequences that show a clear beginning, middle and end and have contrasts in direction, level and speed. This is achieved by providing pupils with opportunities to ask and then find answers to the following four key questions:

- What can we do?
- Where can we move?
- How can we move?
- Who can we move with?

The gymnastics curriculum emerges out of finding increasingly inventive and creative answers to these questions. In the next section we suggest ways in which the teacher can develop a high quality and well-rounded programme of Gymnastics that addresses the aspects of learning. Teaching pupils the skills associated with Gymnastics is made easier when the actions to be introduced are classified. Developing the work of Smith (1994), we recommend a simple classification system as shown in Figure 5.3.

TEACHING TIP

For each new action or combination, ask the pupils to describe where it would fit on the model (Figure 5.2) to encourage them to look for and describe travel, balance, shape and rotation. Placing the names of, or a picture of, the action on a chart in the classroom helps to develop pupils' understanding of gymnastic skills.

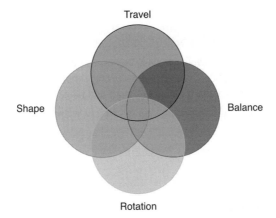

Travel	movement that takes you from one place to another in any direction
Shape	the placement of body parts in relation to one another
Balance	achieving and maintaining stillness in an otherwise unstable position
Rotation	movement about one of the body's axes

FIGURE 5.1 Gymnastics skills

Source: Adapted from Smith (1994)

These are the building blocks of successful gymnastic performances. Each can be rehearsed and developed in isolation from the others but a sequence of many actions is likely to involve two or more domains.

The following charts illustrate some of the skills that pupils should rehearse at Key Stage 1.

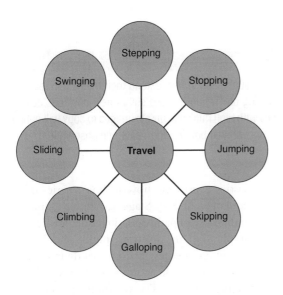

FIGURE 5.2 Key Stage 1 gymnastic skills

After introducing each of the 'travel' actions to pupils, give them time to practise on their own, on the spot or in a small space. Then try the following simple pattern: start from being still, perform the action on the spot to the count of eight and be still again. When they can repeat this consistently, increase the space they are allowed to work in and the length of time they repeat the action for.

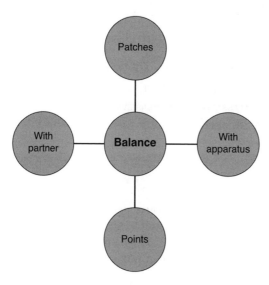

FIGURE 5.3 Developing balance

It is important to provide pupils with a visual guide to help extend their thinking in relation to what body parts they could try balancing on. Trying to keep still in new positions develops pupils' core stability. Presenting pupils with high quality example images to copy will enhance their performance and improve their accuracy in both performance and observation.

One of the key challenges of Gymnastics is learning how to link a series of actions together into a continuous and fluid sequence. At Key Stage 1, helping pupils to link movements together involves developing their use of pathways, direction, level and speed.

Having practised and repeated a simple skill in isolation, pupils should then be encouraged to create an 'action sandwich' where the new action is sandwiched between two others. Pupils will enjoy creating their own simple action sandwiches and can then start to add additional and more challenging 'fillings'. Try variations on the following activity.

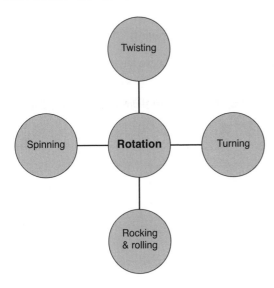

FIGURE 5.4 Developing rotation

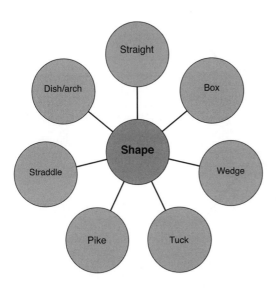

FIGURE 5.5 Developing shape

TEACHING TIP

When helping pupils to remember simple movement patterns it is a good idea to write down the pattern or draw it on a board. Not only does this help to remind pupils what is coming next but it will also help to extend their movement vocabulary.

THE SPECIAL DOUBLE DELUXE GYM SEQUENCE SANDWICH

Using a balance as the 'bread' in your gym sandwich, choose three fillings from this list to squeeze in between:

Turn, slide, jump, roll, twist, hop, skip, gallop, crawl. My Special Double Deluxe Gym Sequence Sandwich:

   Balance
   Slide
   Balance
   Jump
   Balance
   Skip
   Balance

The next challenge is to learn to perform the movement pattern along a specified pathway. Try the following example patterns:

FIGURE 5.6 Movement patterns

Then use recognisable letter shapes:

A K G H Q

Using apparatus to develop pupils' skilfulness and confidence is an important part of Gymnastics. The different surfaces and levels that the introduction of apparatus brings to the working environment helps to extend pupils' repertoire of actions and challenges their composition skills. Pupils need to be taught how to handle mats, benches, trestle tables and climbing frames. While integrating apparatus time into every lesson may not be feasible, within each block of Gymnastics lessons pupils should have the opportunity to try out their skills with low-level apparatus combinations.

By providing pupils with the opportunity to assemble patterns of movement from a series of separate parts they will get better at visually unpicking patterns when they see them performed by others. Thus through the processes of selecting, ordering, reordering, practising and performing movement patterns, pupils will intuitively develop an understanding of composition. The act of observing and then describing individual actions, and then simple patterns of movement, will assist pupils to develop a gymnastic vocabulary. This can be helped by the use of flash cards.

TEACHING TIP

Once pupils are changed for PE but while still in the classroom, show images of gymnasts and ask them to describe what they see. As pupils' gymnastic vocabulary develops hand out large photographs of gymnasts in action to small groups and ask pupils to describe what the gymnast has just done, is doing and will do next.

Once confident in describing movement from still images they can then practise on live action by observing each other. More able pupils can then be challenged to make suggestions for improvement.

Swimming and water-based activities

Bath time at home and early play experiences in wet play areas should provide pupils with experience of pushing and pulling motions through water, developing their knowledge of what floats and sinks, and how water pours, splashes and fills containers. Changing to get into a paddling pool or larger pool of shallow water should be a natural extension of these experiences and provide children with the opportunity to play with water using their legs and feet.

Where swimming is introduced at Key Stage 1, pupils should learn to move in water (for example, walking jumping, hopping and turning, using swimming aids and supports, propelling themselves using different swimming aids, using arm and leg actions and basic strokes). They should be able to float and move with and without swimming aids and feel the buoyancy and support of water and swimming aids.

Pupils will, of course, arrive in Key Stage 1 with varying degrees of water confidence and competence. Following an initial assessment, teachers will need to select appropriately challenging experiences and draw, where necessary, from the curriculum activities planned for pupils in Key Stage 2.

Since only very few Primary schools have their own pool, in the majority of cases going swimming involves a journey to an unfamiliar site, with unfamiliar faces, smells, sights and sounds. For this reason we recommend arranging a 'dry run' class visit to the pool venue prior to starting the swimming programme. If pupils also pack their swimming kit to take with them on this visit, the whole experience provides good practice for the real thing. Pupils will need to know:

■   Where they change
■   Where to leave their clothes
■   Where the toilets are
■   The rules for safety and hygiene at the pool
■   How to get from the changing rooms to the poolside
■   Where to wait prior to entering the water
■   Where the shallow water and deep water is
■   Where to get in and out of the water
■   What equipment they will be using
■   How to behave when in the water
■   What the various whistles, alarms and signals mean
■   Where to congregate at the end of the lesson

TEACHING TIP

Devising a question sheet for pupils to complete during the visit can be a good way to focus pupils' attention on the information they need to know.

Prior to developing pupils' knowledge and competence in the recognised swimming strokes (see Chapter 6), it is important to develop their confidence in the water so that they can relax and allow the water to support them. While many pupils will welcome the opportunity to get into the pool, there will be some for whom it is a frightening experience. For this reason, teachers should try to make the water as inviting as possible. By distributing toys, floats, 'noodles', flips and hoops in the water, pupils will be much more inclined to enter the space. The activities listed below provide some initial ideas for building water confidence in the pool environment. Pupils can work with or without buoyancy aids as necessary.

Walking practices

Holding the rail

■   slide feet along the bottom;
■   lead with only one foot, then alternate feet;
■   try the above while moving up and down in the water.

In pairs

- walk holding a partner's hand;
- walk sideways facing your partner holding both hands (remember to look where you are going);
- holding hands walk around in a circle;
- try the above while moving with your shoulders in the water.

With equipment

- push a ball across the pool with your hands/shoulders/knees/chin/nose;
- push a ball across without touching it;
- pass the ball between you and a partner while walking forwards/sideways/ backwards across the pool;
- climb in and out of a floating hoop (push the hoop down to step in and out).

Regaining feet

- hold a ball/float/noodle for support and practise lifting both feet off the bottom;
- looking down to the bottom of the pool, stretch one leg out behind you (arabesque), lean forwards with your weight on the ball/float/noodle, lift the other leg to meet it. Bend at the knees and at the waist to regain feet;
- as above but start looking up at the ceiling;
- walk forwards/backwards and repeat the above.

Floating practices (use buoyancy aids as necessary)

Keeping shoulders under the water

- hold a float under each arm or wrap a noodle around your back and hop from one leg to the other;
- jump feet off the bottom and hold them up as long as you can;
- jump feet off the bottom and make a tuck/straddle/pike shape;
- with a partner supporting you under your shoulders let your head lie on the surface and look up at the ceiling;
- In this position, can you push your tummy to the surface?
- How long can you keep both feet off the bottom for?
- Can you lie parallel with the side of the pool holding on to the side with the nearest hand and with a float under the other arm? Gently let go of the side and lie still before regaining your feet.

Propulsion with arms

As pupils play these games and move through the water with growing confidence and speed they will automatically begin to rehearse the arm actions similar to those used in breaststroke, front crawl and butterfly. To develop and refine these actions try the following activities:

With shoulders beneath the surface

- walk along the bottom of the pool, pulling yourself along with bent arms/straight arms;
- recover arms out of the water, at first together and then alternately;
- try feeling the difference when fingers are closed tightly/spread wide;
- walk sideways with one arm pointing where you want to go and pull with the other arm only, recovering out of the water;
- hop along the bottom, pulling arms together or alternately;
- count how many times your feet touch the bottom.

Having tried 'alternating' and 'simultaneous' actions, label these 'front crawl', 'back crawl', 'breaststroke' and 'butterfly' to extend pupils' vocabulary and for easy reference in the future.

Propulsion with legs

When learning to kick it is fun to make a big splash, but too much splashing can be intimidating for less confident pupils. Pupils should aim to create some 'white water' turbulence where their feet are, bringing their feet up to, but not breaking, the surface. Try the following:

- Hold on to the side of the pool, look down towards the bottom of the pool and kick your feet up and down with bent legs. Try the same but with straight legs. Which feels harder?
- Wrap a noodle around your back (or hold a float under each forearm) and push your tummy up towards the surface. Try drawing big circles with your heels, first one way and then the other way. Can you do the same but with your feet turned away from each other?

As with the arm actions, having tried 'alternating' and 'simultaneous' actions, label them accordingly.

Games

Once pupils have gained experience of moving in the water, playing games is a good way of consolidating their movement skills and provides them with opportunities to select and apply skills. The following examples are good to start or conclude lessons:

- The Lighthouse Keeper's Lunch – In groups of three or four, spread out in a line across the pool and, on the signal, pass items from one side to the other without them getting wet.

- Lifeboats – spread a range of floating toys/swimming aids on the surface. Pupils have to 'rescue' one item at a time and place it on the side.

- Overboard! – like 'Simon Says' but using actions with a nautical theme such as 'climb the rigging', 'scrub the decks', 'duck the boom', 'bail out', etc. On the command 'Overboard!' pupils have to jump up, submerge, resurface and wave both arms in the air.

Before and after swimming lessons, encourage pupils to talk about how they feel when they are in and around the water. Sharing thoughts about their feelings can alleviate concerns and can also ensure that pupils are supportive of each other when in the water. Show pupils pictures of different water sports (swimming, sailing, scuba diving, water skiing) and talk about what is happening. Ask pupils to set personal targets for each lesson and share them with their swimming 'buddy'. Ask buddies at the end of the lesson if the target has been achieved.

Developing knowledge and understanding of fitness and health

Key Stage 1 pupils should know:

a)   how important it is to be active;

b)   to recognise and describe how their bodies feel during different activities.

From getting to know their bodies through naming and labelling body parts to recognising that lots of energetic activity makes us tired, there are a number of opportunities in any PE lesson to focus pupils' attention on the impact of activity on their bodies.

> **TEACHING TIP**
>
> It is a good idea to establish a regular warm-up/cool-down 'routine' that pupils can be introduced to in stages and which provides them with an opportunity to learn and improve a simple movement pattern.

As the lesson draws to a conclusion, pupils should be offered opportunities to show what they can do. Allowing time for showing and sharing provides a natural slowing down of pupils' activity rates. Following brief discussion of a range of performances, pupils could repeat a variation on actions carried out in the warm-up at a reduced intensity. Engaging pupils in warming-up and cooling-down activities provides good opportunities to discuss how exercise makes us feel different. Recognising and being able to describe the changes that take place is one of the key indicators that pupils are developing knowledge and understanding of fitness and health appropriate to the key stage.

Chapter summary

This chapter has provided a rationale for the inclusion of the practical areas making up the PE curriculum experience for pupils at Key Stage 1. Through identifying the distinctive nature of these we have sought to demonstrate how each makes an important contribution to a pupil's initial experience of physical education. By outlining a framework of understanding for them we hope to have contributed to your understanding of the potential for learning about, in and through each domain and that this provides coherence to what may otherwise appear to be a rather eclectic set of experiences. Keeping this in the forefront of your thinking is the key to moving beyond occupying pupils in activities to helping pupils to learn through those activities. Furthermore, we have encouraged you to think about ways, just like in classroom-based activities, you can differentiate the level of challenge in each of the activity areas in order to address the needs of all pupils. We hope that the suggested activity ideas are useful and serve as a catalyst to inspire further thinking, discussion and planning.

Questions for reflection

- Do you think that the activity areas suggested for inclusion at Key Stage 1 represent a complete PE experience? If not, what would you add/take away?
- What do you identify as the key barriers, if any, to delivering the recommendations for PE at Key Stage 1?
- How well does your teaching in PE accommodate the needs of pupils with different levels of experience?

References

Bunker, D., Hardy, C., Smith, B. and Almond, L. (1994) (eds) *Primary Physical Education – Implementing the National Curriculum*. Cambridge: Cambridge University Press.

Douglas, M. (1999) *Primary PE: Dance*. London: Hodder and Stoughton.

Fisher, R. and Alldridge, D. (1994) *Active PE*. London: Stanley Thornes.

Hardy, C. (1994) 'Swimming'. In D. Bunker, C. Hardy, B. Smith and L. Almond (eds) *Primary Physical Education: Implementing the National Curriculum*. Cambridge: Cambridge University Press.

Hardy, C. (2000) 'Teaching swimming'. In R. Bailey and T. MacFadyen (eds) *Teaching Physical Education 5–11*. London: Continuum.

Reynolds, T. (2000) 'Teaching Gymnastics'. In R. Bailey and T. MacFadyen (eds) *Teaching Physical Education 5–11*. London: Continuum.

Smith, B. (1994) 'Gymnastic activities'. In D. Bunker, C. Hardy, B. Smith and L. Almond. *Primary Physical Education: Implementing the National Curriculum*. Cambridge: Cambridge University Press.

6

Physical education in Key Stage 2

Chapter objectives

By the end of this chapter you should be able to:

- Understand the breadth and scope of PE at Key Stage 2.
- Develop knowledge of delivering successful learning experiences in dance, games and gymnastic activities.
- Develop knowledge of delivering successful learning experiences in athletic activities, outdoor and adventurous activities and swimming.
- Include the information relating to fitness and health into practical teaching.

PE in the National Curriculum at Key Stage 2

Common sense would suggest that PE at Key Stage 2 builds upon the movement experiences at Key Stage 1, but with a greater level of challenge, providing pupils with the opportunity to consolidate and extend their repertoire of skills.

In this key stage pupils should continue to implement and develop a broader range of skills, learning how to use them in different ways and to link them to make actions and sequences of movement. They should enjoy communicating, collaborating and competing with each other. They should develop an understanding of how to succeed in different activities and sports and learn how to evaluate and recognise their own success.

Pupils should be taught to:

- use running, jumping, catching and throwing in isolation and in combination;
- play competitive games, modified where appropriate, such as football, netball, rounders, cricket, hockey, basketball, badminton and tennis, and apply basic principles suitable for attacking and defending;

■ develop flexibility, strength, technique, control and balance, for example through gymnastics and athletics;

■ perform dances using a range of movement patterns;

■ take part in outdoor and adventurous activity challenges both individually and within a team;

■ compare their performances with previous ones to achieve their personal best.

All schools must provide swimming instruction in either Key Stage 1 or 2.

Dance activities

Davies (2000) suggests that Dance makes a unique and distinctive contribution to pupils' physical education, posing the performer the challenge of finding meaning in movement. Douglas (1999) argues that dance is not only interactive but also an integrating medium in which pupils are provided with the opportunity to increase their movement vocabulary, practise decision-making and problem solving and exercise aesthetic judgement.

Through their dance experiences in Key Stage 2 pupils should be encouraged to develop an awareness of quality and beauty in their immediate environment, to describe what they see, to discuss how they feel and to enjoy objects and events for what they are, 'the way they look, sound or feel . . . for their qualities of line, pattern, dynamics, colour, texture and shape' (Davies, 2000, p. 127). Since Dance is the only art form in the PE curriculum, through creating, performing and evaluating dances pupils experience what it is to be an artist. Just as all art forms evolve over time, the Dance curriculum in school is able to draw upon a wide range of traditional and contemporary styles for inspiration. We contend that the dual location of Dance, in the PE curriculum and in the expressive arts domain, represents an opportunity to explore movement from a dual perspective. On the one hand, pupils can enjoy the physicality of dance as a movement form and experiment with the mechanics of motion, the challenge to their physical fitness, control and co-ordination and the discipline of choreography that any dance performance demands. On the other hand, pupils can enjoy the intellectual and emotional demands of the creative process through devising, performing and appreciating dances. Approached from either direction, in our experience, teaching Dance is an exciting, stimulating, infinitely varied process that is full of surprises and which so often produces truly memorable results. The four key components of movement in dance are action, space, dynamics and relationships.

Building on their experiences in Key Stage 1, at Key Stage 2 pupils should be encouraged to increase their use and understanding of each component and in so doing become more confident, skilful and appreciative dancers.

The three key phases in this process are composition, performance and appreciation. Dance composition involves the selection, ordering and pacing of movements to communicate an idea or story to an audience. During performance, the dancer attempts to present their work to an audience. Prior to this, plenty of practice is essential. Practising a performance enables the dancer to refine the movements, the quality of expression, the use of space and each other to convey their ideas most effectively. Showing dances, or parts of dances, to the rest of the class is an important experience and serves as a useful stepping stone to developing the confidence to perform in school assemblies, to parents and the wider public.

TEACHING TIP

It is a good idea to increase the frequency of performance opportunities in Dance lessons as a Dance unit progresses. An audience can consist of one other pupil and need not be a large group.

At Key Stage 2 pupils should learn how to create and perform dances using a range of movement patterns, including those from different times, places and cultures. They should also be able to respond to a range of stimuli and accompaniment. To help here, Robertson (1994) helpfully sees four clear stages to work through:

- Learning to tell stories.
- Developing those stories.
- Composing and performing dances.
- Experiencing other styles of dance.

The first stage requires that pupils acquire and develop an extensive movement vocabulary.

A precursor to effective communication in any new language is accurate pronunciation. When learning the language of movement this equates to learning to use the body, as a whole or in part, to convey a word or idea convincingly. This takes much practice and will always be open to misinterpretation. In order to minimise error, dancers use repetition and amplification. By exaggerating and repeating key aspects of a movement idea, the novice dancer increases their chances of being understood.

Dance lessons should provide opportunities for pupils to rehearse each of the four key components through a range of stimulating themes (see Table 6.1).

TEACHING TIP

Before introducing a theme with pupils, complete a table such as Table 6.1 with specific terms that relate to your theme. This will provide you with a bank of ideas to help pupils when their ideas dry up.

Each time you introduce a new theme to your pupils add their ideas to a word wall (see Figure 6.1). This will help pupils to develop an ever-expanding movement vocabulary.

TABLE 6.1 Components of movement applied to dance

Action	Dynamics	Space	Relationships
Whole body – jump, leap, hop, skip, shiver, fall, shake, collapse, roll, stamp, twist, spin, twirl; Body parts – hands, feet, head, knees, elbows, above waist, below waist.	Time – hurried, quick, hectic or relaxed slow, calm; Weight – heavy, firm, strong, powerful or light, fine, gentle, delicate; Pathway – direct and decisive or indirect and faltering; Flow – the rhythm or continuity of a movement, predictable or unpredictable.	Direction – forward, backward, sideways; Level – high, medium, low; Proximity – near to, far from; Pathway – curling, angular, diagonal; Size – big, small.	Solo, duo, duo + 1, trio; Unison or canon; 'Question and answer'; Mirroring/shadowing; Symmetry/asymmetry.

During Key Stage 2, pupils should be challenged to compose longer dance phrases that:

- have a clear beginning, middle and end;
- can link to other dance phrases;
- show progress along the four key components.

Stimulating pupils' imagination, creativity and storytelling capability relies on the selection of appropriate themes (see Table 6.2).

TEACHING TIP

Make mini whiteboards available for pupils to sketch and record their ideas. This helps them remember what they were doing and can be a useful focus for discussion with a partner, small group or the teacher.

Where	What			
Straight	Freeze	Hop	Stride	Spin
Square	Shudder	Melt	Writhe	Cower
Diagonal	Heave	Flick	Crumble	Expand
Triangle	Turn	Twist	Rise	Slide
Curling	Scamper	Spiral	Leap	Fall
Circle	Roll	Zip	Swoop	Pounce
Zig-zag	Glide	Wheel	Contract	Skip
Spiral	Drip	March	Float	Extend
Crescent	Envelop	Retreat		
Jagged	Who		How	
Smooth	Alone		Effort	
Forwards	In pairs		Strong Light	
Backwards	In groups		Heavy Weak	
Sideways	Lead and follow		Smooth Free	
In front	Together		Jerk Hesitant	
Behind	Meeting		Sudden Sustained	
Alongside	Parting		Speed	
Above	Going around		Accelerating	
Below	Encircle		Decelerating	

FIGURE 6.1 An example of a word wall

Drawing on a range of dance styles from different times and cultures adds a further dimension to pupils' dance experience. This will also provide an opportunity to discuss similarities and contrasts between dance styles and the significance of costume, staging, makeup and music to dance experience.

TABLE 6.2 Stimulus and movement ideas for KS2 dance

Theme	Movement ideas	Stimulus ideas
Work	Farmer – driving, stacking, milking, fencing;	Pictures, toy animals;
	Mechanic – lifting, hammering, winding and washing;	Toy cars, lorries;
	Fire fighter – cleaning, sliding down the pole, hosing down, chopping;	Fireman Sam;
Seasons, e.g. autumn	Gusts of wind, leaves detach, fall, tumble, drift, settle, swept up;	Dried leaves, sweeping brush, dustbin bags;
	Fireworks – patterns created by different types of firework – rocket, Catherine wheel, Roman candle;	Tchaikovsky's 1812 overture, patterns;
	Halloween – witches bent over cauldrons, making potions, curious cats, swooping on broomsticks, gliding ghosts, flapping bat's wings;	Pumpkins, masks, witches hat, rubber bats;
The Olympic Games	Faster – higher – stronger;	Video excerpts from an opening/ closing ceremony;
	Preparing, competing, celebrating;	Olympic picture icons for each sport.
	Different activities at different sites – makes for a good whole class dance.	

TEACHING TIP

By selecting a theme with the potential for multiple activities performed simultaneously, the teacher can choreograph an effective whole-class dance, as in the Olympic Games example below.

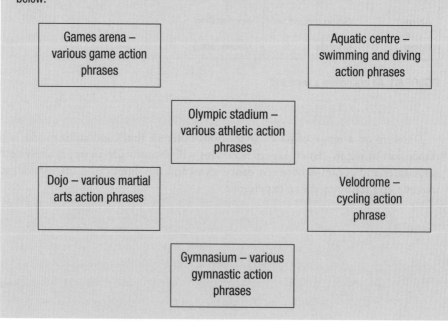

TEACHING TIP

Show pupils pre-recorded dance performances of professional dance artists or companies. This will motivate pupils and help develop the skills of observation and appreciation (see key questions below), as well as being a source of compositional ideas.

Key questions for the audience

- Does the dance have a clear beginning, middle and ending?
- Is there variety in the movement?
- Does the dancer control their movements well?
- Does the dancer show good extension of the body?
- Can you see shapes in the movement – in the body or in the pathways used?
- Do the movements flow from one to the other?
- Is the dancer convincing?
- How does the dance make you feel?

Games activities

Across the ages many games have appeared, been developed and become popular. Where some have endured and now enjoy long histories and rich traditions, others have disappeared only to be replaced by new games. Amidst all this change one thing remains constant – our insatiable desire to play! Through the energetic use of large muscle groups and the subsequent heavy demand on the cardiovascular system, games can provide excellent opportunities for physical growth and development. The requirement to cooperate, compete and abide by rules and conventions in the pursuit of arbitrary goals have also long been associated with the development of social and emotional skills. At Key Stage 2, pupils should play and make up small sided and modified competitive net, striking/fielding and invasion games and use skills and tactics and apply basic principles suitable for attacking and defending.

At Key Stage 2 pupils should build upon their learning of skills in Key Stage 1, then experience and create games drawn from selected categories or families of games. Games can be classified into different groups in many ways. The most common approach, however, classifies games according to their structural features and presents us with several family groups that include combat, invasion, net/wall, striking/fielding and target games. By developing our understanding of how games work, we should be better placed to help pupils develop an understanding and appreciation of games play, in addition to helping them to play well.

All games have structural, strategic and technical components. The game structure determines the overall aim, playing boundaries, time limits, number of players, the equipment to be used and the playing rules. Structural components are usually fixed and upheld by independent officials.

Specific game strategies evolve over time and determine how the game is played. Players selectively employ strategy to try to outwit their opponents and be successful in achieving their aim.

Players put into practice their game strategy through employing techniques at the appropriate time. Some techniques are very complex and highly specific to individual games (such as the golf swing) but others are more generic and are useful in a multitude of games (such as running, catching, throwing).

Thus, while several games may share common rules, apply common strategies and certain generic techniques, it is in the unique mix of structure, strategy and technique that each named activity remains distinct.

As pupils enter Key Stage 2, they are still developing consistency and accuracy in sending, receiving and travelling skills. In invasion games, however, pupils are denied sufficient time and space to rehearse and refine these skills in context. Thus, games experiences should be selected on the basis that they provide an environment where pupils have as much time and space as they need, and in which they can be protected from interference. In this context, pupils are more likely to be successful and develop a sense of achievement. Whole-class invasion games (such as bench ball) break all of these rules and consequently are unlikely to be productive in helping pupils to develop their skilfulness or strategic thinking.

With this in mind, we suggest that during Years 3 and 4 children are exposed in equal measure to target, striking and fielding and net/wall games. Having had the opportunity to rehearse and combine their sending, receiving and travelling skills in these formats, children should be sufficiently skilful to try simple small-sided invasion games towards the end of Year 4. Throughout Key Stage 2, children should be encouraged to make up, revise and adapt their own games in order to assist their understanding of how games work. Rather than teaching and refining pupils' technical proficiency in isolation, we advocate developing pupils' proficiency in games through the 'games for understanding' model.

The traditional approach to teaching games involves teaching 'how' followed by teaching 'why'. In other words, pupils are taught games skills in small, progressive steps and then asked to put these into practice in games. Learning technique takes precedence over learning tactical or strategic understanding. The Teaching Games for Understanding (TGfU) model (Bunker and Thorpe, 1982) uses sequences of game-like scenarios in which pupils can work on game strategies and on the skills needed for the task, in a developmentally appropriate manner. TGfU follows six basic steps:

Step 1: Learners are introduced to the game and allowed to play.

Step 2: Following play, the conventions of the game are explained.

Step 3: Learners reflect on their experience of playing the game and think about the major tactical problems that the game presents.

Step 4: Learners practise using game-like tasks to develop their tactical knowledge and to learn to apply strategies to specific situations.

Step 5:   Learners are encouraged to use new and existing skills/tactical awareness in game-like situations.

Step 6:   Learners refine their skills so that game play is based on tactical knowledge, game appreciation and game strategies.

This process encourages pupils to develop higher-order cognitive skills and social skills through problem solving, analysing, evaluating, decision-making, and social interaction, which are crucial to success in game play. The learning of skills, while no less important, is relegated to later in the process.

In Tables 6.3 and 6.4, which show some examples, the review questions are designed to start conversations in lessons about what makes a good performance and how performances can be improved.

When using the TGfU model, teachers and pupils can work together to create games that develop understanding of the principles of game play. At a later date, the strategies employed in these games can be put into practice in modified versions of adult games. Pupils will not be disadvantaged by delaying their introduction to adult games in curriculum time. On the contrary, their performance in these games is likely to be enhanced by their increased understanding of how the game works. Table 6.6 identifies key features of families of games that could be used as a starting point in creating new games.

TABLE 6.3 Games involving travelling activities

	Adaptations	Technical tips	Signs of success
Stuck in the mud Nominated 'catchers' tag 'runners'. Caught runners stand still until tagged by free runners.	Number of catchers. Playing time.	'Catchers' plan how to work together. 'Runners' change speed and direction.	Catchers working as a team. Runners avoiding being caught.
Raiders In a divided playing area, 2 teams of 4 players try to 'raid' beanbags/balls from their opposition's end zone. Defenders are not allowed in their own end zone. Having captured a beanbag the 'raiders' have to return to their own half, avoiding being tagged by the opposition.	Number of players. Court size.	Plan strategy before a raid.	Continuous game.
Review questions		Can you describe three ways of avoiding someone trying to catch you? How do you use your feet when changing direction?	

TABLE 6.4 Games involving striking, throwing and catching activities

Striking, throwing and catching activities	Adaptations	Technical tips	Signs of success
See 'Kicking rounders' p. 97 but add a striking implement.	Size of bat/ball. Strike from tee.	*Batters* Stand sideways on to ball. Take bat back. Swing through the ball to follow through in the direction of travel. *Fielders* Line up with direction of ball. Scoop ball with both hands. Stand sideways on to target for throw.	Consistency of contact. Accuracy in direction.
1, 2, 3, 4 Number players 1–4. Pass ball in order whilst moving around a nominated space. Score 1 point every time the ball gets back to No. 1 without being dropped.	Playing time. Number of players.	Move near to passing player. Show a target for thrower to aim at.	Number of dropped passes decreases.
Review questions		Give three tips to help a partner throw/hit with accuracy.	

TABLE 6.5 Features of games at KS2

Game type	Distinctive features	Common features
Striking and fielding	Players take turns to accumulate points. Consistency of hitting/throwing for distance and accuracy. Speed around bases/over short distances.	Players use/invent strategies to outwit opponents.
Net/wall	Barrier divides court. Consistency of hitting for accuracy/power. React quickly to opponent's hit to develop a rally (repeated 'turn-taking').	Players use/invent strategies to dominate the playing space. Players try to anticipate what opponents will do next.
Invasion	Players share same playing space. Gaining and retaining possession. No 'turn-taking'.	Players make decisions individually and collectively.
Review questions	In a striking and fielding game how do fielders decide where to stand? In a net game what are the advantages and disadvantages of playing close to the net? When you have possession in an invasion game, when should you run and when should you pass?	

Gymnastics activities

Four core themes underpin all skill development in Gymnastics activities – travel, balance, rotation and shape. Even when performing very complex tumbling combinations the most accomplished gymnast draws on these same fundamental principles. Thus during Key Stage 2, pupils should be encouraged to consolidate their performance and understanding through revisiting these themes, through repetition and through differentiated challenges. At Key Stage 2, pupils create and perform sequences on the floor and using apparatus that include variations in level, speed and direction.

With such broad guidance, identifying what pupils should be taught, and in which order, can be a perplexing problem. The key performance goal of Gymnastics activities is to enable pupils to create and perform aesthetically pleasing patterns of movement that use the whole body. In the Early Years Foundation Stage pupils will establish basic movement and control competencies. In Key Stage 1 these will be refined and consolidated. As pupils become more experienced in Key Stage 2, their knowledge, performance and composition skills will develop further along what we refer to as the PACE continuum (see Table 6.6).

TABLE 6.6 The PACE continuum

P	Presentation	Developing awareness of an audience and performing movements in an aesthetically pleasing manner for that audience.
A	Accuracy	Developing greater control over the body and accuracy in movement through repetition.
C	Combination	Linking movements together in increasingly inventive and challenging ways.
E	Extension	Building an ever increasing repertoire of repeatable actions using both floor and apparatus.

Teachers can identify that learning in gymnastics is taking place when they see evidence of pupils' progression along the continuum in Table 6.7.

Using the PACE continuum is one way in which teachers can help pupils to remain focused on producing high quality work in gymnastic activities.

The structure of a Gymnastics lesson should normally consist of:

■ Warm up – gentle preparation for thinking and moving with control and poise;

■ Floor work – exploration of a theme with open-ended and skill-based tasks;

■ Apparatus work – development of movement ideas from floor work section on and around apparatus;

■ Conclusion – reflection and review of achievements, revision of some aspects of floor work.

TABLE 6.7 Examples of progress

	Examples of progress		
PACE	**KS1**	**Early KS2**	**Later KS2**
Presentation	Little or no awareness of audience, occasional use of starting or finishing position.	Regularly uses starting and finishing positions for a movement sequence.	Performer is conscious of the audience throughout all stages of a movement sequence.
Accuracy	Movements performed differently each time.	More consistency in the way in which some movements are performed.	Consistently accurate in the performance of the movement repertoire.
Combination	Can link two movements together smoothly in a repeating pattern.	Can remember and link up to four movements together smoothly in a repeating pattern.	Can remember and link more than four movements together smoothly.
Extension	Work on the floor and mats only.	Performs floor work on apparatus.	Uses apparatus to develop and extend floor work.

Shorter lessons, however, may be structured differently, as shown in Figure 6.2.

Lesson 1	Lesson 2	Lesson 3	Lesson 4
Warm up	Warm up	Warm up	Warm up
Floor work	Apparatus work	Floor work	Apparatus work
Conclusion	Conclusion	Conclusion	Conclusion

FIGURE 6.2 Structuring shorter lessons

When pupils are regularly challenged to learn new skills, to incorporate those skills in ever-expanding sequences of movement and given regular opportunities to perform, their hunger for new material grows and their enthusiasm for the activity increases. Teachers should not shy away from challenging pupils to work at their skill threshold and this will require a seamless blending of open-ended tasks with formal (named) skill teaching (see Table 6.8).

Remembering to adhere to the principles of differentiation, outlined in Chapter 7, individuals and groups should be working at a level of challenge that is appropriate. Thus, while all pupils will be working on the same theme in a lesson, some will be working on open-ended tasks while others will be learning specific named skills under closer supervision.

Once pupils have developed a repertoire of movement ideas, they should be challenged to pick and mix these actions to create interesting patterns and combinations. Providing an action word bank is a really useful device to both develop pupils' vocabulary and their organisation skills. Doing this collaboratively (in small groups or as a class) adds a further interesting dimension in which pupils learn to share their movement thoughts and pick up ideas from each other. To begin with, pupils should be encouraged to copy and repeat appropriately challenging patterns that have been devised for them. Once they are sufficiently experienced in remembering and repeating patterns with consistency and accuracy they can start to assemble their own from an action word/image bank. This not only encourages pupils to develop, then select and apply their knowledge of actions and sequences, but also provides a sound framework for beginning to describe and comment on the performance.

TABLE 6.8 Blending open-ended tasks with named skills

Theme	Open-ended challenge	Named skill(s)
Travel	Find three ways of leaping from one foot to the other.	Stag leap
Balance	Find three ways of balancing on two body parts.	Handstand
Rotation	Find three ways of rotating close to the floor.	Forward roll
Shape	What shapes can you make in the air when you jump from a bench to a mat?	Straddle, pike and tuck jumps

Integrating the use of apparatus in Gymnastics is vital for pupils' progression. Not least, teaching pupils how to lift, carry and place large objects are important transferable skills. Through the process of planning, assembling, using and dismantling apparatus pupils will develop their confidence and awareness of safe practice in Gymnastics.

TEACHING TIP

Distribute apparatus around the edge of the school hall to make it accessible and reduce assembly/dismantling time.

Check that apparatus:

- is complete (rubber feet, plastic knobs, etc.);
- can be placed on a firm footing;
- is clean and nonslip (including mats);
- coverings are not ripped or surfaces splintered;
- locking devices can be fully secured;
- can be accessed easily;
- can be assembled by the pupils.

TEACHING TIP

Encourage pupils to visualise the layout of separate apparatus 'stations' and to work together in assembling apparatus through the use of apparatus cards (see examples in Figures 6.3 and 6.4).

Take the time to teach pupils how to carry and place equipment. It is helpful to establish simple guidelines for the pupils to follow:

■ Always face the direction of travel.

■ Ensure sufficient pupils are in position to lift the apparatus easily.

■ Lift with bent legs and a straight back on a count of '1, 2, 3, lift'.

■ Move to new position and place apparatus on the count of '1, 2, 3, down'.

■ For each apparatus 'station':

• Large items out first (boxes, benches, tables and frames);

• Small items out last (mats, skipping ropes, hoops);

• Ensure adequate entry and exit points to avoid queues;

• Encourage use of space around apparatus;

• Encourage planning the route across the apparatus;

• Set specific challenges for each apparatus formation.

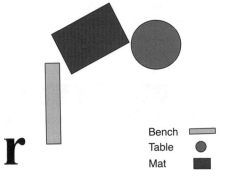

Bench
Table
Mat

FIGURE 6.3
Key Stage 1 apparatus
station card

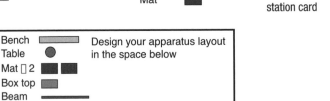

Bench   Design your apparatus layout
Table   in the space below
Mat 2
Box top
Beam

Apparatus challenge:

In the space above write an appropriate challenge for your equipment layout

FIGURE 6.4
Key Stage 2 apparatus
station card

Planning the layout of the room

■ Ensure apparatus 'stations' allow sufficient travelling proximity between them (enough to accommodate 'rolling out', 'walking away' or 'jumping from' space).

■ Allow up to 2m between apparatus and walls/windows.

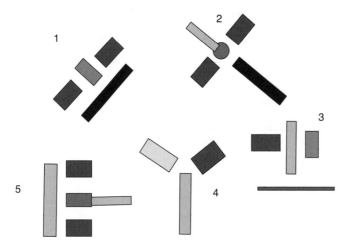

FIGURE 6.5 Plan the layout of the room

TEACHING TIP

Organise pupils into apparatus groups. Each group can assemble and dismantle the same apparatus station each week. Appoint a different group leader on a weekly basis to organise assembly and dismantling.

To begin with, pupils should be restricted to working at a single station. After sufficient time to explore the theme at that station there may be time to move to another station. To evaluate and improve sequences of movement on floor and apparatus requires an ability to appreciate quality in technique and composition. This will develop through regular opportunities to see and discuss high quality gymnastic performance. Working from task cards (see example in Figure 6.6), viewing images, and watching video recordings and live performance in class will help to develop an appreciation of what is possible and raise pupils' expectations of performance. Not least, the opportunity to talk about Gymnastics with their peers provides another opportunity to develop speaking and listening skills and extend their vocabulary.

Forward roll

Teaching points	Extension ideas
Take weight on hands. Tuck chin to chest. Push with legs, tuck tight and reach forward to stand up.	Try different starting and finishing positions. Try rolling **on** apparatus. Try rolling **from** apparatus.

In pairs

Watch your partner's attempt and describe to them what they do well and what they might improve (use the teaching points and extension ideas above).

Try adopting a variety of balance positions and practise rolling into or away from them.

Devise a short sequence with your partner where both of you perform and which includes a forward roll from one or both of you.

FIGURE 6.6 Example of a KS2 task card

Swimming and water-based activities

The requirements for Key Stage 2 state that pupils should be taught to:

■ swim competently, confidently and proficiently over a distance of at least 25 metres;
■ use a range of strokes effectively such as front crawl, backstroke and breaststroke;
■ perform safe self-rescue in different water-based situations.

Being able to swim is a prerequisite for a wide range of other water-based activity experiences such as sailing, canoeing, water-skiing and snorkelling. The pool environment offers such diverse potential that it can be used to encourage pupils to develop and extend their thinking skills in other practical activity areas. In water, pupils can try to outwit their opponents through playing games; they can strive to replicate movements as in Gymnastics; they can race as in athletics; they can solve problems as in outdoor and adventurous activities; and they can choreograph expressive, rhythmical movement phrases as in Dance. Swimming is both vital and versatile, so much so that the requirement remains that pupils should be taught to swim at least 25 metres. Hardy (2000) suggested that the presence of the 25 metre target in the previous programme of study, rather than leading to an enhanced swimming experience for pupils, ironically can lead to a narrow curriculum focused exclusively on meeting the distance. In so doing, he warned, pupils may not fully develop the basic skills and understanding of safety around water that the target was introduced to guarantee. Many would argue that swimming is a natural activity and that the earlier children are introduced to water, the sooner they will acquire the confidence and co-ordination required for efficient and effective propulsion. Many schools will no doubt choose to introduce pupils to swimming as early as possible.

Robertson (1994) argues that the swimming curriculum should address three core skill themes:

- Confidence building
- Personal survival
- Whole stroke techniques.

Confidence building is essential, and here are some suggestions for activities:

- Water entry and exit; travelling through water; bringing water to the face; submerging to collect items from the bottom.
- Changing shape in the water (including prone and supine positions); floating (using buoyancy aids as appropriate); regaining feet from prone and supine floating positions.
- Playing travelling games involving moving arms and legs to change speed and direction in the water.

Once pupils have developed water confidence, rapid progress can be made with developing new techniques.

Personal survival skills include pushing off; gliding; swimming under water; turning; rolling; treading water; feet and head-first surface diving; entering and exiting the water without the use of steps. For whole-stroke techniques, practical experience of a range of propulsive techniques on the front, back and side, using a 'whole part whole' methodology, is an effective way of improving pupils' skills and their knowledge and understanding of how the strokes work.

> **TEACHING TIP**
>
> Create and laminate task/information cards about stroke development practices for pupils to use independently, in pairs, or in small groups.

Water-confidence activities

- 'What's my name?' Think of a name, take a breath, put your head in the water and say the name. Your partner has to lip-read your name through the bubbles!
- 'Jellyfish'. Divide the group into two. One half of the group spread out in the water, each holding on to a buoyancy aid to practise floating. The rest of the group have to cross to the other side without touching one of the 'jellyfish'. Jellyfish can only reach out with their tentacles if they are floating. If you are touched, join the jellyfish.

Personal survival activities

After some initial practice at the specified techniques pupils may be ready to take on challenges such as:

How long can you keep going around a personal survival obstacle course without touching the ground? Try to keep going for set lengths of time, e.g., 5 minutes, 12 minutes. The course should involve:

- swimming on the surface
- swimming under water
- carrying equipment
- floating or sculling for a set period of time
- retrieving equipment from the bottom of the pool.

A circuit of different challenges around the pool might take the form shown in Figure 6.7.

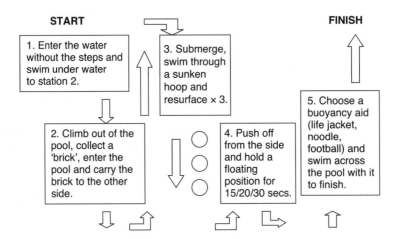

FIGURE 6.7 Different challenges around the pool

Whole-stroke development activities

To avoid the monotony of simply swimming endless widths and lengths, keep pupils motivated by providing them with the opportunity to use their developing techniques in challenging tasks, and reflect on the outcomes of those tasks. Try using activities such as timed swims, distance swims, medley swims, team relay swims. For each of these activities pupils should be encouraged to compete against the clock and keep a record of their personal best times.

Evaluating and improving performance

Pupils rarely get the chance to view their swimming technique or to compare their technique with another. For this reason, it is advisable to establish a buddy system where one pupil swims while their partner observes their effort. It is now possible, through using digital technology, to show pupils video footage of their performance or compare still images of their technique with that of their peers or elite swimmers.

Through the effective use of demonstrations, video extracts and a buddy system, pupils will develop their knowledge and understanding to help develop their own and others' techniques.

TEACHING TIP

Use a buddy system to encourage pupils to observe and talk to each other about their technique. Use technique cards to help the observer focus on specific features of the stroke, as shown in Figure 6.8.

Back crawl

Things to look for

Legs
- Floppy ankles
- Keep knees below the surface
- Imagine you're kicking a ball off the surface of the water
- Avoid too much splash.

Arms
- Lead with the thumb
- Arm brushes ear
- Reach for the top of the catch
- Little finger enters first.

FIGURE 6.8 An example of a technique card

Athletic activities

Whether as observers or participants, by the time they enter Key Stage 2 pupils are likely to have gained some personal experience of an athletic event. Across the country, the raw material of track and field athletics is practised informally in the playground on a daily basis. As pupils challenge themselves, and one another, to run faster, throw further and jump higher they are engaging in a rudimentary form of athletics, at the heart of which lies a burning curiosity to find out what they are capable of and an intrinsic desire to compete. Primarily concerned with the pursuit and fulfilment of individual potential, rather than the measurement of success in specified technical events, the athletic experience in the Primary school should be viewed as a means to an end, not an end in itself. In Key Stage 2, pupils should take part in and design challenges and competitions that call for precision, speed, power or stamina. They demonstrate running, jumping and throwing skills both singly and in combination and pace themselves in these challenges and competitions.

Almond (1989) and O'Neill (1996) agree that the traditional teacher-centred approach to teaching athletics, which privileges 'events' and the learning of recognised techniques, represents a narrow and exclusive method. A broader and more inclusive approach, in which the child is at the centre of the process, they argue, is more likely to ensure that pupils remain motivated to learn, regardless of their athletic prowess. A pupil-centred approach demands that we rethink the roles of pupil as 'athletic performer' and teacher as 'event coach'. In pupil-centred athletics the content and presentation of lessons should be such that all pupils are encouraged to strive to improve, fulfil their potential and enjoy the athletic challenge. This is unlikely to be realised using the traditional model in which we may find pupils running against one another over set distances to establish a rank order. Through planning a progressive programme, in which pupils learn to gather information about their performance through measuring, recording and comparing, their focus is shifted from, 'Who is best?' to 'What is my best?' and 'How much better can I get?'

Track and field athletics represents only one form of athletic endeavour. Athletic events include all of those activities in which objective measurement, such as time, distance and weight, determines the winner. Thus rowing, cycling and weightlifting fall into the same broad sport category as pole vault, javelin and 100m sprint. In athletic events, participants strive to maximise their performance to finish ahead of their opponents, improving their chances through dedication to training in preparation for competition. It is usually through participating in activities linked to individual track and field events, however, that pupils get their first taste of the athletic experience.

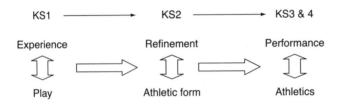

FIGURE 6.9 The progression in athletic activities

Through measuring, comparing and evaluating their efforts in the fundamental movement patterns of walking, running, jumping and throwing, pupils will be made aware of their physical capacity, begin to understand and develop a love of competition, and enjoy the sweetness of success. As O'Neill (1996) points out, through careful planning and structured teaching, competition and success become compatible for all pupils, not just the physically gifted. The challenge for all teachers is to set a range of differentiated tasks that serve to motivate all pupils to strive to improve. In our experience, most Primary pupils will approach such tasks with vigour and enthusiasm, making the teaching of athletic activities a pleasure.

Pupils' earliest exposure to athletic challenge is through play. The core skills of athletic activities, running, jumping and throwing, are also integral to Gymnastics, Games and Dance. Improvement in co-ordinating these actions will arise as a natural consequence of regular opportunities to practise. During Key Stage 2, these movements can be isolated, explored and refined. At Key Stage 3 and beyond, these movements are further developed according to the structures and rules of specific events (see Figure 6.8).

A pupil-centred athletics curriculum will centre around running, jumping and throwing in many different ways. Having practised these within other activities at Key Stage 1, at Key Stage 2 these actions need to be isolated to be improved. The following lists the types of activities that might be included in an athletics programme, under each of these headings:

Running

- Technique
- At different paces
- Over different distances
- Acceleration and deceleration
- Starting and finishing
- Around the bend
- Over obstacles
- In relays
- Tactics

TECHNICAL TIPS

- Run on balls of feet
- Slight lean in the direction of travel
- High knee lift
- Vigorous forwards and backwards movement with the arms

SAFETY: Make sure pupils' shoes are secure and properly laced.

TEACHING TIP

Show pupils images of runners and ask them to comment on their technique. This will highlight the key points and help them to improve their running.

Jumping

- Phases
  - Preparation
  - Take off
  - Flight
  - Landing
- For height
  - scissor technique
  - roll technique
- For distance (single jumps)
  - standing start (one- or two-footed take off)
  - running start
- For distance (combination jumps)
  - standing start
  - running start
- Assisted – using springboards or low platforms.

TECHNICAL TIPS

Standing broad jump – to show use of arms swinging backwards and then forwards at take off.

Scissor technique – stand sideways to the bar. Take-off foot is the one further from the bar. Kick lead leg upwards and over the bar. Take-off foot follows behind.

Roll technique – stand sideways to the bar. Take-off foot is the one nearer to the bar. Swing leg up and over the bar, causing the body to turn to face the bar. Take-off leg follows.

SAFETY: Always land on your feet.

Throwing

- For accuracy
- For distance
- Using different techniques
  - Underarm
  - Push
  - Pull
  - Sling
  - Heave

TEACHING TIP

When planning to improve pupils' skills in athletics lessons, always include activities for at least two of the three core skills. Select a focus activity (e.g., running) and a secondary activity (e.g., throwing).

Pupils will enjoy practising the core athletic skills through problem solving. Try the following:

Running

How far can you run? Pupils work in pairs to mark and measure how far they can run in 3 secs, 6 secs, 12 secs. Vary the task by changing the starting position – lying, sitting, kneeling, standing. Collect distances for each time and place the data in a graph when pupils return to the classroom. Repeat the exercise over different times, e.g., 1 min or 3 mins.

Jumping

Can you jump your own height? Pupils work in pairs to mark on the ground their body length. Using different jumping techniques, can they jump equal to or exceed their own height?

World record jumps. How many jumps do you need to take to match the world record high jump, pole vault, long jump and triple jump? Measure and mark out all the distances on the field/playground and ask a partner to count your jumps.

Throwing

Which goes furthest? Using three different objects (large ball, quoit, small ball) conduct an investigation with a partner to find out which ball goes furthest. Each athlete throws each ball three times using each technique. Each athlete completes a table like the one shown in Table 6.9.

TABLE 6.9 Which goes furthest?

Object/technique	Sitting push			Kneeling push			Standing push		
Attempts	1st	2nd	3rd	1st	2nd	3rd	1st	2nd	3rd
Large ball									
Quoit									
Small ball									

Discuss your results with your partner.

Which was the furthest throw?

Which technique proved best for distance?

Which object travelled the shortest distance?

Can you explain your answers?

While measuring and recording performance data provides opportunities to reflect on the magnitude of performance, it is equally important to encourage pupils to develop their observation skills and identify quality in performance. Pupils' knowledge of performance will accumulate through looking at live demonstrations, still images or diagrams and video of the core actions. Older pupils can even be encouraged to develop their own performance task cards as a guide for one another when watching their partner's performance. Figure 6.10 shows an example.

Overarm throw

When your partner throws, check to see if they:	First attempt	Second attempt
• Stand sideways on to the target		
• Start with their opposite foot forwards (right arm thrower should have left leg forwards)		
• Take their throwing arm back behind their body but keep their hand above their shoulder		
• Lean slightly backwards using their other arm to balance		
• Turn their hips and chest towards the target		
• Move their weight forwards on to their front leg		
• Move their arm quickly		
• Keep both feet on the floor		
• Keep looking at the target		

FIGURE 6.10 An example of a performance task card

Outdoor and adventurous activities

The experience of moving in different, challenging and changing environments has, for many years, been acknowledged to contribute to pupils' personal, moral, social and emotional development. The outdoor and adventurous experience has been designed therefore to provide opportunities for pupils to develop physical, psychological, cognitive and emotional skills, such that they can draw upon these resources when faced with unforeseen challenges.

Martin (2000) helpfully draws the important distinction between outdoor and adventurous (O&A) activities and outdoor pursuits. Whereas managing learning in outdoor pursuits will normally require additional qualifications, reduced pupil–teacher ratios and take place away from the school site, he argues that O&A activities can be taught by the class teacher, using existing facilities on the school site and to the whole class at the same time. O&A activities are process-oriented and designed to engage pupils in developing the necessary thinking skills to solve problems, and to build trust, confidence and co-operation. The success of O&A activities thus relies heavily on the teacher's skilfulness in evoking a sense of adventure for their pupils. Pupils' tolerance of adventure, or their adventure threshold, will shift as they experience new situations. It remains vital, therefore, that teachers are sensitive to the range of adventure tolerance in any class and avoid setting challenges that will cause pupils' adventure threshold to be lowered rather than raised. Well-managed O&A activities will provide pupils with feelings of exhilaration, accomplishment and pride. At Key Stage 2, pupils should take part in outdoor activity challenges, including following trails, in familiar, unfamiliar and changing environments; use a range of orienteering and problem-solving skills and work with others to meet the challenges.

O&A activities in Key Stage 2 can therefore be broadly categorised into three areas, focusing on the development of:

1 Orientation skills

2 Communication/collaboration skills

3 Problem-solving skills

Acquiring and developing skills in O&A activities

The skills identified in Table 6.12 could be introduced at any stage from Year 2 onwards. In addition to trying these activities during lesson time, pupils should be encouraged to practice these skills during active playtime and at home. The review questions identified at the foot of each table focus on evaluating and improving performance.

The skills identified below are best learned through application in a range of activities in different contexts. Try the suggestions shown in Tables 6.10 and 6.11.

Since much of the learning that takes place through these O&A activities is associated with personal development rather than technical proficiency, the thinking, talking and reviewing that takes place after the event is an important part of the process. There are numerous ways in which activity reviews can be conducted. Since not all pupils will be

TABLE 6.10 Outdoor and adventurous activities at KS2

Activities	Adaptations	Technical tips	Signs of success
Orientation Orientating a map Identifying features on a map Finding where you are Planning and walking on a short route along a trail	Simple/complex maps. Large/small landmarks. More/less distance between signposts on a trail. Familiar/unfamiliar terrain.	Hold map parallel to ground in front of chest. Move feet rather than the map to line up key features/landmarks.	Pupils talk to each other about how to orientate a map. Able to locate position on map. Able to navigate around a marked trail unaided.
Communication/ collaboration Giving instructions Listening to instructions Trusting your partner/ earning your partner's trust Being sensitive towards others	Simple/complex instructions. More/less 'risk'. More/less confident partners.	Think about what to say before speaking. Always be polite. Reassure partner with positive talk.	Groups start working quickly without argument. Pupils place trust in one another.
Problem solving Assessing risk Decision making Analysis of outcome and process Reviewing and target setting	Simple/complex problems. Provision of more/less verbal guidance.	Use planning time before acting. Listen to a range of views before deciding on course of action. Prioritise action.	'Blameless' post-activity discussion. Constructive thoughtful analysis.
Review questions	Can you explain how to set a map to one of your parents? Can you describe the qualities of a good team leader?		

TABLE 6.11 Orientation – finding your way

Activities	Adaptations	Technical tips	Signs of success
Treasure hunt In pairs or small groups, collect items from a list.	More/fewer items.	Encourage pupils to stay together and plan where to go to collect items before they start the hunt. Encourage the use of directional terms – right, left, ahead, behind.	Pupils co-operate in planning.
Follow a trail In pairs or small groups, pupils follow a picture trail collecting a letter at each location. Make as many words as possible with the letters collected.	More/fewer photos. Easier/harder to locate.	Use digital photos of landmarks around the school campus for the location of clues.	Pupils listen to each other's ideas and take it in turns to lead.
Orienteering Using a map to locate and visit a series of points on a permanent orienteering course.	Familiar/unfamiliar terrain. More or fewer control points. Work in small groups/pairs.	Decide on the order of points before setting off.	Collecting all control points. Speed of completion.
Review question	Can you identify any potential hazards on your journeys around the school?		
What next?	Work from simple maps to follow trails in unfamiliar locations.		

confident to express themselves openly, it is good practice to vary the way in which pupils are asked to reflect and share their feelings about participation. The following suggestions are worth considering and can be conducted as a whole class or in smaller groups:

■ After any activity, pupils sit down with the teacher for a whole-class question and answer session on what they liked or disliked about the activity and how it made them feel.

■ Make a large circle with skipping ropes (sometimes referred to as a 'racoon circle'). All pupils start inside the circle. Pupils are encouraged to say something about the experience in order to step outside the circle. The review is complete when the circle is empty.

■ The teacher writes down on a whiteboard key words that relate to the activity. Using their own mini whiteboards, pupils are encouraged to write down one of the key words that relates to how they did or how they felt during the activity. Pupils then search among the class for anyone else who has the same word. They sit together and explain why they chose that word.

TABLE 6.12 Communication/collaboration activity and problem solving

Activities	Adaptations	Technical tips	Signs of success
Alphabet soup Groups of six pupils create large letter shapes on the floor.	More/fewer pupils to accommodate.	Take a picture of the shape for pupils to review and improve their position.	Accurate letter shapes. Effective collaboration.
Stepping stones Groups of six pupils cross the hall using only hoops to stand in.	More/fewer hoops. Larger/smaller hoops. More/less time.	Make sure the gap between the hoops can be straddled.	Evidence of planning before setting off.
Jungle trek Groups of six pupils collaborate to travel over each of the obstacles on their jungle adventure.	More/fewer attempts. More/less time.	Obstacle course around the school hall to include: stepping stones, rope swing, climbing frame, sloping bench bridge.	Pupils can describe how they feel when they are successful as a group. Pupils can describe how they could improve their group performance.
Review questions	What did your group do really well? What could your group do to work together even more effectively? Did you break any of the rules? What should happen if rules are broken?		
What next?	Mix the groups. Take similar tasks outdoors. Take similar tasks to unfamiliar environments.		

Developing knowledge and understanding of fitness and health

During Key Stage 2 pupils should know how exercise affects the body in the short term; to warm up and prepare appropriately for different activities and know why physical activity is good for their health and wellbeing and why wearing appropriate clothing and being hygienic is good for their health and safety.

Short-term effects of exercise

Lay out a line of markers at the side of the activity space to act as a guide to temperature, breathing rate or heart rate as follows:

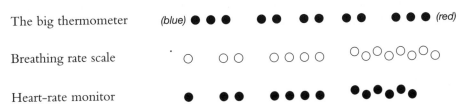

Ask pupils to position themselves on the scale at the start of an activity, in the middle, and at the end. This provides a good start to a conversation about the immediate impact of exercise.

Warming up (and cooling down)

The warm up (and the cool down) are important features of any lesson and should be part of a seamless movement experience for the pupils. Introducing pupils at Key Stage 1 to the concept of getting ready for action, and for inaction at the end of the lesson, is vital to establish good habits for the future. At Key Stage 2 a typical warm up will combine the mobilisation of joints and pulse-raising activity in whole body actions performed with control, often under the direct command of the teacher. This should be followed by some held stretched shapes, or stretching 'moments', in which pupils enjoy what should be the pleasant and comfortable sensation of stretching groups of muscles in combination. By Years 5 and 6 pupils should be able to independently identify warm-up routines for particular activities and be able to perform appropriate stretches for specific parts of the body – upper arm, front and back of upper leg, back of lower leg, chest and back.

The cool down phase of the lesson provides an opportunity to review progress, observe and comment upon performance, share ideas, thoughts and questions and to look forward to the next lesson. During the discussion the pupils should be encouraged to revisit some of the stretches that they performed during the warm up and to discuss with 'talking partners' what they have learned and what their personal targets for improvement are. This should ensure that the more sedate pace of activity prepares pupils both physically and mentally for the transition back to the classroom.

Engaging pupils in conversations about the short-term effects of exercise will lead to discussions about why they should change for PE, the different types of clothing used in different activities and the importance of preparing the body prior to and following any kind of exertion. Encouraging pupils to examine the extent to which exercise is both a normal and pleasurable part of their daily lives will provide opportunity to reflect on their personal responsibility for maintaining their health. PE provides a useful link to science programme of study and offers good potential for making cross-curricular links.

Chapter summary

This chapter has provided an introduction to the activity areas making up the PE curriculum experience for pupils at Key Stage 2. We have sought to demonstrate how to build upon the work carried out in Key Stage 1 and develop pupils' knowledge, skills and understanding. Providing pupils with a coherent programme of accessible and age-appropriate experiences in which they can enjoy success is the key to nurturing a lifelong love of physical activity. Underpinning our approach is an emphasis on playful experiences that do not steer pupils into adapted forms of adult sporting activity too soon. Take your time and have fun with your pupils.

Questions for reflection

- Is the Key Stage 2 PE programme in your school pupil-centred or activity-centred?
- Does your PE curriculum include all the areas of activity? Is there a balance between these so that pupils receive as broad a PE curriculum as possible?
- Does your curriculum enhance the practical activities discussed in this chapter, by including activities such as mountain biking, martial arts, street dancing or other games?

References

Almond, L. (1989) (ed.) *The Place of Physical Education in School*. London: Kogan Page.

Bunker, D. and Thorpe, R. (1982) 'A model for the teaching of games in the secondary schools'. *Bulletin of Physical Education* 10, pp. 10–16.

Davies, A. (2000) 'Teaching dance'. In R. Bailey and T. Macfayden (eds) *Teaching Physical Education 5–11*. London: Continuum.

Douglas, M. (1999) *Primary PE: Dance*. London: Hodder & Stoughton.

Hardy, C. (2000) 'The school experience as a working laboratory'. *British Journal of Teaching Physical Education* vol. 31, no. 3.

Martin, B. (2000) 'Teaching outdoor and adventurous activities'. In R. Bailey and T. MacFadyen (eds) *Teaching Physical Education 5–11*. London: Continuum.

O'Neill, J. (1996) *Athletic Activities for Juniors*. London: A & C Black.

Robertson, E. (1994) *Physical Education: A Practical Guide*. London: John Murray.

Planning, teaching, assessment

7

What happens *before* the lesson?

Planning and preparation

By the end of this chapter you should be able to:

- Understand the principles and purposes associated with effective long-, medium- and short-term planning for physical education.
- Develop knowledge of differentiating learning experiences in PE to accommodate a spectrum of pupils' needs.
- Know how to organise pupils and resources for effective learning.
- Critically reflect on your own planning for all practical activity areas in the subject.

Planning can be considered as a process in which decisions are taken about how to reach a specified destination. If we think about being 'physically educated' as the destination, we can plan the journey accordingly:

- Where do we want to go?
- When do we want to arrive?
- How will we get there?
- How do we know when we have arrived?

Inevitably, however, the journey towards being physically educated will be long and complex, with no clear ending and no specified route. When planning a long and unpredictable journey such as this, it makes sense to break it up into manageable stages, where key milestones along the way can be marked and celebrated and used to measure progress by. During each stage of the journey, to avoid being knocked off course, potential hazards must be anticipated and avoided. By embracing the challenges and opportunities that such journeys inevitably bring, both leaders (teachers) and travellers (pupils) will emerge more knowledgeable, confident and skilled than when they embarked. Teachers charged with planning the physical education journey for their pupils have the additional challenge, however, of ensuring that every pupil's passage is smooth, continuous and progressive, despite moving from one key stage to the next and, in so doing, often moving schools. This inevitably means that colleagues will need to share with others information about the pathway they have been following and that pupils will need to be knowledgeable about their own progress on this journey. For this reason, teachers' planning needs to be both well thought through and clearly documented.

While planning is one of the most significant factors affecting teacher effectiveness (Bailey, 2000), preparing detailed plans to support teaching and learning is often considered more of a chore than a pleasure. Where plans are in place, OFSTED (2005) reports that teachers appear to focus more on what activities will take place than on the learning outcomes associated with those activities. While focusing on the detail of events at the micro level is commendable, and should contribute to high quality outcomes, taking one's eye off the big picture can lead to a disjointed and ad hoc experience for the pupils. Thus it is important to recognise that all planning must be placed in context and that to plan for the entire physical education journey necessitates consideration of the process at a number of different levels. Raymond (1998) identifies these interdependent and mutually supportive layers in the planning process:

> **Whole school**: how does PE contribute to the overall school aims and mission? Does the PE curriculum address and develop cross curricular themes? Is the PE curriculum appropriate and does it facilitate progression and continuity?
>
> **Key stage**: What aspects of knowledge, skills and understanding are developed through which activity experiences at each key stage? How much time will be allocated to each activity area in each key stage?
>
> **Class:** Which activity experiences will be used as the focus for each of the four aspects of learning? How will pupils' progress be monitored?
>
> (Adapted from Raymond, 1998, p. 139)

For each layer to serve its purpose and usefully contribute to the achievement of the ultimate goal – the physically educated pupil – different questions need to be asked at each stage. Broad, strategic questions steer the thinking at the whole-school level while detailed operational questions govern what happens during lessons. Both the questions and the answers are to be found in the school's PE planning documentation, which is usually organised hierarchically as follows:

- School PE policy – the big picture
- Schemes of work – long-term plans
- Units of work – medium-term plans
- Lesson outlines – short-term plans

The rationale for connecting the layers of planning in this way is to ensure that both teachers and their pupils are mindful of the fact that each activity within each lesson contributes in a small way to achieving the overall goal. The following section explains the layers in more detail.

The lexicon of planning in PE

School PE Policy

This is a summary statement setting out the aims and objectives for PE in the school. This document describes the purpose, nature and management of PE in the school. It sets out the unique contribution of PE to the development of the whole child and draws connections between PE and other areas of the school curriculum. To be formally adopted by the school it should be agreed by all the staff and approved by the school governing body. All policy documents should be subject to review on a regular basis.

Scheme of work or PE curriculum map

This is the long-term plan for PE across the key stage or the school as a whole. This document provides an 'at a glance' illustration of the allocation of curriculum time to specific activity experiences across one or more key stages. It represents the school's interpretation of the National Curriculum in its local context. The curriculum map is used to balance pupils' entitlement within the constraints of the school's access to facilities and resources. It is particularly helpful to colleagues if, in addition to naming the activity area and/or venue, the scheme indicates the central theme and key resources to use in developing the learning experience for pupils (i.e. published schemes which might be particularly helpful).

Unit of work

Each cell in the PE curriculum map represents a unit of work. This is the medium-term planning stage and provides further detail regarding what will take place over a half-term period (usually between five and eight weeks). This is a very important level in the planning process in which the aims and objectives for whole school PE are located within activity-based experiences. A well-organised unit plan will make the planning of individual lessons much easier, will provide coherence and context to those lessons and should ensure good progression. While each school tends to adopt a template for medium-term planning that suits their purpose, common features of the headings found on unit plans include: learning objectives, expectations of the pupils, core or target tasks, outline content (sometimes presented as a weekly itinerary), resources, curriculum links, assessment opportunities.

Lesson plan

This is the short-term plan that details the distribution of learning activities within the allocated lesson period. The format for lesson planning varies between teachers and schools but should include: learning objectives, appropriately differentiated learning activities, class organisation and management, deployment of resources, the role of additional adults and guidance on assessment (what to look for). Space should be provided at the end of the template for making notes, evaluating the lesson.

Learning objectives

Learning objectives (LOs) communicate what the teacher is trying to teach; what the pupils are expected to know, understand or be able to do (that they couldn't do before); how their achievement will be measured; and what is deemed to be good evidence that the intended outcome has been achieved. In short, LOs describe what the learner will know, feel or be able to do, under specified conditions and to a specified standard.

Learning activities

These are the activities that are devised, selected and presented to help pupils achieve the learning objectives. A range of progressive learning activities should be planned in order to challenge all pupils appropriately. Teachers should be able to vary the presentation of the learning activities to appeal to different pupils' learning preferences.

Teaching points

These highlight important details in the learning activities that might relate to safety, technique or quality of movement. These can be presented in a number of different ways: orally, in print, through diagrams or images. While there may be many teaching points for any particular learning activity, the teacher needs to be selective in the amount of information provided at any one time.

Initiating the planning process: three scenarios

The scenarios presented below provide a context for initiating the planning process at different stages. Consider each in turn and reflect on the nature of the questions posed at each stage. What would be your advice to Sophie, Alice and John?

Next year – thinking about the long term

Sophie has just been appointed as PE co-ordinator in her school. She has been teaching for three years, is confident in her own teaching (particularly in games, athletics and swimming) and is very enthusiastic about her new role. Following her first meeting with colleagues Sophie starts thinking about how PE at Key Stage 2 contributes to pupils' physical education. What sorts of experiences do pupils need in order to become 'physically educated'?

Next term – thinking about the medium term

Alice has just been appointed to her first post as a newly qualified teacher in a large urban Primary school. She is keen to get organised and wants to make a positive start but she is a little nervous about teaching PE in Key Stage 1 independently for the first time. The curriculum map for PE suggests that, for one of their two PE lessons in the autumn term, her pupils will be 'doing' gymnastics. When Alice asked to see the planning documentation for PE she was directed to a published scheme that had recently been adopted by the school. While this provides broad guidance about themes and content that would be appropriate for her year group, Alice is still confused. How does she convert these ideas into a series of progressive lessons that are appropriate and challenging for all of the pupils in her class?

Next week – thinking about the short term

John is in his second year of teacher training and has just taught his first PE lesson (Year 3 games activities) on school placement. He is a very competent footballer and he thought his knowledge of the game and his own skills would see him through. Very early on in the lesson he realised that his broad outline plan was insufficient to ensure that all pupils had a useful learning experience. The pupils were enthusiastic at the start but, because they didn't understand what he wanted them to do, some of them started misbehaving. It took longer than expected to organise the groups, the playing areas and the equipment.

TASK: PLANNING FOR PURPOSE

To resolve their problems, Sophie, Alice and John need answers to some key questions. While there may be many different answers to the questions posed, it is important to ask the right questions. Some of the key questions to consider are suggested below. Can you identify any others?

Long-term planning

- What should the pupils know, understand and be able to do in PE by the end of Key Stage 2?
- What should they know, understand and be able to do at the end of Years 3, 4 and 5?
- How much curriculum time should be devoted to PE to achieve these targets?
- What activities will pupils need to experience to reach these targets?

Medium-term planning

- What should the pupils know, understand and be able to do at the end of this Gymnastics unit of work?
- How much activity time will they have to reach this target?
- What resources will be needed in order to get them there?

Short-term planning

- What should the pupils know, understand and be able to do by the end of the next lesson?
- How will the pupils be organised?
- In what order will pupils attempt the tasks set?
- How will their performance be assessed?

The demonstrations didn't work and his explanations were too complex. In the short time the pupils were active they made no progress. His expectations about the pupils' ability to cope were unrealistic. After the lesson, feeling disappointed, he reflects on his plan and tries to identify what he needs to do to improve things for next week, when his university tutor will observe the lesson.

What these familiar scenarios reveal is that planning for progress in PE is a multi-layered, complex and challenging activity. When planning for the long, medium or short term, the issues that need to be considered may vary but what remains common is the need to think carefully about what you are seeking to achieve. Visualising the goal – an effective demonstration; a purposeful and safe lesson; a stimulating and inspiring unit of work; or a physically educated child – is an essential first step in the process of deciding how to get there.

Thinking about planning – planning for pupils' thinking

Teaching is a professional thinking activity and what is actually done in the classroom is largely dependent upon the teacher's thought processes that have gone on before the lesson.

(Mawer, 1995)

Mawer's (1995) attention to teachers' thinking is an important starting point when considering how to plan for effective learning experiences in physical education. The fact that physical education lessons are designed to engage pupils in active, practical experiences in direct contrast to the sedentary, non-practical 'classroom' lessons that occupy much of the school day, does not render the former 'thoughtless' and the latter 'thoughtful'. Often movements are controlled automatically and we only become aware of the thinking that controls movement when it gets in the way of doing it well. Helping pupils to refine their movement performance requires that teachers give due consideration to the thinking required to underpin effective performance, i.e., to teach effectively we have to understand the 'thinking' behind the 'doing'. This means that we need to understand the essence of an activity and the demands that each domain makes on pupils' thinking if we are to plan effectively for improvements in their understanding.

It is a common misconception that being able to do something well is a prerequisite to teaching it well. This reveals a basic confusion of knowledge of 'doing', with knowledge of 'teaching'. Knowledge of 'doing', what we call 'content knowledge', is acquired through personal practice and experience, and it can be extremely valuable to teachers, even initiating the desire to want to teach. In order to teach effectively, however, experienced practitioners continuously draw upon a wealth of other knowledge – knowledge of learners, of curricula, of pedagogy and of context. The synthesis of all of this knowledge – which Shulman (1987) refers to as *pedagogical content knowledge* – enables the teacher to transform personal, practical experience into powerful and effective learning experiences. This takes a great deal of careful thought and planning.

In addition to the accumulated personal and professional experience teachers bring to any teaching/learning episode in PE, the way in which teachers think about PE is, to a greater or lesser extent, determined by a number of factors:

- Statutory curriculum requirements (the National Curriculum);
- Local Authority policies and guidance
- School aims/mission
- School architecture
- School development plan
- School PE policy
- Pupils', parents' and other teachers' (particularly headteachers') expectations.

While each of these factors help to shape our perceptions, since its introduction in the early 1990s, the original National Curriculum has become, by far, the most significant. The way in which the National Curriculum defines PE imposes frameworks for thinking about how activity experiences should be organised and presented to pupils.

TABLE 7.1 Linking practical PE and pupils' thinking

Activity area	Pupils learn to think about:
Dance activities	how to express and communicate ideas, emotions and concepts.
Gymnastic activities	how to replicate actions, agilities and sequences as accurately and precisely as possible.
Games activities	how to outwit the opposition.
Athletic activities	how to produce the best possible performance in relation to fastest, longest, highest, nearest.
Outdoor & Adventurous activities	how to solve problems and overcome challenges for a successful outcome.
Swimming	how to develop all of the above but in water-based contexts.

Table 7.1 illustrates how each activity area of the original PE National Curriculum encourages pupils to think in different ways and reminds us that this should underpin the plans we make. The simple truth is that effective teaching rarely occurs by accident. Teachers have to think through a host of issues prior to delivering a practical learning experience to ensure that the challenges set are meaningful, purposeful, safe and appropriate and meet the expectations laid down in the National Curriculum.

In the early stages of teaching, planning a coherent learning experience that adequately addresses all of these issues can be quite daunting. Some of the questions that these issues present would include: What are the pupils going to do? What will my role be? What do I want the pupils to learn? How will I share this with them? How do I get the level of challenge right? How will I keep everyone safe? How will I keep control of the pupils in the space? What equipment/resources will I need? When should I get the equipment out? How much space will each pupil/group need? What if there isn't enough equipment to go around? How do I get the apparatus out? How should I group the children? Who should work with whom? How much time should they have on each activity?

How do I know when they are making progress? Who should I spend my time with? Who can help? What if the pupils know more about the activity than I do? Who should I get to demonstrate? How will I involve all of the pupils when there is such a wide range of ability?

To help impose some kind of order on this cascade of questions, we suggest that thinking in categories can be helpful. Initially these might be as follows:

- Content-related questions – what will happen?
- Process-related questions – how will it be organised?
- Timing-related questions – when will it take place?
- People/resource-related questions – who will do what, with which equipment?

TASK: CATEGORISING ALL THE QUESTIONS

Categorise the series of questions into those related to content, process, timing or people. Then try adding other questions of your own.

While it is very easy to become singularly focused on content-related issues, it is equally important to continually ask:

- Why am I asking the pupils to do this?
- In what way does this contribute to the overall aim?
- What will pupils learn as a result of this experience?

These questions serve to remind us that in physical education we deploy physical activity as an educational tool and that the central purpose in doing so is pupil, rather than activity, development. While we cannot necessarily predict precisely what every pupil will learn in every situation, by identifying explicit learning objectives we do at least acknowledge a rational purpose behind the selection and ordering of lesson activities. Thus we now turn our attention to the identification and articulation of learning objectives.

Planning for pupils' learning

We know that pupils are learning when we see changes in what they can do, their attitudes, and the ways in which they think and behave. Regardless of the timeframe for which you are making plans (long, medium or short term) it is vital that you set out clear and challenging expectations for pupils that look beyond becoming competent performers in sporting activity and consider the development of the whole person. Casbon and Spackman (2005) suggest that it is sensible to start by looking at:

- What pupils have already learned, experienced and achieved.
- What they already know, understand and can do.
- What they need to learn next in order to improve, make progress and achieve more.

Given that it is unusual for there to be a wealth of existing data about pupils' progress in PE, it is important to seek out information in order to establish a benchmark. This can be done by:

- Talking to the pupils' previous class teacher to check what they have already experienced and achieved.
- Asking the pupils questions, to check their level of knowledge and understanding.
- Setting the pupils physical tasks to determine what they can do.

Once you have been able to identify your pupils' needs, the next step is to set out clear expectations. Using the national expectations set out in the National Curriculum, by the end of Key Stage 1 most pupils can be expected to achieve level 2, improving to level 4 by the end of Key Stage 2. The key to rendering these expectations meaningful and achievable is to communicate these clearly to the pupils. Sharing with your pupils the goals you have set for them can be a very powerful device in ensuring that they are met. To return to the travel analogy, when you know where you are going, you are better placed to identify the landmarks on the way. Giving pupils direction through setting clear targets helps them to make connections between individual activities, lessons and groups of lessons and see a coherent path towards progress.

The planning gap

For many teachers, however, establishing benchmarks and setting expectations are often thought of as collaborative activities, discussed in working parties and subsequently agreed and adopted by the whole staff team. A more pressing individual planning issue is the selection, ordering and organisation of the activities that pupils will undertake – 'What are my pupils actually going to do in the lesson – tomorrow, next week and thereafter?' While these are legitimate concerns, we need to remember that a preoccupation with devising discrete activity-focused lessons, and blocks of lessons, can militate against continuity and progression (Ofsted, 2005). While many teachers have devoted a great deal of time and effort to thinking about and articulating, in PE policies and schemes of work, the ways in which pupils can and should benefit from a stimulating, challenging, relevant and connected physical education, the programme that is delivered to the pupils, in many cases, has continued relatively unchanged over many years. This is what we refer to as the planning 'gap'.

The planning 'gap' exists where broad, age-appropriate and inclusive goals are in place but are not effectively translated into practice. While this may occur for any number of reasons, our concern here is to help teachers to recognise and close the gap.

Target learning tasks

One key strategy for making more explicit connections between the long-term policy aims and the short-term lesson experience is to adopt a system of progressive 'core' or 'target' learning tasks.

By assembling a 'staircase of tasks' to mark progress in knowledge, skills and understanding, the problem of connecting the PE policy goals with the individual units, and the learning activities undertaken within those units, is made more explicit and, in so doing, the planning 'gap' closes. If a staircase of tasks can be established in each area of activity, teachers can exercise choice in deciding which route to follow to achieve their goals.

Figure 7.1 shows a staircase leading to a physically educated pupil. Each riser represents a target/core task. The 'zoom view' shows a single riser consisting of a series of smaller steps – individual lessons.

Thus rather than adopting a bottom–up approach to planning the PE curriculum, we argue that working backwards from the main goal, or a top–down approach, is better suited to mapping progression towards the goal of the physically educated pupil. By sharpening our focus on pupils' development of knowledge, skills and understanding, and establishing landmarks (in the form of end of school, end of key stage, end of year, end of unit targets) to monitor their progress by, we give direction and purpose to the PE experience. Within this structure, devising appropriately challenging and progressive target learning tasks takes on critical significance.

When choosing or designing target learning tasks to help your pupils to achieve a particular intended outcome, keep the outcome clearly in mind and include activities that specifically address the intent of the outcome. It is particularly important to use learning activities that are appropriate and inclusive, and that motivate the pupils. A target learning task should describe, in pupil-friendly language, a challenge that will enable pupils to show what they have learned over a series of lessons.

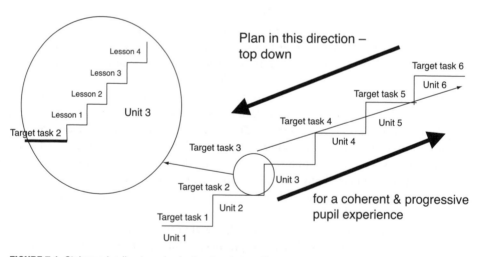

FIGURE 7.1 Staircase leading to a physically educated pupil

Example: Gymnastics unit of work

Choose two ways of travelling and link these to make a movement phrase that you can remember and perform on the floor. Make sure you know where you start and finish, and what shapes you will make to start and finish.

When presented to the pupils this might be adapted to:

We will be learning to make our own Gymnastics sequence (our sequence will include: a clear starting shape, two different ways of travelling and a clear finishing shape). Practise your sequence until you can link these movements smoothly and then show it to a partner.

We will be looking for:

- stillness at the start and at the end

- clear movements and shapes

- smooth links from one action to the next.

To accommodate the pupils' different levels of experience, variations to the level of challenge could be made as follows:

Level 1	Level 2	Level 3
1 Start in a Y shape.	1 Start in a Y shape.	1 Choose a starting shape.
2 Jump forwards three times.	2 Choose a travel.	2 Choose a travel.
3 Lie down.	3 Choose a turn.	3 Choose a turn.
4 Roll back to your starting position.	4 Choose a different travel.	4 Choose a different travel.
5 Lie on your back in a star shape.	5 Lie on your back in a star shape.	5 Choose a finishing shape.

TASK: TARGET LEARNING TASKS

Can you think of further ways to challenge more able pupils?

In our experience, when pupils know what is expected of them and are successful in meeting the challenges set for them, their progress picks up momentum.

By now your head will be spinning with the sheer number of issues to take into consideration. We've reached the point therefore when we need to think about how to commit thoughts, ideas and solutions to paper.

Planning in writing

It's not so much the planning itself that many teachers find mundane, it's the process of committing your thoughts to paper that often proves to be less appealing! Bailey (2000) points out, however, that a clearly laid-out lesson plan serves several purposes. It helps to:

1   remind the teacher of important teaching points;

2   identify gaps in knowledge and stimulate further research/development of additional resources;

3   warn of potential 'crisis' points in the lesson;

4   provide a record of what has taken place.

While this is true for a teacher working alone, the written record becomes even more important where teachers work collaboratively and share their planning ideas. The articulation of thinking (Williams, 1996) that the preparation of a lesson plan demands, enables the teacher to address the immediate organisational issues of the lesson. However, we should continually remind ourselves that lessons, and the activities within them, form a small part of an interconnected web of experience. Figure 7.2 provides a schematic view of the different components of the 'planning web'.

In the next section we present example templates, which can be adapted to suit individual school needs in order to illustrate what information should be captured at each layer of the planning process.

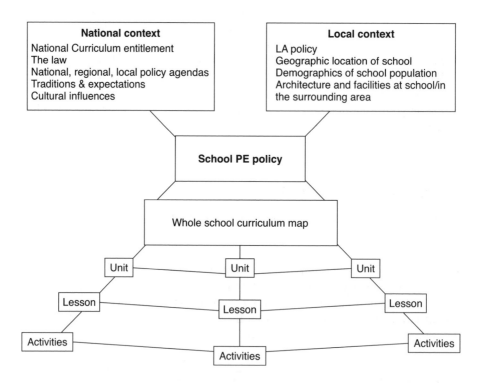

FIGURE 7.2 The PE planning web

Examples of units of work

The following examples show two different medium–term planning templates. The plans have been selected to show different year groups in different activity contexts.

Structuring the learning experience

As the examples of medium–term and short–term planning templates demonstrate, giving due consideration to the order in which the activities selected to deliver the objectives are presented is of vital importance. Establishing a natural flow to the learning experience, whereby pupils are introduced to, assimilate, consolidate, apply and then adapt new knowledge and skills, will increase the likelihood of the lesson objectives being successfully met.

Planning the phases of the lesson

Having experienced PE as a pupil, you will be familiar with the traditional approach to the structure of lessons. Table 7.2 illustrates what might be planned for in each phase and the way in which this structure can be used to focus on different aspects of learning.

TABLE 7.2 Phases of the lesson

Lesson structure	Plan to	NCPE aspect of learning
Introduction	Outline the objectives, the success criteria, the ways in which pupils will be assessed and the range of activities that will take place.	
Warm up	Prepare pupils physically and psychologically for the activities to follow. This should be consistent with the nature of the experience in the rest of the lesson. Warming up for gymnastics by playing a game of tag will not appropriately prepare pupils for what will follow.	Knowledge and understanding of fitness and health
Development	Introduce new knowledge and skills through relevant and challenging practical tasks.	Acquire and develop skills/Evaluate and improve performance.
Application	Provide opportunities for pupils to show what they can do, what they know and understand. This might be through showing a dance phrase, playing a small-sided game or solving a problem.	Select and apply skills, tactics and compositional ideas/Evaluate and improve performance.
Conclusion	Summarise what has been learned, celebrate success and look forward to the next lesson. Cooling down through low-intensity activity and stretching will help to calm pupils down for their return to the classroom.	Knowledge and understanding of fitness and health/Evaluate and improve performance.

Examples of units of work

The following examples show two different medium-term planning templates. The plans have been selected to show different year groups in different activity contexts.

Example 1

Weekly activities for:	Subject:	Classes:	Years:	**Half**	
PE	Athletics	1 and 2	R, Y1, Y2	**Term:**	Summer A 2004

Learning objectives

- to be able to run confidently over different distances;
- to be able to throw, kick or roll and catch an appropriate object;
- to be able to jump in different ways.

Week	Outline	Details
Week 1: Focus: moving feet to position body appropriately	**Each week the children will warm up in a broadly similar pattern, jogging first and then stretching gently, with exercises to make sure that joints are properly warm. They will then rotate in groups to take part in various activities, some of which will be in teams.** a) potato race, putting out or retrieving beanbags; b) rolling and receiving balls down a line; c) standing long jump; d) longer distance, run in pairs, with rests.	Each week there wil be markers, spots, cones, canes, a variety of balls, beanbags, hoops, skipping ropes and bats. Playground chalk will be needed.
Week 2: Focus: using the opposite hand to foot when throwing	Half group coaching on a) throwing activities – beanbags, tennis balls, foam balls, footballs; b) jumping over little cane hurdles in a row. The other half of the group will be improving fitness by doing scout's pace around the edge of the field.	

Week 3: Focus: swinging arms to enable a higher jump	Half group coaching on a) throwing/rolling/kicking and catching/retrieving using balls of different weights and sizes; b) jumping up to touch a weighted band suspended from a netball ring. The other half of the group will participate in a variety of short relay activities.
Week 4: Focus: transferring weight when kicking	Children to work in groups, taking it in turns to lead warm-up exercises for the others to follow. Ch to evaluate the exercises and suggest improvements. a) skipping with a rope static/swaying/turning; b) batting a ball along a course on the ground; c) kicking a ball against the kicking wall from markers; d) running and walking a longer distance.
Week 5: Focus: pointing hand in direction of target when throwing	Three groups to work on relay races of various kinds whilst one group performs an obstacle course which will include: walking along benches, going through hoops, in and out of cones, over and under canes, throwing beanbags into a basket and running back to the start. Ch to suggest ways of improving performance and try them out. Everyone to help clear up and talk about what they have enjoyed.
Week 6 Competition in groups using a carousel	■ Potato race* ■ Long run taking turns in pairs ■ Throwing a beanbag ■ Jumping over little canes or hurdles* ■ Kicking a ball at a target ■ Rolling a ball into a basket ■ Running to hoop, through and on to collect a bean bag, reverse* Children coached on * activities, and encouraged to work co-operatively, helping to coach one another by making helpful comments. Plenary: children to make suggestions about improving performance in different areas.

Example 2

Unit No: 3	Key Stage: 2	AREA OF ACTIVITY: O&AA	Title of Unit: Intro to O&AA	Year 5	Target Level(s): 3/4
		X-curricular links : Geography	Core task: QCA unit 20 task 1	Time: 6 x 50	Venue: Outside/Hall

Unit objectives	Assessment opportunities
Acquiring and developing skills/techniques/ideas	Selecting and applying skills/strategies/ideas	■ Performance of orienteering skills and basic compass work.
To practise and perform different trails and orienteering activities focusing on map orientation and basic compass work.	To solve simple group problems using basic navigation and communication skills.	■ Ability to communicate with others in pair and group tasks to solve problems.
Understanding health and fitness	Evaluating and improving performance	■ Evaluation of own and group performance.
Understand how preparation for O&AA may differ from other activities.	To discuss and evaluate the effectiveness of pair and group performance.	■ Performance of core task.

Structure	Lesson 1	Lesson 2	Lesson 3	Lesson 4	Lesson 5	Lesson 6
Intro	Introduce pupils to the O&AA unit. Explain that the focus is on working within the school environment to solve challenges in groups. Explain core task.	In the hall unless weather is nice. Do the numbers warm-up. Encourage non-friendship groups. End up with pairs.	Star orienteering. In pairs pupils are allocated a map of the school site and a control card. Allow some discussion of the map for familiarisation.	Point to point orienteering. In groups of 3. Each group is allocated one map with controls marked and a control card.	Introduce a compass and teach/review the 8 cardinal points. Play the compass game warm-up.	Introduce pupils to a compass. The red part of the compass always points North. Teach how to take a 'bearing'.

Develop 1	In 3s. Pupils have to find the 'photo place' in 10 photos of the school site. When they find the place there should be a control there so that they can record that they have been there.	'Beanbag' challenge. Each pair has 3 hoops and must move around the hall collecting beanbags. They must only step in their hoops and must carry beanbags with them. Discuss how pupils solved the problem.	Look at the key on the map to identify features. Pupils have to find the different controls marked on the maps (one control marked on each map) and return to the central point each time for a new map.	Allow pupils 5 minutes to plan their route. Ask different groups to go to different controls first so that they can all go at the same time. Perform core task.	Pupils follow a route between cones laid out in a grid square and record the letter code for each cone on their control card. North needs to be clearly marked. Try core task on different course.	Practise walking on a bearing. Start from a small marker, walk on a bearing for 30 paces, after 30 paces add 180 degrees to the bearing and walk 30 paces back. Where should you be?
Develop 2	When each group has seen and visited each photo place discuss the route pupils took to each photo. Was it the shortest? How did they identify each location?	Play number warm-up again. End up with 4 groups of 7. Two groups work while two groups evaluate. Aim is to make a square with the rope while blindfolded. Let all 4 groups have a go before sharing evaluations.	Discuss how to set a map, how to plan the shortest route, and the importance of recording the control information clearly.	Each group follow their own route finding the controls. They only return to the start after finding and recording all the identification letters/numbers on their control card.	Pairs design a route for another pair to follow. They can use the control signs from task one and rearrange them. Pairs complete each other's courses.	Repeat above but walk three sides of a triangle. Follow a short route marked on a map as compass bearings. Use key features to check accuracy.
Conc.	How did each group work together? Any communication or leadership issues?	Discuss communication and organisation within groups.	Discuss reasons for any mistakes. What helps teams to be successful?	Discuss how they decided which way to go. How did they find their way? How well did they work together?	How easy was it to: a) Design a course? b) Follow instructions? c) Meet the core task?	Discuss evaluate progress made against LOs. Set targets for improvement.
Key Vocab	Control marker, control card.	Safety, listening, co-operation.	Route, star orienteering, key, symbols.	Point to point orienteering, map orientation.	Cardinal points, compass.	Compass needle, bearings, pacing.

Swimming lesson plan

Pupils:	Yrs 5/6	Main theme:	Front crawl arm action	Equipment:	Float each, sinkable objects (10), sinking hoops, task cards
No.:	24 (HA:6, MA:10, LA:8)	Contrast:	Underwater search		
Time:	30 mins in water	Lesson:	5th of 10	Adult support:	TA to work with LA group.
Learning objectives:		a) to refine the performance of front crawl arm action b) to be able to describe and comment on a partner's front crawl arm action c) to understand the principles of safe practice when working under water.			

Time	Gp	Learning activity	Teaching points	Organisation
3m	LA MA HA	Introduction/warm up Enter pool 4 x width any stroke Enter pool 6 x width any stroke Enter pool 8 x width any stroke	i) Long body, face down ii) Reach for half width glide iii) Breathing to minimum.	In gps working in pairs, x completes and y follows.
2m	All	Group stretch Tricep stretch, pectoral stretch	i) Demonstrate position and describe what to do ii) Stay low in the water iii) Hold for 8s.	All in standing depth
		Main Theme		
3m	All	Front crawl – whole stroke Continuous swim for 3min	Think about arm action: 'big pull'	In pairs, work/rest Select demonstrators

12m	All	Demonstrations of action	i) Fingers enter first	Organise head-on and profile demonstrations (4 pupils)
		Gp watch several demonstrations using task cards for guidance	ii) Elbow high on recovery	
			iii) Pull along centre line of body	Still working in pairs
		Gp stand in shoulder depth and imitate action	iv) Hand exit at hip.	T advise individually and encourage observer to describe swimmer's arm action. Reinforce TPs with observer.
	LA	Single arm pull ½ W + change arm (using kick board)	LA Can walk on bottom	
	MA	Single arm pull ½ W + change arm (using kick board)	MA Use legs to kick	
	HA	Single arm pull ½ W + change arm (no kick board)	HA No kick board	
		Introduce whole stroke again as appropriate		
		Contrasting activity		
8m	LA	Collect objects thrown by partner (seen)	Attempt feet- and head-first surface dives.	Gps A + B use single channels.
	MA	Collect objects thrown by partner (unseen)		Gp C use deep water
	HA	Collect objects thrown by partner (unseen) but must swim through sunken hoop to search and collect		
2m	All	Scull on back, float and slowly complete 360°		

Assessment: a) ability to describe and imitate correct arm action in FC; b) ability to observe and communicate accurately with partner; c) demonstrating awareness of, and concern for, others.

Evaluation:

> **PLANNING TIP**
>
> While the transitions between phases should ideally be seamless, careful planning of critical moments in the lesson – such as the organisation/reorganisation of groups, the distribution/retrieval of equipment and the provision of important information – can make all the difference.

Differentiation in planning

Just as all good teachers adjust the level of challenge in classroom activities according to the needs of their pupils, in PE teachers must ensure that pupils are challenged appropriately. Guiding principles on differentiation include the following:

1   assume that learners are different;

2   adjust the nature of tasks not just the quantity;

3   adopt multiple approaches to content, process and product;

4   focus on students to render learning engaging, relevant and interesting;

5   blend whole-class, group and individual instruction in a natural flow;

6   learn with pupils.

Using the STEP framework to differentiate

The acronym STEP (space, task, equipment, people) can be a useful reminder to help teachers differentiate activities to enable all pupils to achieve their personal targets. Table 7.3 is an example of applying STEP in gymnastics.

TABLE 7.3 Differentiation of a task, using STEP

Devise, practise and perform a sequence that includes a balance, a roll, a jump and a turn.

	Easier	Harder
Space	In own space	Sharing the space around the room
Task	Copying a set routine	Devise your own routine
Equipment	On the floor only	Using a mat and a bench
People	Working on own	Working alongside or with a partner/group

TASK: APPLYING STEP PRINCIPLES

In teams of four, find out ways of running:

- the fastest time as a relay team over a shared distance of 60m;
- the longest distance as a relay team over times of 1 minute, 2 minutes, 3 minutes.

Chapter summary

In this chapter we have highlighted some of the key issues to take into consideration when planning for pupils' progression in PE. We have considered the context in which planning takes place and the key questions that need to be answered at different levels in the planning process. Above all we have stressed the importance of being committed to purposeful planning, namely, planning for pupils' learning. We have made the case for plotting pupils' progression through meaningful authentic target tasks, which provide purpose and direction to any PE programme.

Planning, like teaching, will improve with practice. In the early stages of teaching for learning, it is likely that you will remain heavily reliant on your written plans. As you gain more experience and grow in confidence, your repertoire of strategies for promoting high quality learning will inevitably improve and consequently you will become less plan dependent. While experienced teachers still plan carefully, the focus of their planning changes. No longer preoccupied with content, organisation and class-management issues, experienced practitioners can direct their energies elsewhere and use their plans to explore new ways of challenging pupils to reach new heights.

Questions for reflection

- Look at your school PE policy alongside some examples of your short- and medium-term plans for PE. Are these documents as well 'connected' as you would like them to be?
- Look at two examples of medium-term planning from different activity areas. To what extent do they reveal a focus on 'doing' activities compared with pupils' learning?
- How favourably does differentiation in PE compare to differentiation in other subjects?
- What changes would you need to make to your PE planning to address pupils' learning preferences more effectively?

References

Bailey, R.P. (2000) Teaching Physical Education: *A Handbook for Primary and Secondary Teachers*. London: Kogan Page.

Casbon, C. and Spackman, L. (2005) *Assessment for Learning in Physical Education*. Leeds: Coachwise/BAALPE.

Mawer, M. (1995) *The Effective Teaching of Physical Education*. London: Longman.

Ofsted (1994) *Primary Matters: A Discussion on Teaching and Learning in Primary Schools*. London: Office for Standards in Education.

Ofsted (2005) *Annual Report of Her Majesty's Chief Inspector of Schools*. London: Office for Standards in Education.

Raymond, C. (1998) *Co-ordinating Physical Education across the Primary School*. London: Falmer Press.

Shulman, L. S. (1987) *Knowledge and Teaching: Foundations of the New Reform*. Harvard Educational Review 57, pp. 1–22.

Williams, A. (1996) *Primary School Physical Education: A Guide for Mentors and Students*. London: Falmer Press.

8

What happens *during* the lesson?

Teaching a lesson

Chapter objectives

By the end of this chapter you should be able to:

- Know the characteristics of effective teaching in PE.
- Appreciate the need to use a range of teaching strategies.
- Appreciate the need to use a range of teaching approaches.
- Understand that flexibility in teaching is vital to meet the individual needs of all pupils.

This chapter begins with a question. What is meant by quality teaching in PE? Some might say that this is something that cannot be defined, while others will talk about teaching lessons where pupils are active for the majority of the time. Others relate it to enjoyment or the reproduction of skilled movements. When you watch a really good PE lesson, regardless of the activity or indeed age of the pupils, there is one aspect that sets it apart. That is the amount of learning that takes place because of that teaching. Quality teaching is simply teaching that leads to more pupil learning. The literature on teaching in PE is confusing, with words such as good, effective or high quality, and the search to pin this down has been going on for many years. Research tells us a lot about the ways in which teachers teach in PE and the effect these have on what and how much pupils learn in lessons. An interesting and comprehensive review of studies into teacher effectiveness in PE is given by Mawer (1995). Drawing upon research from notaries (such as Metzler, 1990; Siedentop, 1991; Silverman, 1991), we offer what amounts to key characteristics of effective teachers in PE. A summary is provided in Table 8.1.

Teaching children is complex. You may regard teaching as an art and might agree that the endeavour involves an application of one's knowledge both educationally and ethically to the everyday reality of teaching (Schwab, 1969). Or you might agree it is about being reflective and modifying this knowledge according to the requirements of the practical situation in ways that are much more than being technical experts (Carr, 1989). Alternatively, you may agree that teaching PE is a science (Siedentop, 1991) and about having a set of skills that build up from basic to more advanced. While there is

TASK: WHAT IS QUALITY TEACHING IN PE?

What do you understand by 'quality teaching in PE'? Make a list of skills and qualities necessary to teach effectively in PE.

TABLE 8.1 Characteristics of effective teachers of PE

Characteristics of effective teachers	Descriptions
They plan work effectively.	Know what it is that they wish to accomplish and have clear instructional goals.
	Design effective class-management procedures.
	Provide realistic and attainable goals for pupils.
	Progress work in sequence.
They present new material well.	Explain new concepts with clarity.
	Have effective communication skills.
	Make use of modelling and demonstrations.
They organise and manage pupils and learning experiences.	Have management structures, routines and class rules.
	Make their expectations clear.
	Create business-like environments.
	Use resources effectively.
They are actively involved in teaching.	Have developed observation skills.
	Give feedback relating to learning objectives.
	Demonstrate skills. Explain clearly.
	Monitor pupil progress.
They provide supportive learning environments.	Individualise guidance.
	Are enthusiastic and positive.
	Plan lessons that involve pupils in decision-making.
	Provide greater time for pupils to learn.
They possess a repertoire of teaching styles.	Possess them and know when to use them for best effect.
They teach for understanding.	Use a variety of skills/strategies to develop discussion.
	Provide opportunities for pupils to apply their learning.
	Scaffold tasks appropriately.

obviously no correct answer, the stance taken in this book is a middle one. We acknowledge that effective teachers in PE demonstrate flexibility, intuition and creativity (in
sympathy with the teaching as an art form notion) and they are also self-reflective and
constantly reflect on the professional teaching (Hellison and Templin, 1991). We also
believe that good teachers are disciplined and systematic in their approach and although
they have inevitably developed personal styles, they have a thorough knowledge and a
composite set of teaching skills (in sympathy with the teaching as a science). This would
seem to encompass the best of both worlds. Our view is that:

Knowledge (of children's development and of the subject) +
pedagogical skills = quality teaching!

As outlined in Chapter 1, the goals of PE are multifaceted and therefore for pupils to
achieve these goals is no easy task. The skilled teacher of PE requires a sound toolkit of
teaching skills because how we teach is just as important as what we teach. Although it
is not possible to present all teaching skills here it is possible to identify some of the
important ones, and this is the focus of the next section.

A toolkit of teaching strategies

First, consider Martin's story. Martin was a good classroom teacher. He had just completed
his course in teacher training and passed it well. He was conscientious and had read the
recommended books on his course and had observed several teachers 'doing' a PE lesson,
yet he himself had never taught a whole lesson. It was the second week into his teaching
career when he was timetabled to teach Year 4 PE in the school hall. A little nervous
but confident he could do it, this is how the lesson went – and went wrong.

He entered the hall behind the class, his mind on the maths lesson he was to teach
later in the day. With his mind preoccupied he had forgotten to get himself changed.
The class entered the hall to his rather feeble instruction, 'Find a space everyone'. Looking
up he saw children running everywhere. Chaos reigned. Eventually gaining order he set
them a task he had written down from his teacher training course. An observer watching
the lesson would have concluded that the lesson was dull. He lacked sparkle. He taught
in one style only. He did not question or challenge. Children were unclear about what
to do. He told them nothing after the set tasks were completed. The time dragged on:
twenty minutes seemed an eternity. His first PE lesson was a disaster.

Afterwards Martin was puzzled. The content of his lesson surely was OK, so what was
wrong? He reflected some more and realised that it was in his delivery and teaching skills
that the problems lay. Martin had not understood that the 'how' of teaching is just as
important as the 'what' of teaching. He needed a toolkit of teaching tools.

Be a positive and enthusiastic role model

This is simple but immediately effective! Share your enthusiasm for PE with your class.
Teaching is much more than instructing children how to perform a forward roll correctly
or execute a short corner in hockey. Evidence to support being an enthusiastic role model

exists in the literature (Rosenshine and Furst, 1973; Rolider *et al.*, 1984) and readers are referred to the descriptors of enthusiasm advanced by Behets (1991) whose list comprises vocal intention, articulation, word selection, encouragement, gestures, body movements and overall energy level.

Take the advice of Smith and Cestaro (1998) and lead by example. If your pupils see you living the active lifestyle you teach about and not just talking about it, no motivation is stronger to want to participate in and enjoy your PE lessons! Ensure you dress appropriately for every PE session and are always enthusiastic. Raise awareness of PE events on noticeboards around the school. Create a display in the hall. Make pupils aware of the role of nutrition and healthy eating. Bring PE and the promotion of health into your classroom. Class topics such as 'Ourselves' and 'My body' offer many possibilities for cross-curricular learning and show how health and PE pervade the curriculum. You might wish to offer to run an after-school club. Bring in experts to give instruction in activity areas where you feel less confident. Broaden the curriculum in your school by offering new activities such as baseball or pop-lacrosse. Organise trips to other facilities that offer physical activities, such as a local climbing wall. Be interested and actively promote children to become involved in all sorts of physical activity outside school. This can range from skateboarding in the local area to street dance and martial arts. Children look to you for encouragement and reinforcement. Show this in what you say and how you say it, with words and with body language. Facial expressions are especially powerful communicators of enthusiasm, as are signals like thumbs up and hand claps. Use lots of smiles. Unlike Martin, if you make your lessons interesting, varied and fun and you enjoy them, so will your pupils!

Giving explanations and instructions

Good teachers are also very good communicators. A recipe for disaster is to become the teacher who spends most of the lesson talking and rambles on, oblivious that the children are bored. Research has found that pupils spend much of their time waiting, listening to the teacher and being organised for activities instead of actually doing them (Siedentop and Tannehill, 2000). Children are normally extremely well motivated in PE and what they want above everything else is to do some! When giving explanations or instructions, make use of the KISS principle, which is 'Keep it short and simple'. The younger the child, the shorter the attention span, so it is imperative that the teacher captures the attention of the group at once. Make eye contact with the group. You could consider having a signal to signify that you have important things to communicate. Speak clearly and politely at just above a normal speaking voice. Establishing a regular routine is advised. Due thought must be given to the positioning of the group you are going to talk to. Explain to children why an activity or an aspect of it is important. Avoid over-elaborate explanations and remember to match the language and complexity of your instructions or explanations to the age and ability levels of your class. Play–teach–play is a useful technique, and one that is especially effective with pupils who just want to play a game. In this, pupils begin by playing games then practise relevant skills in context and then put these back into their games. In this way the connection between skills practice and playing games is solid because pupils see a direct relevance of the skills they are practising and their purpose in a game.

Giving instructions is the process of providing information, and generally instructions are delivered orally. For instructions to work well, pupils need to know what they have to do and how they should go about it. This requires decisions relating to the size and formation of a group, equipment to be used, starting and stopping and any relevant conditions to the activity. (The conditions, for example, might include changing player roles in a game or specifying the number of passes before shooting at goal.) Readers may find the three factors in successful explanations identified by Perrott (1982) as useful: continuity referring to the way the explanations connect across a lesson; simplicity – the match between language and the learner's ability and age; and explicitness, which relates to assumptions that pupils understand more than they actually do. Check understanding by using a phrase such as, 'Does everyone understand? Are you sure?' These are sound guiding principles for both types of teacher–pupil interactions.

Barrett defined this skill as 'the ability to perceive accurately both the movement response of the learner and the environment in which the response took place' (1983, p. 22). To a novice teacher the task of trying to observe everything and everybody in a PE lesson is daunting. It is also impossible. We offer three pieces of advice. First, acquire the skill of scanning a group. This is similar to a lighthouse beam sweeping across the sea. It does not stop but continues from one side to the other.

With experience this skill is soon acquired and will be of great value in all environments where PE takes place. Second, focus in on one component. For example, you watch a Year 5 pupil trying to serve a tennis ball. No easy skill for the pupil but you as the teacher are aware that things are obviously badly amiss. Linked to feedback (which we will cover shortly), you are advised to concentrate your observations on the element that is most in need of rectifying. This might be the swing plane of the racket up to the point of impact with the ball. You would then provide the necessary feedback to the learner based upon your observations.

Observation is an important tool when the class is working on a variety of tasks within a lesson, such as when working on various pieces of apparatus in Gymnastics. Good observation skills need to employed here but once again a focus can be most helpful. The teacher may have decided to focus on whether the class have answered the task set, how well it is being answered or may wish to observe an individual or group at work. A third technique in observation is to have a third person to observe with you. A colleague not involved in teaching a group can be an invaluable aid and if this person is briefed in advance and knows exactly what to look at, there are many benefits to be accrued.

In order to observe, you must be in the right place. Positioning is an important consideration and is directly linked to the purpose of the observations. To observe a pupil's technique it is necessary to be close enough to see it in detail, whereas in order to scan the whole group working in the hall, a position in the centre of the space is ineffectual. For this purpose, adopting a position on the periphery, essentially with one's back to the wall, is much better. Observation offers much benefit when the focus is on pupil behaviour or assessing how much time pupils spend on task. Observation schedules designed to measure 'time on task', or academic learning time (Berliner, 1979) or ALTPE can be quite revealing. Somewhat alarming statistics reported in Mawer (1995) show that pupils spend only about 15 per cent of their time engaged on tasks during lessons.

Observation is also closely linked to analysis. In fact it may be thought of as the first stage of analysis. If we take the common skill of rolling, what should the teachers look

TASK: WHAT TO LOOK FOR WHEN OBSERVING A FORWARD ROLL

Observe a pupil performing a forward roll at least once. Then answer the following questions:

- What was the initial position?
- Can you describe the pupil's body shape at the start, during and at the end of the movement?
- Where were the pupil's hands?
- Did you notice what the head position was like?
- Was the final position balanced or not?
- Can you describe the roll's speed/direction?
- What was the level of proficiency – beginner, intermediate or advanced?

for when a child is performing it? Using a forward roll as an example, the following task requires you to identify what to look for in a proficient performance.

Demonstrations

Social learning theory (Bandura, 1977) proposes that we learn from copying the behaviour of significant others. This has immediate and powerful implications for teaching physical education: what you do as the teacher gives a reference for pupils and this is immediately evident when using demonstrations. As suggested by Bailey (2001), demonstrations rely upon the sharing of visual information, and PE has many visual features such as shape or form in dance that lend themselves more to seeing than to verbal explanations. This being said, the combination of demonstration followed by explanation is a highly effective teaching tool. Don't talk during the demonstration. Let pupils watch, then talk afterwards.

Demonstrations by pupils can be used to showcase pupil work, and celebrating work in Gymnastics and Dance is common in Primary school assemblies. Demonstrations have powerful motivational qualities too by encouraging other pupils to imitate what they have just seen. Readers are referred to *Teaching Physical Education: A Guide for Mentors and Students* (Williams, 1996) for an accessible account of the purposes of demonstrations in PE. Children quite naturally learn from watching others. A 3 year old will watch an adult balancing on one leg and try to copy the movement. A 6 year old, watching others playing hopscotch in the playground, will quite naturally imitate the same movements. Although demonstrations are recognised as important aspects of presenting information, other evidence suggests that many motor tasks are presented to learners without a visual demonstration (Werner and Rink, 1989). The old adage of 'a picture paints a thousand words' is certainly true and remains so for pupils at all stages in their learning. Beginners are provided with a mental picture of the movement overall, while more proficient performers benefit from specific points being highlighted, helping them both to remember and reproduce the movement (McCullagh, 1993). Who demonstrates is an important consideration. The obvious choice is the teacher, provided that an accurate representation of the skill or movement can be given: 'Watch me while I demonstrate . . .'. Ideally demonstration is followed by an oral explanation that focuses attention on key elements. There are times when pupils should demonstrate, and the advice is to share this around the class so that not the same few children get to demonstrate all the time. There is some evidence (Darden, 1997) that learning will occur if a demonstration from a peer is less than perfect because children perceive the movement to be similar to their own and are motivated to try it. Pinpointing is a technique used after a demonstration where the teacher asks a pupil with good technique to demonstrate, allowing relevant points to be emphasised. In a Reception class where children are learning to jump for height, the following might be heard: 'Look everyone how Jodie bends her knees to land. They are really squashy. Let me see you all try this now'. The use of verbal cues such as 'squashy' helps pupils to attend to the critical features of a skill in a relevant way and has received much support in the literature (Housner and French, 1994; Roach and Burwitz, 1986). A number of such cues exist for many physical activities that get pupils to create a mental image associated with a component of a skill. With advanced performers this may take the form of mental rehearsal strategies where performers create images of themselves performing the skill or routine (such as in Gymnastics), or with beginners using cue phrases. When helping children to achieve a streamlined body shape in swimming to push and glide, a phrase like 'See yourself sliding across the top of a polished table' is often helpful. There are many such phrases and you may want to compile a list for future reference. The use of charts, diagrams and DVDs are also effective ways to provide visual information accurately and are instructional and motivating (Melville, 1993). Digital and camcorders are highly effective, provided these are used in short episodes, and downloading clips from the internet and YouTube will serve the same purpose. As with all demonstrations, careful thought should be given to viewing arrangements. Should the demonstration take place before, during or after the children have experienced the movement skill? Consider viewpoints so that all children see the demonstration from different angles, and if appropriate, being performed with both sides of the body (such as in throwing techniques or in Gymnastics). The use of DVD enables the movement to be frozen or shown at a slow speed, which is particularly helpful in dynamic actions such as hitting with a bat or throwing.

Questioning

Questioning is a potent teaching strategy and one that is important to master. Questions in PE can be used for a number of purposes and findings from Brown and Edmundson (1984) show that these range from allowing pupils to express their feelings to encouraging thinking and understanding of ideas. Four of the main purposes of questions are given below, with examples:

Questions to focus attention

- In Sarah's demonstration, what do you notice about her body shape in her forward roll?
- Look at Karla's hands before she catches the ball? What are her hands doing?
- Watch this short video clip of Tony's group playing our basketball game. Can you tell me why the place Mark is standing in to receive the pass from Sally is so good?

Questions to test knowledge

- Who can tell me why it is important to warm up before we do any exercise?
- How many points are in contact with the floor in a headstand?
- In athletics, what was the little phrase we used to help get us into the right positions for throwing?

Questions to develop deeper understanding

- Why do we use our arms to run fast? How does it help?
- Remember we talked about centre of gravity? Can you tell me why the first balance you did was better than the second one?

Questions to encourage reflection

- What have you learned from today's lesson?
- Think about what I have just said about safety. Why is this so important in the swimming pool?

Questioning is such a powerful tool that it not advisable to leave it to chance or use questions in an ad hoc way in lessons. Planning is the key. It is always a good idea to make the precise questions to be used in a lesson explicit on a lesson plan and record at what phase of the lesson they can be put to best use. Questions that require pupils to observe and comment upon their own or another's performance might occur during the main part of a lesson, whereas those requiring pupils to reflect might appear at the end of the lesson. Brown and Wragg (1993) developed their 'IDEA' approach to planning for questioning and there is much merit in adopting this approach:

> I – identify what key questions are needed in relation to lesson objectives
> D – decide on the level and timing of your questions
> E – use extensions and supplementary questions too
> A – analyse the answers you are likely to receive.

When questions are planned in advance and have a specific purpose, they invariably have clarity and precision. Consider the language you use to ask the questions, and relate this to the age and ability of your pupils. Brevity is best. Avoid jargon and make the question audible to the group. Make sure also that those receiving the question know that it is a question! One well-planned and precise question is much better than a stream of questions fired out by the teacher that do not allow the class time to respond or are not even perceived as questions.

In addition, the literature refers to different levels of questioning. Although there are endless questions to ask, the types of questions can be categorised to correspond with different levels of thinking (King, 1992; Thorpe, 1992). There is evidence (Galton et al., 1980) showing that low-level questions in lessons require pupils merely to recall information (e.g., Who can remember what we did in last week's lesson?) or deal with basic organisational issues (e.g., Which group is collecting the balls today?) but that higher-order questioning can produce higher-order thinking in pupils (Schwager and Labate,

TABLE 8.2 Higher-order questioning mapped against Bloom's taxonomy of higher-order thinking skills

	Foundation Stage	Key Stage 1	Key Stage 2
Analysis	Everyone watch my jump. (Teacher performs.) What did I do to jump up high in the air?	Watch how players in this group use space in this mini game. What do you notice?	Observe the DVD showing the front crawl arm action. Can you tell me three things about how it was performed?
Synthesis	How could you make your first shape and your second shape different?	Make up a partner game to improve dribbling a ball with a hockey stick. How will you go about this?	Can you as a group generate ideas to solve the problem-solving challenge set up for you?
Evaluation	Balance on one leg and hold it until I count to three. Which was the best way to do this for you?	I want this group to observe Group B's dance. Can you judge it against the three points we decided on earlier?	Can you come up with a way of marking technique for throwing the foam javelin?

1993; Tishman and Perkins, 1995). Higher-order questions stimulate pupils to seek out information for themselves, engage in problem solving and encourage them to think deeply and critically. Examples of the kinds of higher-order questions that teachers might ask are shown in Table 8.2, mapped against the processes of analysis, synthesis and evaluation that Bloom (1956) equated with higher-order thinking in pupils.

Giving feedback

If you were asked to wear a blindfold and then kick a football to a goal a reasonable distance away, with no one to give you advice, you would probably not do very well. Hardly surprising, and yet this is not dissimilar to how many youngsters feel when they are performing movement skills in PE lessons. Although they can usually see what their movement has been like, what they also need is someone to tell them what exactly to look for in their performance and/or what they need to do now to improve it. This is why giving feedback is an important teaching skill because without it, systematic learning is not going to happen. So what is feedback?

Feedback is the information received about one's performance. This can take one of two common forms. Intrinsic feedback is what we receive through our senses naturally. In the example above you would receive information from sensors in your muscles and joints about the kick. So, for example, you would obtain new knowledge about your leg position prior to the kick, the feel on impact and, if you were not blindfolded, the flight of the ball in the air and where it landed relative to the target. Extrinsic feedback, also known as augmented or enhanced feedback, is provided by someone or something external to the situation. Normally this will be the teacher (hence its use as a teaching tool), but it can also be a displayed time, score of a judge or a DVD replay of the performance. There are two categories. Knowledge of results (KR) informs about the movement's success. You will hear phrases like, 'Goal! Great shot Sally', or simply, 'Missed', that give little information. Knowledge of performance (KP) is more effective and gives information on the movement itself. Phrases like, 'OK. Your shot went high. Try to keep your hands closer together in future', provide information on the goal but also important information on the quality of the movement.

The properties of external feedback make it a useful pedagogical tool because:

- It motivates pupils to continue to practise when improvement is slow.
- It provides specific information on how to perform the action effectively.
- It reinforces correct performance and decreases performance that is incorrect.
- It allows the teachers to assess how quickly a skill is being learned for individuals or a whole class.

The literature on teacher effectiveness (Boyce, 1991; Silverman *et al.*, 1992) and motor learning (Magill, 1994) are generally positive about teachers' use of extrinsic feedback in enhancing pupil learning. What we see as the next step is to embed this into practical teaching to make most use of it. Here are six suggestions as to how this might be accomplished:

1   Avoid general statements like 'Good' and increase your use of specific feedback statements. While general phrases may have an effect on promoting a positive environment, especially with younger pupils (Sharpe, 1992), older children will benefit from specific feedback such as 'Next time I want you to hold the balance slightly longer. Hold it and count to three.'

2   Get children to focus on a small number of points in any task you set them and give feedback in relation to these.

3   Keep what you say simple and match your language to the age and ability of the class (or individual pupils).

4   Use positive feedback on most occasions such as, 'Carrie, I like how you showed both curled shapes and the long stretched shapes on the apparatus' and avoid negative statements (Kniffen, 1988) like, 'That is not a proper throw Darren'.

5   Give feedback as soon as possible after the action is observed and decrease its use as learning progresses so as not to make pupils dependent on having it.

6   Make sure you give feedback to all pupils (Sharpe, 1992).

Extrinsic feedback is a valuable teaching tool chiefly because it lets your pupils know how they are performing by providing them with information about correct and incorrect aspects of their performance.

Teaching movement concepts and skills

The movement concepts and skills described in Chapter 3 in this book operate as organising centres, giving cohesion to the EYFS and Primary curricula in a sequential and progressive way. In this next section we present some specific examples of how to teach movement concepts and skills, using dance to illustrate. In the chapter, a hierarchical model of movement skills based on the work of Gallahue (1982) was presented. We believe that this offers a good basis for teaching movement skills progressively from the EYFS through to the end of Key Stage 2. Pre-school and Primary-age children need to acquire and develop fundamental movement skills in the categories of stability, locomotion and manipulation described in that chapter. This builds upon the rudimentary skills they have acquired in the first two to three years of life and enables them to apply these and learn specific sports skills in a progressive manner. Teachers of children from 5 to 11 should concentrate their efforts on the first three elements of the model: exploration, discovery and combinations.

Teachers should allow pupils time to get an idea of what the movement is all about. Proper technique is less important as pupils experiment with different ways of executing the movement in an almost unlimited range of possibilities. There is no 'best' response, only different ones. In teaching, seek to guide pupils to achieve success within their own limits and avoid presenting the correct model to novice learners.

After the teacher provides some guiding principles, the class engages in finding out for themselves. Teaching hopping in Foundation Stage, the teacher should encourage pupils to try hopping on different legs, to hop various distances and heights and explore what part the arms play in the movement. By using fun games and challenges, the child will learn some fundamentals of the movement in a broad sense.

Discovery

This second tier also involves skills being taught indirectly. The teacher sets the problem for pupils to solve. It differs from movement exploration because this latter method has a limited range of possibilities. The teacher restricts the possibilities of movement responses that allow for several solutions to be acceptable. Observing the movement responses of the pupils allows the teacher to prompt and guide and the pupils to assess and reassess their performance. In teaching in Key Stage 1, the teacher may pose the problem, 'What is the best way to throw a tennis ball for distance?' Through observation and a series of prompts, the teacher gradually moves the children to adopt several techniques that 'they have discovered for themselves'.

Combinations

Normally this requires teaching indirectly and directly (this concept is expanded upon in the next section) and involves pupils in combining skills already acquired. Skills may be taught indirectly by continuing with the exploration and discovery methods previously described, and extending them by putting several of the skills together. In a gymnastics lesson warm up in Key Stage 1, the teacher might say, 'I want you to run and then jump' or in Key Stage 2, 'Run, stop, roll sideways and continue running'. A more direct teaching approach requires a model of what the performance should look like, and this is presented to the class using strategies such as explanation and demonstration. Pupils then seek to replicate this model, based upon their individual capabilities. After a practice period, the teacher presents the model again and comments upon the observed responses from the class. An example of this might appear in an athletics lesson with Key Stage 2 pupils that is focused on jumping for distance. The class have already learned skills such as running, hopping, leaping and jumping, and the teacher sets the task: 'Combine any three skills

TABLE 8.3 Movement concepts and skills in Dance lessons

Movement concept	Specific concept	Activity
Body awareness	Body parts	*Skeleton dance* Isolate different body parts in turn. Explore how the arms move, then the legs, feet, fingers, the head.
	Shapes	*Letters* Make letters with the body (sitting, lying, kneeling and standing): solo (e.g. T, Y, A); with a partner (e.g. C, W, O) or threes (e.g. B, Q).
	Non-locomotor actions	*Turning!* Use the action words *spin*, *twist*, *spiral* to create a short dance motif. Make up other turning words. Combine turning with other actions.
	Supports	*Shape dance* Small groups create short motifs based on meeting and parting; forming diamonds and squares by contacting and supporting each other's bodies.
Space awareness	Location	*Statues* Class tiptoe into space. Freeze on a signal. Change travelling action. Play musical statues.
	Directions	*A foggy day* Imagine getting lost in a fog. Moving forward, backward and sideways. Add balance shapes and jumps.
	Levels	*Volcanoes* In one spot, move and show level changes to represent a volcano bubbling, spurting, showering. Extend into small group dance.
	Pathways	*Kites* Move around as if following a kite on a piece of string. Emphasise a variety of pathways, straight, curvy and zig-zag. Include level and speed changes.
	Extension	*Butterflies* Represent the lifecycle of a butterfly from caterpillar to emerging butterfly. Combine actions and levels. Begin in a curled shape and end with a stretched butterfly shape.
Effort	Time	*Minibeasts* Moving like different insects. Slow like snails, fast like ants. Show a parade with groups moving like the different insects.

TABLE 8.3 *continued*

Movement concept	Specific concept	Activity
	Force	*Strong and light* Strong – stamping, stepping, clapping. Light – tiptoeing, floating. Move like an elephant. Float like a cloud.
	Flow	*Balloon dance* To accompany music, children use balloons to make a flowing dance.
Relationships	Body parts	*Dancing feet!* Stamp out rhythms with flat feet and heels. Tap dancing. Pointed toes and high knees (Irish dancing). Spinning on heels (Kathak). Steps in traditional folk dances.
	Objects	*In the box* Explore a large box. Skip around it. Jump into it, peep out. Travel in it. Leap out. Compose a short dance.
	People	*Follow my leader* Children march around behind the teacher. Vary actions. Change the leader, once confident.

to jump as far as you can'. Typical responses involve combinations such as hop, jump, jump; leap, hop, jump or hop, hop, leap. Such a scenario is ideally set up for the teacher to circulate among the class and provide individual feedback as pupils perform their movement combinations.

Direct and indirect teaching approaches

It seems there has always been a good deal of interest in what might be termed 'teaching approaches' in PE. What is clear from both professional and research literature is that a characteristic of an effective teacher is having a repertoire of instructional approaches and knowing when to use them to facilitate pupil learning and understanding (Mawer, 1995). Although different writers employ terms such as 'teaching style' or 'strategies', for the purposes of this book we prefer to use the broader term of 'teaching approaches' since it combines both these elements together. Mosston and Ashworth's landmark work, the Spectrum of Teaching Styles (1986) describes the extent to which decisions in lessons are taken by pupil or teacher. In the model, decisions made by teachers define their teaching behaviours and those made by learners define their learning behaviours. Both teachers and learners make decisions in each of the category sets defined within the spectrum. What varies is the involvement and the shift in decision-making, moving between direct and indirect teaching. At the extreme end of direct teaching is the 'command style' in which all decisions are made by the teacher. At the other end is indirect teaching, the 'learner initiated style' where pupils may ask and answer their own questions regarding the work context. Direct teaching, according to Mawer (1995) is one of the most popular modes of teaching and continues to receive much support empirically. It involves telling or showing pupils what they have to do, supervising progress and evaluating it. It is the teacher who chooses the lesson content, communicates the task and designs content progression. Pupils play little part in any of the decisions concerning the lesson. Teaching approaches that involve pupils much more in the decision-making process in their lessons are located at the opposite end of the spectrum and are allied to indirect teaching. Such approaches involve pupils in taking the initiative and creating or solving problems and encourage them to be more independent and self-reliant in their learning (ibid., p. 196). What follows is a broad interpretation of the spectrum styles, including both direct and indirect teaching, based on the work of Williams (1996) but with examples given relevant for the 5–11 age range.

However convenient, it would be wrong to assume that certain teaching styles might be associated with particular activities in PE, for example that games is better taught in a practice style, whereas dance benefits from instruction in an inclusion style. Findings from the BAALPE study (1989) confirm that teaching in different activity areas of PE was most effective when various styles were utilised. The spectrum was never envisaged as a straitjacket wherein teachers work in a constrained way. Effective teaching of PE is about using the spectrum's inherent mobility, and moving along it in both directions. Certain teachers may appear to be able to switch from one style to another instinctively, but this ad hoc approach is not desirable (Coates, 1997). The spectrum provides a way of analysing one's own teaching in a rational way, of identifying the effects of that teaching and assessing the competency of it.

The importance of adopting variety in teaching PE is inherent in the documentation from the first National Curriculum in 1992. This confirmed that a single teaching approach would be insufficient as more was becoming expected of pupils in terms of thinking about their work and developing skills in communication, problem solving and decision-making. The need to seriously consider how content is delivered to pupils and the need for flexibility in delivery to cater for pupil abilities and needs is less evident in the recent National Curriculum but nevertheless is essential for good teaching and learning.

TASK: IDENTIFYING YOUR PERSONAL TEACHING STYLES

Refer to your teaching plans for five PE lessons. Match them with the teaching styles in Mosston's spectrum to identify your predominant styles.

■   What are your most common teaching styles?

■   How successful do you think your lessons were when you used these styles?

■   Could you have included other styles alongside these?

■   Can you see any advantages in adding or substituting other teaching styles?

TABLE 8.4 Characteristics of Mosston's Spectrum of Teaching Styles

Spectrum style	Teacher–Pupil characteristics	Learning intentions	PE tasks
Style A Command	Teacher makes decisions. No allowance for pupil individuality.	Motor skill acquisition.	Learning a dance motif by copying the teacher.
Style B Practice	Individuals work at own pace. Some individual feedback given.	Motor skill development.	Solo practice dribbling a ball around cones.
Style C Reciprocal	Pupils work in pairs. One performs, the other gives immediate feedback.	Working with others. Observation and analysis.	In twos, observe each other's swimming technique.
Style D Self-check	Pupils assess their own learning against set criteria.	Assessing their own performance. Making judgements.	Throwing in athletics. Success criteria are provided on a teaching card.
Style E Inclusion	Allows for individual practice. Assumes motivation and awareness of limits.	Maximising involvement. Helping others to succeed.	Using hurdles set at different heights and distances in athletics.
Style F Guided discovery	Pupils are involved in discovering a pre-determined learning target. A discovery process.	Discovery learning. Matching response to question or stimulus.	Pupils find the best way to cross climbing apparatus using hands and feet.
Style G Divergent	Problem-solving. Pupils are encouraged to find alternative solutions. Creative.	Independent thinking. Group work.	Devising a new co-operative game using a range of equipment.
Style H Individual	Teacher decides on area for study. Acts as adviser to pupils.	Planning. Increasing levels of understanding via performance.	Making individual decisions about a dance routine.
Style I Learner initiated	Learner takes initiative on content and process of learning. Teacher is adviser. Limited relevance to Primary PE.	Understanding through selection/application. Taking personal responsibility.	Discussion with teacher about a project on keeping healthy.
Style J Self-teach	Learner is fully independent. Very limited relevance to Primary PE.	Understanding and application.	Little application in schools below KS4.

Chapter summary

Teaching physical education in the National Curriculum is complex. We began this chapter by describing the key characteristics of effective teaching and offered our own definition of quality teaching in PE. In order to achieve the multiple aims in the subject, highly developed pedagogical skills are required, a number of which have been outlined in the chapter. A variety of teaching approaches are also required, as discussed with reference to Mosston's spectrum (1986). There is no single way of teaching. Deciding on what teaching tools or approaches to use varies from class to class and will also vary according to the age of the pupils. In any PE lesson the teacher is involved in adjusting and reviewing tasks according to the needs and responses from pupils. Being able to use a teaching approach that is matched to the learning intentions of a lesson allows teachers to set high standards of achievement and facilitate pupils' learning and thinking effectively.

Questions for reflection

- After reading this chapter, has your idea of what makes quality teaching in PE changed? Would you define it any differently?

- What additions would you make to the toolkit of teaching skills offered in this chapter?

- Think of a lesson you have taught or observed recently. How was feedback used in the lesson? How effective was this?

- With reference to Mosston's spectrum, what are your predominant teaching styles? Do these change according to the activity areas you are teaching? Does it matter what age range you teach?

References

Bailey, R. (2001) *Teaching Physical Education: A Handbook for Primary and Secondary School Teachers.* London: Kogan Page.

Bandura, A. (1977) *Social Learning Theory.* Englewood Cliffs, NJ: Prentice Hall.

Barrett, K. (1983) 'A hypothetical model of observing as a teaching skill'. *Journal of Teaching in Physical Education.* 3, 1, pp. 22–31.

Behets, D. (1991) 'Teacher enthusiasm and effective teaching in physical education'. *Physical Education Review Spring,* pp. 50–5.

Berliner, D. (1979) 'Tempus educare'. In P. Peterson and H.Walberg (eds) *Research on Teaching: Concepts, Findings and Implications.* Berkeley, CA: McCutchan.

Bloom, B. (1956) *Taxonomy of Educational Objectives.* New York: Longmans.

Boyce, A. (1991) 'The effects of an instructional strategy with two schedules of augmented feedback upon skill acquisition of a selected shooting task'. *Journal of Teaching in Physical Education* 11, pp. 47–58.

British Association of Advisers and Lecturers in Physical Education (BAALPE) (1989) *Teaching and Learning Strategies in Physical Education.* Leeds: White Line Press.

Brown, G.A. and Edmundson, R. (1984) 'Asking questions'. In E. C. Wragg (ed.) *Classroom Teaching Skills.* London: Croom Helm.

Brown, G. and Wragg, E.C. (1993) *Questioning*. London: Routledge.

Carr, W. (1989) (ed.) *Quality in Teaching: Arguments for a Reflective Profession*. London: Falmer Press.

Coates, B. (1997) 'Refining your style'. *Sportsteacher*, Spring, pp. 18–19.

Darden, G. (1997) 'Demonstrating motor skills: rethinking that expert demonstration'. *Journal of Physical Education, Recreation and Dance* 68(6), pp. 31–5.

DfEE (1999) *The National Curriculum for England and Wales*. London: QCA.

Gallahue, D. (1982) *Understanding Motor Development in Children*. New York: John Wiley.

Galton, M., Simon, B. and Croll, P. (1980) *Inside the Primary Classroom*. London: Routledge & Kegan Paul.

Hellison, D. and Templin, T. (1991) *A Reflective Approach to Teaching Physical Education*. Champaign, IL: Human Kinetics.

Housner, L.D. and French, K.E. (1994) (eds) 'Expertise in learning, performance, and instruction in sport and physical activity'. *Quest* 46, p. 2.

King, A. (1992) 'Facilitating elaborative learning through guided student generated questioning'. *Educational Psychologist, 27*(1), pp. 11–126.

Kniffen, M. (1988) 'Instructional skills for student teachers'. *Strategies* 1, pp. 5–10.

McCullagh, P. (1993) 'Modeling: learning, developmental and social psychological considerations'. In R.N. Singer, M. Murphy and K.L. Tennant (eds) *Handbook of Research on Sports Psychology*, pp. 106–26. New York: Macmillan.

Magill, R.A. (1994) 'The influence of augmented feedback during skill learning depends on characteristics of the skill and the learner'. *Quest* 46, pp. 314–27.

Mawer, M. (1995) *The Effective Teaching of Physical Education*. London: Longman.

Melville, S. (1993) 'Videotaping: an assist for large classes'. *Strategies, 6*(4), pp. 26–8.

Metzler, M. (1990) *Instructional Supervision in Physical Education*. Champaign, IL: Human Kinetics.

Mosston, M. and Ashworth, S. (1986) *Teaching Physical Education*. Columbus, OH: Merrill.

Perrott, E. (1982) *Effective Teaching: A Practical Guide to Improving your Teaching*. London: Longman.

Roach, N.K. and Burwitz, L. (1986) 'Observational learning in motor skill acquisition: the effect of verbal directing cues'. In J. Watkins, T. Reilly and L. Burwitz (eds) *Sports Science: Proceedings of the VII Commonwealth and International Conference on Sport, Physical Education, Dance, Recreation and Health*. London: E and F Spon.

Rolider, A., Siedentop, D. and Van Houten, R. (1984) 'Effects of enthusiasm training on subsequent teacher enthusiastic behavior'. *Journal of Teaching in Physical Education, 3*, pp. 47–59.

Rosenshine, B. and Furst, N. (1973) 'The use of direct observation to study teaching'. In R. Travers (ed.) *Second Handbook of Research on Teaching* pp. 122–83. Chicago: Rand McNally.

Schwab, J.J. (1969) 'The practical: a language for curriculum'. *School Review* 78, pp. 1–23.

Schwager, S. and Labate, C. (1993) 'Teaching for critical thinking in physical education'. *Journal of Teaching in Physical Education, 64*(5), pp. 24–6.

Sharpe, B. (1992) *Acquiring Skill in Sport*. Eastbourne: Sports Dynamics.

Siedentop, D. (1991) *Developing Teaching Skills in Physical Education*. Palo Alto, CA: Mayfield.

Siedentop, D. and Tannehill, D. (2000) *Developing Teaching Skills in Physical Education*. Palo Alto, CA: Mayfeld.

Silverman, S. (1991) 'Research on teaching in physical education'. *Research Quarterly for Exercise and Sport, 62*(4), pp. 352–64.

Silverman, S., Tyson, L.A. and Krampitz, J. (1992) 'Teacher feedback and achievement in physical education: interaction with student and practice'. *Teaching and Teacher Education, 8* pp. 333–44.

Smith, T. and Cestaro, N.G. (1998) *Student-centred Physical Education*. Champaign, IL: Human Kinetics.

Thorpe, J. (1992) *Methods of Inquiry Programme*. Toronto: Ryeron Polytechnic Institute.

Tishman, S. and Perkins, D. (1995) 'Critical thinking and physical education'. *Journal of Physical Education, Recreation and Dance*, August, pp. 24–30.

Werner, P. and Rink, J. (1989) 'Case studies of teacher effectiveness in physical education'. *Journal of Teaching in Physical Education* 4, pp. 280–97.

Williams, A. (1996) *Teaching Physical Education: A Guide for Mentors and Students*. London: David Fulton.

9

What happens *during* and *after* the lesson?

Assessment, recording and reporting

Chapter objectives

By the end of this chapter you should be able to:

■ Understand the principles and purposes associated with effective assessment of pupils' achievement and progress in PE.

■ Develop templates for recording and reporting judgements in PE that are fit for purpose.

■ Be more aware of using digital technology to record and analyse pupils' movement.

■ Devise a process whereby you may reliably and consistently judge evidence of pupils' attainment in PE and use this to construct a coherent report.

This chapter seeks to demystify the whole area of monitoring and assessing children's achievement in PE. It gives straightforward advice on what to look for across the 5–11 continuum. Emphasis is placed on observation of movement with reference to OCM (Tacklesport, 2003), and strategies to develop observational skills of assessment in fundamental motor activities are provided. Integration of technologies to assist assessment is suggested. Finally, examples of reporting to parents are given from the age phase.

What is certain is that everybody involved in education – teachers, pupils, parents and administrators – have a view on what assessment is, its role, and its purposes. What is also certain is that there will be a range of views expressed about its importance. While the views of these different parties will certainly vary, all would probably agree on one thing at least: whether we like it or not, assessment is a central feature of teaching and learning practice and therefore a permanent feature of the school day. It has always been integral to teaching and learning. The Assessment Reform Group (ARG) emphasised its significance:

> The important message now confronting the educational community is that assessment which is explicitly designed to promote learning is the single most powerful tool we have for both raising standards and empowering lifelong learners.
>
> (ARG, 1999, p. 2)

Yet here too it is a time of enormous change. A return to traditional methods of testing, the relentless pressure on school league tables, and escalating floor targets set higher and higher expectations on pupil attainment. Parents are being given more information and schools are in open competition with each other for pupil numbers and standards. Key Stage 1 has seen the introduction of phonics testing and KS2 is grappling to define what it should and should not test. Foundation subjects are being pushed out of the spotlight in favour of the emphasis upon core subjects. But learning and assessment are fundamental to all subject areas and PE is no exception. Effective assessment in physical education is integral to teaching and learning and is important because it provides information on which to base future teaching. It provides information on which judgements are made about the effectiveness of a school, that assists with evaluation of teaching; it provides information that can be shared with parents and gives feedback to pupils that is motivating (Brigg et al., 2003).

For the purposes of this chapter, the term 'assessment' refers to all those activities undertaken by teachers, teachers' assistants and pupils specifically to provide information about the teaching and learning process. We believe that this broad definition articulates the essential principles and purposes of assessment, namely that it is necessary to enable us to access reliable and valid information about our teaching and pupils' learning. There is little consensus however regarding the type of information that we need to access to effect improvements in teaching and learning in PE. Equally contentious is the method(s) we should employ to capture that information. These important topics are the subject of the first section of this chapter. Thereafter, subsequent sections will address the recording and the reporting of assessment judgements.

Perceptions of assessment

The results of a brief word-association exercise conducted recently with physical education teacher trainees revealed that the term assessment is synonymous with 'nerve-racking', 'tests', 'exams', 'coursework', 'stress' and 'failure'! While we recognise that this quick straw poll is hardly robust scientific research, it does reveal a broadly negative perception of assessment and points to assessment being the source of considerable anxiety. In an increasingly standards-focused education system, teachers, pupils and parents are, at some point, likely to experience some degree of assessment anxiety. Further probing, however, reveals that this anxiety stems not from the assessment process itself but from the social consequences arising from the treatment of the information it yields. The current trend in education for creating rank order lists or league tables of performance based on assessment data reflects a simplistic and reductive approach to data analysis. In a social and cultural context, in which success is traditionally associated with rewards and failure brings with it sanctions, one might legitimately argue that the pressure to avoid being labelled as 'failing' renders traditional assessment conditions highly stressful. Consequently, a pupil's performance may not necessarily be representative of their true capability.

Given that it is difficult to predict who is likely to be affected in this way and by how much, it would seem that some forms of assessment will be at best unreliable, or at worst futile. This basic flaw in the assessment process has been recognised for a long time and has been the impetus behind a great deal of research investigating assessment practices in schools. Regardless of the perceptions of any assessment process, one of the unavoidable features of assessment activity is the exercise of judgement. To arrive at a judgement that accurately describes a pupil's current level of knowledge, skill or understanding involves making comparison. Piotrowski (2000) suggests that these comparisons can be made in relation to:

■ Criteria or learning objectives, known as criterion-referenced judgements.

■ The performance of others, known as norm-referenced judgements.

■ The pupil's previous achievements, known as ipsative judgements.

While each form of comparison can be useful at different times, deciding which should be used on which occasion can be a source of tension. McMillan (2000) suggests that this is just one of several tensions that teachers need to discuss during the development of assessment policy. Other sources of tension include the purpose, timing, type, focus and the scope of assessment (see Table 9.1).

TABLE 9.1 Possible sources of tension in assessment

Assessment tensions	Debate
Purpose	Assessment for learning v assessment for auditing
Type	Traditional v alternative; authentic v contrived
Timing	Formative v summative
Focus	Added value v absolute standards
Scope	National tests v local tests

Having engaged with these debates, teachers should be in a better position to determine what kind of activities they need pupils to participate in to collate the evidence necessary for consistent and accurate evaluation of achievement.

Assessment in PE

Given that assessment is a complex process, it is not surprising that assessment in PE is frequently reported as one of the areas of professional responsibility in which practitioners feel most vulnerable. QCA (2005, p. 15) report that 'assessment and recording remain problematic in Key Stages 1 and 2'. Evidence from school inspections report that assessment is one of the weakest aspects of practice across the UK. Ofsted (2009) in their survey of 99 Primary schools found that the procedures to assess, record and track pupils' progress in physical education over time were a relatively weaker aspect of provision in the Secondary and most of the Primary schools visited. They were not used systematically to improve standards. Subject leaders in the Primary schools did not have suitable data to know precisely how well pupils were doing and in which areas of learning they were underachieving. Such monitoring was often better developed in the Foundation Stage, where staff kept comprehensive records of children's progress in physical development. In many schools, systematic assessment procedures for PE are either not in place or they are highly complex. Either way this is not conducive to teachers making accurate judgements about the standard and quality of their pupils' work. This is compounded by the fact that the vast majority of teachers in Primary schools feel that they do not have the subject knowledge required to make valid judgements. Consequently, the use of assessment to inform planning in PE is a considerable weakness. One of the key reasons why this has remained the case for over a decade with relatively little progress evident (see DES, 1992; OFSTED, 1998; QCA, 2005) is that teachers' attention has been focused elsewhere, principally on raising standards of pupils' performance in core subject standard assessment tests (SATs). Given that the overall judgement about a school's effectiveness does not weight performance in PE particularly heavily, there has been little impetus to address this issue. However, times are changing and our attention is shifting. With a growing body of evidence suggesting that high quality PE can effect whole-school change and contribute to the raising standards agenda across the curriculum (QCA, 2005), increasingly schools are recognising that a commitment to good assessment practice across all subjects can improve pupils' motivation and engagement with learning. Not least, growing public concern about the health of children in the UK and the subsequent changes in legislation, has extended schools' accountability in these areas. It is hoped that these subtle shifts will cause assessment in PE to move up the order of priorities.

There are many examples of excellent practice in assessment taking place in schools. In their survey, *Working towards 2012 and beyond*, Ofsted (2009) reported that in the sample of schools inspected in 2007/08, two thirds of the teachers seen were consistently observing pupils' progress. A small number of schools used the outcomes of high quality physical education and sport effectively to assess pupils' progress or evaluate provision. They made timely interventions to set more challenging tasks or to help pupils understand what they needed to do to improve their work. The following example from the survey of a school illustrates effectively how assessment may be used to help pupils to learn and make progress.

> Teachers assessed through carefully observing pupils' performances. They questioned pupils about what they thought they were doing well, why, and what they thought were the main characteristics of good work. Teachers praised pupils appropriately; specific feedback helped them to move forward in a task. For example, the teaching assistant in a Year 1 lesson contributed significantly to supporting assessments by taking digital images of performances, watching the playback immediately with the pupils to evaluate the strengths and identify what could be improved. This immediate feedback helped pupils to make instant changes in their performances, such as improving their use of space, their co-ordinated timing of their dance movements within the group and their use of gesture to emphasise the meaning of their dance. It also helped to develop their vocabulary when they used specific terminology to

evaluate their own performances in a structured and realistic way. At the end of the lesson the teacher and teaching assistant discussed and agreed which pupils had made progress and who needed support in future lessons.

(Ofsted, 2009)

If we were to adopt a *laissez-faire* approach to the organisation and management of learning, we might choose to provide pupils with opportunities to acquire new knowledge, skills and understanding without ever attempting to track their progress or determine their success. In this mode of instruction pupils may be learning, but without tracking their progress we would never know. Equally, without embedding any monitoring process into our teaching we would not know the extent to which our selected methods were working. This is not good teaching. One of the distinguishing characteristics of a good teacher is their capacity to use assessment to promote learning and improve their own teaching. To confirm this view the literature is replete with lists of the specific purposes of assessment (see Hopper *et al.*, 2000; Piotrowski, 2000; McMillan, 2000; Casbon and Spackman, 2005), arguing that, among other things, assessment enables teachers to:

■ establish what pupils already know, understand and can do;

■ identify pupils' specific needs;

■ give pupils feedback about their progress;

■ set appropriate targets for pupils;

■ motivate pupils to continue to improve;

■ level pupils' achievement;

■ evaluate teaching;

■ improve curriculum planning (in the short, medium and long term);

■ gather information for distribution (to parents, colleagues, inspectors, governors);

■ assure the quality and fitness for purpose of the programme.

What this list reveals is that good assessment practice relies on collating a range of information from a number of sources. PE has a tradition of collecting quantitative data (e.g., personal bests, school records, fitness scores). Sometimes this information can be particularly useful and serve to motivate pupils. For more complex actions, where changes in the outcomes of performance may be less obvious, shifting the focus to qualitative indicators of performance can be equally revealing. Table 9.2 distinguishes between these different forms of assessment information.

While some of these improvements may not have been originally planned for, a vigilant and reflective teacher will be sensitive to these changes and adapt their practice to suit the needs of their learners accordingly.

In order to be able to answer the question, 'What have the children learned in PE today?' with any degree of confidence, we need to develop a range of tools that will provide us with information about how our pupils are progressing. Despite a wealth of activity and learning taking place in any lesson, compared with other subject areas, PE has traditionally been a relatively 'data poor' environment. This is not due to a lack of learning but an absence of effective strategies for capturing what learning has taken place.

TABLE 9.2 Examples of quantitative and qualitative assessment data

Quantitative data	Qualitative data
■ Claire can do 100 skips in 3 mins.	■ Imogen can describe how to throw for distance.
■ 18/28 children completed the task.	■ Pupils are showing more creativity in their dance compositions.
■ 65% of pupils obtained level 2 at the end of Key Stage 1.	■ Since introducing pupil referees in games lessons, pupils seem to play more fairly.
■ 20 pupils asked about attending gym club after school.	■ Using task cards in swimming has improved pupils' knowledge of how to do front crawl well.
■ Class 3B are now able to stay active for 20 mins which represents an improvement of 5 mins.	■ After doing problem solving activities in O&AA, pupils' planning skills have improved.
■ Since introducing sport education in PE, Yr 6 attendance has improved by 12%.	

The process of making judgements in PE is hampered by the nature of the activity. Maude (2001) sums up the difficulties well,

> Movement is not easy to observe analytically because it leaves no trace, as writing and painting do. Movement is transitory and in most children's experience is not repeatable.
>
> (Maude, 2001, p. 79)

While this point is well made, it should not be taken as cause for abandoning any efforts to collect information about pupils' performance in PE. On the contrary, it should be the catalyst to urge us to explore other possibilities. There are of course many ways to capture pupil progress. Whatever methods are used the main aspects to be assessed are knowledge and understanding (i.e., facts, concepts, themes, and ideas, relationships and connections); skills (i.e., techniques); attitudes and values (i.e., about learning, behaviours and beliefs) and behaviour (i.e., social; relationships, personal characteristics and competences) (Wragg, 2001). For example:

Observation

Questioning

Child discussions

Teacher–child discussions

Matching of key concepts with definitions to show understanding

Reports

Tape recordings

Graphs, models, photographs, computer print outs

Role play

Quizzes

Demonstrations

Labelled diagrams

Problem-solving questions

Games

Presentations

To make reliable judgements about a pupil's physical competence, from observation alone, requires that teachers hone their observation skills and develop their knowledge of performance expectations. This takes a great deal of time, effort and practice and will inevitably lead to some errors, particularly where the teacher is trying to assess the whole class at the same time. The number and impact of such errors, however, can be minimised by employing a range of other strategies, no different to those already used in classroom contexts. Raymond (1998) suggests the following strategies:

- Talking to pupils, individually or in groups as they are working or reflecting on their work.
- Listening carefully to what they say as they discuss tasks or evaluate their own or others' work.
- Observing children throughout the process and during the performance of their work.
- Looking at videos of the children planning/composing and performing their work.
- Analysing written work in children's personal diaries, the class log book, or written notes, diagrams and records of their work.
- Reflecting on relevant information contained in the children's profiles and records.

Jefferies *et al.* (1997) suggest that there are many ways to assess a pupil's knowledge of the key parts of an action or skill, aside from actually demonstrating them to a teacher or peer. Allowing pupils to communicate their knowledge about an action/skill in non-physical ways is a more inclusive approach to gathering information about learning. For the pupil who understands the principles and practise of a skill but cannot yet perform that skill, cognitive assessment techniques provide a means through which their learning can be acknowledged and rewarded. Thus while direct observation will always lie at the heart of good assessment practice in PE, this should be supported by a framework of other assessment methods to enable practitioners to justify their judgements.

Observation in PE in the digital age

Meaningful assessment in the EYFS and during the Primary years should be benchmarked against the ages and stages of fundamental movement ability and motor skill development (Piotrowski, 2000). In the Early Years, *Development Matters* provides benchmarks of development between birth and age 5 and reported in the EYFS Profile in the Reception year (Early Education, 2012) where children's progress is gauged principally through observational assessment. Developing a thorough understanding of the stages of progression for certain key motor skills (running, dodging, balancing, stopping, twisting, bending, stretching, pulling, jumping, climbing, catching, throwing, kicking, dribbling and striking with an implement) is beyond the reach of many generalist practitioners. However, the assimilation of new technologies into teaching continues to facilitate the development of new resources to support practitioners' knowledge of motor development *in situ*. One such resource is the CDROM 'Observing Children Moving' (Tacklesport/PEAUK, 2003), which has been developed with three core principles in mind. These are that:

1   Movement observation involves seeing, knowing, understanding and analysing.

2   The more that is known about what is seen, the more informed the response can be.

3   The outcome of effective observation can be to raise standards for children in movement education and physical education.

This resource represents a landmark in guiding practitioners' observation and assessment of movement. The integration of video footage alongside guidance for the observation and assessment of 12 selected movement capabilities (run, gallop, strike, write, climb, roll, block build, throw, jump, catch, kick and moulding clay) for the first time provides practitioners with the opportunity to see what early and later motor patterns look like. These can then be used with confidence as a benchmark against which observations and assessments of pupils can be made. Furthermore, working through this sort of material with colleagues will promote professional dialogue and will assist teachers in moderating

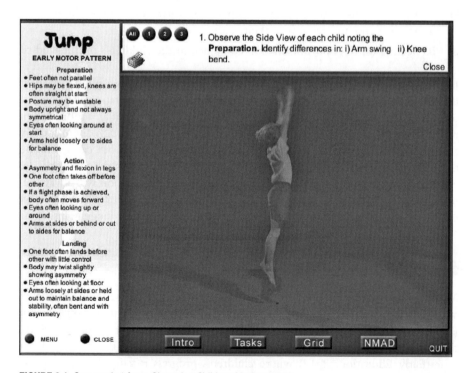

FIGURE 9.1 Screen shot from *Observing Children Moving* (2003)

Source: Tacklesport (2003): *Observing Children Moving.* Worcester: Tacklesport Consultancy Limited/PEA UK

the judgements of their pupils' performance. Designed primarily as a resource for professionals working with pupils in the 3–7 age range, the more recent *Observing and Analysing Learners' Movement* (Tacklesport/PEAUK (2006) has been targeted at those working with pupils in the 7–14 age group. The trend towards integrating technology into everyday teaching in the Primary school is likely to lead to a growth in both the demand for, and the availability of, such resources.

The guiding principles of assessment

We have considered the principles, purpose and the practicalities of assessment in PE. The guiding principles that have emerged can be summarised as follows:

- Build in regular assessment opportunities.
- Assess pupils in different ways.
- Reduce the number of pupils being assessed at any one time.
- Practise the skill of observing pupils in motion.
- Moderate assessment judgements with colleagues.

TASK: REFLECTING ON THE GUIDING PRINCIPLES OF ASSESSMENT

Consider the guiding principles in turn. Try to list ways in which you could embed each one into your current practice.

Planning for assessment – assessment for learning

Thus far, our analysis of the assessment process has demonstrated that assessment and planning are separate yet inextricably linked activities. The explicit planning of assessment opportunities to facilitate pupils' learning is known as assessment for learning (AfL). The Assessment Reform Group (2002) defined assessment for learning as:

> The process of seeking and interpreting evidence for use by learners and their teachers to decide where the learners are in their learning, where they need to go and how best to get there.

According to Leitch *et al.* (2005), AfL is a way of planning activities in lessons so that both the teacher and the pupils know what they are learning and how well they are learning it (p. 6). The deployment of pupil-centred learning processes, such as effective feedback, clear learning intentions, quality questioning, dynamic group work and self and peer assessment has led to suggestions that AfL contributes to raising standards and improving pupils' self-esteem. In AfL classrooms, teachers

- involve pupils in decision-making;
- convey a sense of progress;

- place less emphasis on grades;
- make learning goals explicit;
- develop pupils' self and peer assessment skills;
- promote learning goal orientation rather than performance.

(Leitch *et al.*, 2005)

Applying the principles of AfL to the PE 'classroom', Casbon and Spackman (2005) show that AfL leads to:

■ Improvement – in performance, skills or ability to think;

■ Progress – by enabling pupils to work in more demanding and complex situations;

■ Achievement – by enabling pupils to achieve high quality outcomes;

■ Confidence – by increasing pupils' belief that they can perform well in PE;

■ Positive attitudes – by increasing pupils' motivation, self-esteem and independence.

These outcomes are achieved through the cyclical process of planning, teaching and assessing, and reviewing for improvement.

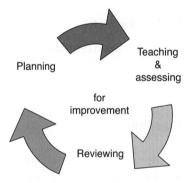

FIGURE 9.2 The cyclical process of assessment for learning

It is important not to confuse this process with the more commonplace plan–teach–review cycle that operates at the macro level and may help steer the annual review of the curriculum map for PE or the content of units of work. The assessment for learning cycle functions at the micro level, in which the teacher works with their pupils through a continuous process of teaching and assessing in pursuit of specified goals. Embedding this continuous process into our everyday practice provides opportunities to adjust the teaching approaches employed and the tasks set in order to make steady progress towards agreed targets. The key differences between the plan–teach–review cycle and the assessment for learning cycle is that the former takes place at the end of a programme and is conducted by teachers for pupils while the latter is a continuous process that involves the teacher and pupil working collaboratively to develop a learning conversation.

Developing the learning conversation with pupils involves:

- Explaining or agreeing the learning objectives for lessons or activities;
- Asking questions that prompt pupils to show their knowledge, understanding and skills;
- Sharing and explaining observations, analysis and interpretations;
- Supporting pupils in self-assessment, helping them to become aware of how they learn best and what they are learning;
- Supporting pupils in peer assessment, encouraging them not to draw comparisons between each other;
- Making judgements about how well pupils are doing and what needs to be improved.

(Casbon and Spackman, 2005)

Feedback

Just as teachers need to gather and interpret information to assess whether their teaching is effective, pupils need to have access to a constant stream of information providing feedback about how they are progressing. In the Early Years, teachers will need to help pupils tune in to what information is available and what it means in order for them to make sense of what is going on around them. As pupils gather experience, teachers can begin to increase the expectations on pupils to begin to gather and use this information for themselves.

Using questioning to enhance feedback

Questioning is an important process in the learning conversation. The right questions, asked at the right time, of the right pupils, can elicit responses that help to reveal how far pupils have progressed in their learning. Questions are used for a number of different purposes:

- As a prompt, e.g., What should we remember to do in this situation?
- As a challenge, e.g., Do you think you can do it more quickly?
- To develop thinking, e.g., What are your options from this position?
- To check knowledge, e.g., Can you explain why this happens?

What pupils do or say in response to this sort of questioning can be used as evidence of learning. The assessment of the quality of these responses, when evaluated against expectations, will act as a reference point for determining the next steps to continue to make progress. Prior to the introduction of the curriculum guidance for the EYFS and the National Curriculum, teachers and other practitioners were left to their own devices to determine what was worth assessing in the physical domain. Often this resulted in devising long lists of age-appropriate physical tasks, which, in theory at least, would be used to judge whether or not pupils were making acceptable progress in their physical

TASK: TEACHING STRATEGY ASSESSMENT

Reflect on the strategies you use to maintain the flow of feedback in PE, and complete the table. Tick the column that corresponds to the frequency of use in your teaching.

Strategy			Always	Sometimes	Rarely
Sharing the learning objective with pupils					
Sharing the criteria for success in a task					
Providing examples of good performance	Live demonstrations				
	Using video / DVD / internet				
Giving ample opportunity for repeated practice	Providing extra time				
	Providing extra information that can be accessed independently	Task cards			
		Image cards			
		Teaching points and/or questions			
Reminding pupils of the learning objective as the lesson progresses					
Suggesting improvements rather than giving complete solutions					
Asking questions about what pupils are doing and how they are making progress					
Using plenary time to pause, look back and look ahead	During lessons				
	At the end of lessons				
Discussing assessment information	With the class				
	With groups of pupils				
	With individual pupils				
Agreeing targets for progress	With the class				
	With groups of pupils				
	With individual pupils				

Now set yourself the target of increasing the number of 'always' ticks.

(Adapted from BAALPE, 2005 p. 18)

competence. As we have already identified, however, the process of becoming physically educated involves more than simply learning physical skills. A physically educated child develops knowledge and understanding that can be applied and adapted to suit new situations. The tools for assessing the development of these characteristics therefore need to be more sophisticated than lists of discrete skills.

Recording assessment judgements

In the absence of any statutory requirement to maintain records of pupils' achievements in PE, teachers have been free to develop recording systems that suit their own requirements. Prior to adopting a system for recording attainment, it is worth reflecting on its role and purpose. In consultation with trainee teachers and colleagues in school, when asked 'What do you need your assessment profile to provide?' a number of common features emerge. These are that an assessment profile must be:

- simple, clear and easy to use;
- informative and meaningful to a range of audiences;
- related to, and helpful in developing, planning;
- helpful in levelling pupils' achievement;
- helpful in constructing reports.

We should therefore abandon recording systems that do not satisfy each of these criteria.

TASK: EVALUATING THE USEFULNESS OF RECORDING TEMPLATES

Using the five given criteria as a guide, evaluate the fitness for purpose of the following recording templates (pp. 194–196).

Recording pupil voices in PE

One of the features absent from any of these recording templates is the opportunity for pupils to contribute to the assessment process. Giving voice to pupils has the potential to transform teacher–pupil relationships from passive or oppositional to more active and collaborative (Leitch *et al.*, 2005, p. 3). Consulting pupils can be a valuable additional source of information for use in judging progress in the development of knowledge and understanding, recognising added value in learning and targeting future action. Maude (2001) provides good examples of the use of both pictorial and written reflective devices.

In addition to written and pictorial records, the increasingly widespread availability of technology in schools opens up a number of possibilities for developing a system of profiling pupils' progress in PE through a range of materials (see Table 9.3).

Template 1

PE assessment for Unit					
Class		**Yr(s)**			
Learning objectives					
1. Acquiring and developing skills: 2. Selecting and applying skills: 3. Evaluating and improving performance: 4. Knowledge and understanding of fitness and health:					
Name		**LO1**	**LO2**	**LO3**	**LO4**

Symbols should be inserted as follows

w   means that the pupil is working towards the learning objective
✓   means that the learning objective has been achieved
ex   means that the pupil has exceeded expectations

Assessment carried out on   **by**

Review of Template 1

Criteria	Rating	Comments
Simple, clear and easy to use	✓✓✓✓✓	This template represents a traditional track-record for PE. On it, the teacher is able to note the extent to which each pupil meets each key objective. For a class of 28 pupils this could involve the teacher making 112 separate judgements for each unit of PE taught! There is no space for making additional notes which might provide evidence of what the pupil was seen doing or heard saying to warrant the judgement made and therefore it will be of limited value for levelling pupils' performance or informing subsequent reports.
Informative and meaningful to a range of audiences	✓✓	
Related to, and helpful in developing, planning	✓✓	
Helpful in levelling pupils' achievement	✓	
Helpful in constructing reports	✓	

Now try a similar excercise with the following two templates.

Template 2

CLASS	Unit Topic
Pitched at Level 2	**Games Unit 2, Year 1**
Acquiring and developing skills	1. Perform a range of rolling, throwing, striking, kicking, catching and gathering skills, with control. 2. Show a good awareness of others in running, chasing and avoiding games, making simple decisions about when and where to run.
Selecting and applying skills, tactics and compositional ideas	1. Choose and use tactics to suit different situations. 2. React to situations in a way that helps their partners and makes it difficult for their opponents. 3. Know how to score and keep the rules of the games.
Evaluating and improving performance	1. Watch and describe performances accurately. 2. Recognise what is successful. 3. Copy actions and ideas, and use the information they collect to improve their skills.
Knowledge and understanding of fitness and health	1. Understand and describe changes to their heart rate when playing different games. 2. Begin to anticipate what they will feel like after playing games.
Opportunities for assessment	

	Children who do not meet the criteria	Children who exceed the criteria
Date:		
Date:		
Date:		
Date:		

Northamptonshire County Council (2005)

Template 3

Physical Education Assessment Framework for Gymnastics

Class/Year group: **Date:**

LEVEL 4 EXPECTATIONS

	Level descriptors	Examples
A&D	Link your gymnastic skills and techniques together and use them accurately and appropriately on the floor and apparatus. Perform your gymnastic skills precisely, showing control and fluency.	Put together in sequence combinations of agilities and actions introducing changes in direction and level to add variety. Aim for stillness in held balances and smooth links between actions.
S&A	Show an understanding of the use of speed, level and direction in creating and performing gymnastic sequences.	
E&I	Compare and comment on gymnastic skills, techniques and ideas used in your own and others students' work. Use your comments to improve gymnastic performance.	
F&H	Explain and use basic safety rules in preparing for gymnastics. Describe what effect gymnastics has on your body. Know and describe how gymnastics is valuable to your fitness and health.	Pupils explain why exercise helps them to take a more active role, keeps them fit and makes them feel good.

Children not reaching level 4	Children exceeding level 4	Specific comments

Source: Adapted from Cambridgeshire County Council (2000) 'Assessment Framework'

By initiating a tracking system in the EYFS, which could evolve into a profiling system for Key Stages 1 and 2, the problems of transition and sharing of information between key stages disappear. It will not be long before such a profile can be stored and maintained solely through electronic means, facilitating easy access and transfer to interested parties. By sharing with pupils the responsibility for maintaining and updating an individual pupil's profile, the assessment and recording process can take on new significance and is likely to have a significant impact on pupils' motivation to learn (Rudduck *et al.*, 2003).

TABLE 9.3 Methods of profiling pupils' progress

Type of record	Maintained by
Personal profile – likes, dislikes, learning preferences, strengths, weaknesses	Pupil
Teacher assessments – including NCPE levels achieved	Teacher, teacher assistant, coach
Self-assessments	Pupil
Peer assessments	Peers
Video recordings	Teacher and pupil/parent
Digital photographs	Teacher and pupil/parent
Personal best performances	Pupil
Personal training programme	Pupil
Extra-curricular participation/representation	Pupil
Significant achievements/awards in PE	Teacher and pupil

Reporting

Teachers are obliged to formally report on a pupil's progress to parents. While the standard of reporting has improved markedly since the days when 'Making satisfactory progress, keep up the good effort' was deemed acceptable, many teachers confess to being unclear about what makes a good summary report for PE. We suggest that good report writing involves compiling a descriptive summary statement that communicates clearly to its intended audience (usually parents) four key themes:

1 The opportunities that have been provided in PE.
2 What has been learned/achieved in relation to the aspects of learning (with supporting evidence).
3 An indication of the current level of attainment and an appropriate end of key stage target.
4 What the next steps need to be to continue to make progress.

While it may be tempting to fill the space provided with a detailed outline of curriculum coverage to meet point 1, this should be a short standardised opening sentence or two, e.g.,

> This year Class 2 have enjoyed learning through Dance, Gymnastics, games and swimming activities. We developed dances to the theme of 'Monsters'; in gymnastics we have developed partner sequences; and in games we have learned about, made up and played our own small-sided net and striking and fielding games.

The bulk of the report should focus on points 2, 3 and 4. The recording template and individual pupil profile should yield statements easily. These and the level descriptors should be the principal guides to constructing positive statements. It is not necessary to comment on how each pupil has progressed in each activity area but referring to at least two different activity experiences will give readers a broader picture of progress made, e.g.,

> Majid has shown increasing control and co-ordination in Gymnastics and Dance activities. He is able to remember short sequences, and links the movements together smoothly. He now needs to practise holding inverted balances for longer and incorporating these into his sequences.
>
> Majid has learnt about tactics in striking and fielding games and now thinks about where he would like to put the ball before he bats. When he is fielding, he needs to watch the batter carefully to anticipate where he needs to move to.
>
> He is always keen to answer questions and makes good suggestions after observing other pupils play. He now needs to listen carefully to other pupils' suggestions about his own work and use their observations to improve his performance.
>
> Majid knows that it is important to warm up and cool down before and after activity. He needs to remember to always put this into practice.
>
> Majid has achieved level 2 standard of attainment which is in line with expectations.

Chapter summary

McMillan (2000) summarises the assessment, recording and reporting process well when he concludes that good assessment:

- enhances instruction
- is valid, i.e., it tests what it sets out to test
- is fair and ethical
- uses multiple methods
- is efficient and feasible
- appropriately incorporates technology.

When we remember that assessment is an integral part of the teaching and learning process, it becomes less of an additional chore. If we remain flexible and open to trying novel approaches, it can even become fun! Assessment should occur naturally and not impede the spontaneity and flow of good teaching and learning. Above all keep things in perspective and remember that if you assess some of your teaching, record some of your assessments, and report some of these records, you will still make a big difference.

Questions for reflection

- Think about the processes through which you currently conduct assessment in your PE teaching. Are you satisfied that your processes result in consistent, reliable and valid judgements?

- How much influence over the assessment process do your current recording templates have? If these were adjusted, what difference would it make?

- Look back at some recent PE reports. Do pupils/parents know what the pupils need to do to improve?

References

Assessment Reform Group (1999) *Assessment for Learning. Beyond the Black Box.* Cambridge: University of Cambridge.

Assessment Reform Group (2002) *Testing, Motivation and Learning.* Cambridge: University of Cambridge, Faculty of Education.

Black, P. and William, D. (1998) 'Inside the black box: Raising standards through classroom assessment'. *Phi Delta Kappan, 80*(2), 139–48.

Brigg, M., Woodfield, A., Martin, C. and Swatton, P. (2003) *Assessment for Learning and Teaching in Primary Schools.* Exeter: Learning Matters.

Casbon, C. and Spackman, L. (2005) *Assessment for Learning in Physical Education.* Leeds: Coachwise/BAALPE.

Department for Education and Science (1992) *Physical Education in the National Curriculum.* London: DES.

Early Education (2012) *Development Matters in the Early Years Foundation Stage.* London: DoE/EE.

Hopper, B., Grey, J. and Maude, T. (2000) *Teaching Physical Education in the Primary School.* London: Falmer.

Jefferies, S., Jefferies, T. and Mustain, W. (1997) *Why assess in PE?* PE Central, 16 April. Available at: www.pecentral.org/assessment/assessmentresearch.html (accessed February 2013).

Leitch, R., Lundy, L., Clough, P., Galanouli, D. and Gardener, J. (2005) *Consulting Pupils on the Assessment of their Learning (CPAL).* Available at www.tlrp. org/dspace/retrieve/1335/ CPAL+TLRP+Conference+paper+26Oct05.doc (accessed February 2013).

McMillan, J. H. (2000) 'Fundamental assessment principles for teachers and school administrators'. *Practical Assessment, Research and Evaluation, 7*(8). Available at http://PAREonline.net/ getvn.asp?v=7andn=8 (accessed February 2013).

Maude, P. (2001) *Physical Children, Active Teaching: Investigating Physical Literacy.* Buckingham: Open University Press.

Ofsted (1998) *Teaching Physical Education in the Primary School: The Initial Training of Teachers.* London: Office for Standards in Education.

Ofsted (2009) *Physical Education in Schools 2005/2008. Working Towards 2012 and Beyond.* London: Office for Standards in Education.

Piotrowski, S. (2000) 'Assessment, recording and reporting'. In R. Bailey and T. Macfayden (eds) *Teaching Physical Education 5–11.* London: Continuum.

Qualifications and Curriculum Authority (2005) *Physical Education 2004–5. Annual Report on Curriculum and Assessment.* London: QCA.

Raymond, C. (1998) *Co-ordinating Physical Education across the Primary School.* London: Falmer.

Rudduck, J., Arnot, D., Fielding, M., McIntyre, D. and Flutter, J. (2003) *Consulting Pupils about Teaching and Learning.* Final report to the ESRC Teaching and Learning Research Programme.

Tacklesport/PEA UK (2003) *Observing Children Moving.* Worcester: Tacklesport.

Tacklesport/PEA UK (2006) *Observing and Analysing Learners' Movement.* Worcester: Tacklesport.

Wragg, E.C. (2001) *Assessment and Learning in the Primary School.* London: Routledge.

10

Physical education in the future

This book began talking about change. As educators, we need to learn to change in order to help our pupils manage change too. These are exciting times for physical education. Things are not standing still. The successes of the Olympics and Paralympics Games in 2012 have left a rich legacy to follow and inspire us. The agenda in 'Every Child Matters' lent support to the physical wellness but is now discontinued. The PESSCL strategy had an enormous impact on the delivery of PE and sport in many Primary schools but is no longer. School Sport Partnerships have altered the structure and functions of how schools work collaboratively with external organisations and offer new horizons for future partnership working with other schools, the local community and with other organisations. A new PE National Curriculum is being introduced and provides a framework for teaching PE in Key Stages 1 and 2 with its emphasis on competitive sport made very clear. Physical development as one of the Prime Areas of learning in a revised EYFS curriculum for children from birth to age 5 years establishes this aspect as crucial for children's overall development and learning. New teachers' standards and revisions in ITT are changing how intending teachers are trained and provide the framework for qualified teachers to work within. A new Ofsted framework sharpens the focus on teaching and learning in all subjects and while inspection evidence reports many examples of good practice in PE in our schools, concerns about Primary teachers' subject knowledge in teaching high quality PE remain.

In this book we have examined physical education and articulated the principles around what quality PE from 5 to 11 is all about. We have offered a new definition of this for readers:

> Physical education, as part of the whole education process is a field of endeavour that is concerned with lifelong physical, intellectual, social and emotional learning that accrues through experiencing physical activities in a variety of contexts.

We have mapped out the boundaries of curriculum PE and argued the unique contribution that PE has to make to the education and lives of all pupils. Underpinning this is the belief in the whole child concept, and in our view of what abilities and characteristics a physically educated learner might possess. Knowledge here is the core business of the physical education community. We strongly urge a return to these core principles. PE teachers need to recognise the values on which their priorities are based and we urge the profession to be clear about what they are attempting to achieve. This is indeed a call to clarify what is at the very kernel of the profession.

How might this best be achieved? We have already urged a return to principles. Once this is clarified and agreed upon, a second way is to focus attention on the methods of delivery of those principles that are most appropriate to the age and ability of pupils – the pedagogy. This is what Almond referred to as the 'missing ingredient' (1997, p. 17) and as Laker explains 'the pedagogy of educational practice dictates how the subject is taught, the values that are promoted and the attitudes and knowledge that are instilled in young people' (2000, p. 113). In order for this to be achievable, however, several other questions are raised. For instance, what structures are needed to support such programmes? What thinking is required for professionals to implement it? For every child still to matter, there is a real need for the workforce to take stock and reflect critically on philosophies and practices. Careful consideration must be given to the goals, the expectations and attitudes of all professionals tasked with promoting this unique area of development and learning. We need to widen the lens away from traditional ideas of the curriculum to one that reflects a changing world and a changing educational climate.

Contemporary issues identified reflect the changing face of curriculum PE and school sport. Physical education must reflect modern society and a society that is also constantly changing. Alongside many programmes of high quality revealed in local and national Ofsted inspections, there have been findings over the last ten years that show the profession is at a crossroads and where changes in thinking are required. What will be the nature of such change? We know that, for many, change is no easy process. Issues such as the perceptions of new teachers into the profession, the role of ITT in equipping future teachers with appropriate knowledge and skills to deliver the PE in schools of the future need to be tackled. There are pragmatic constraints like budget cuts and reduced facilities that have direct resource implications on the practical delivery of the subject. There are changes to be made to alter feelings of de-professionalism and marginalisation among colleagues and countering competency models of instruction that are more concerned with class management than deep learning, to name but a few.

True change comes from within and is about not being distracted or diverted by external factors. Fullan (1991) commented that 'simple changes may be easier to carry out but they may not make much of a difference. Complex changes promise to accomplish more . . . but they also demand more effort, and failure takes a greater toll' (1991, p. 71). (Once again it demands that teachers reflect upon their own practices, beliefs and values.) Critical reflection has a long history in educational practice. It has been associated with professional identity (Beynon et al., 2004) and is linked to quality. As Leeson, comments, 'unless we engage in this process [of refection], the work we do has the potential to be ill informed and possibly dangerous because we may perpetuate practice that is no longer relevant, simply because that is the way it has always been done and no one has questioned whether it is still appropriate' (2004, p. 146). The measure of success of any changes in PE made will be the changes that bring improvements to the learning experiences for every pupil.

If these are the challenges of change, what of solutions? We offer the following ideas of our vision of the future:

- Continued professional development acknowledged as a lifelong process of learning.
- Involvement in professional (PE) organisations.
- School–university partnerships for research and teaching.
- Individual critical reflective practice.
- Work with other agencies (such as sports coaching organisations and health).
- Moving the now trite phrase of 'joined-up thinking' forward.
- Coaching and mentor programmes for Newly Qualified Teachers.
- PE tackling issues of social justice and inclusion in society directly.
- Clarification of the relationship between health and physical activity and PE.
- A position statement of the role of sport in Primary schools.
- A holistic approach to teaching children in PE.
- Rethinking how activity areas in PE can be structured, possibly shifting away from discrete areas to themes in the light of a revised National Curriculum.
- Promotion of learning that moves pupils forward to model of self-responsibility.
- An agreed pedagogy that is consistent and involves teacher and pupils in planning, delivery and evaluation of lessons, is inclusive and provides continuity of learning across key stages.

There is almost universal concern about the future, and in education (and specifically physical education) this is also the case. What will happen next year, in the next five to ten years? As authors of this book we reject the notion of an inevitability for PE in the future, and one in which teachers have little control. We support the idea that the profession can adapt and adjust to external drivers and forces and we champion the idea that the teachers, researchers and university teachers should steer those changes and inform the policymakers.

On reading our book, we hope that we have been able to inform your understanding on the nature and scope of PE in schools and provide knowledge that informs your skills on how PE can be delivered effectively to children aged 5 to 11. We also hope that we have not only answered questions but that this text has prompted you to reflect on your own experiences of teaching PE and to raise some more questions of your own. Most of all, we hope that, whether your teaching is in Key Stage 1 or in Key Stage 2, you are as excited about teaching this unique subject as we are, and are eager to talk with colleagues and try out some of the ideas we offer on practical teaching so that the learning experiences in PE of each one of your pupils will be purposeful, rewarding and memorable. The future starts now!

References

Almond, L. (1997) 'The context of physical education'. In L. Almond (ed.) *Physical Education in Schools*. London: Kogan Page.

Beynon, J., Ilieva, R. and Dichupa, M. (2004) 'Re-credentialing experiences of immigrant teachers: negotiating institutional structures, professional identities and pedagogy'. *Teachers and Teaching: Theory and Practice*, *10*(4): 429–44.

Fullan, M. (1991) *The New Meaning of Educational Change*. London: Cassell.

Laker, A. (2000) *Beyond the Boundaries of Physical Education: Educating Young People for Citizenship and Social Responsibility*. London: RoutledgeFalmer.

Leeson, C. (2004) 'In praise of reflective practice'. In J. Willan, R. Parker-Rees and J. Savage (eds) *Early Childhood Studies*. Exeter: Learning Matters.

Index

Note: page references in italic refer to figures and tables.

ability 50
achievement 66
'action sandwich' 100, 102
Adams, J.A. 52
adventurous activities 132, *133–5*
apparatus 76, *77–8*, 102–3, 121, *122–3*
apparatus station card *122*
Arnold, P.J. 12, 43, 45, 46
Ashworth, S. 175
assessment, recording and reporting 181–200;
    feedback 192–6, *193*; levels statements *193–7*;
    observation 187, *188*, 189; in PE 183–5, *186*,
    187; perceptions of 182, *183*; pupil's voices
    193, *197*; questions for reflection 199;
    recording systems 193, *194–6*; reports for
    parents 197–8; tasks 189, 192; tension in *183*
assessment for learning (AfL) 189, *190*, 191
Assessment Reform Group (ARG) 181–2, 189
assessment templates *194–196*
athletics: jumping 129, 130; Key Stage 2 127, *128*,
    129–30, *131*, 132; levels statements *195–6*;
    progression *128*; running 129, 130; teaching
    tips 129, 130, 132; throwing 129, *131*; units of
    work *154–5*

BAALPE 192
Bailey, R. 12, 45, 46, 142, 151–2, 168
Barrett, K. 167
beanbag ball bash *97*
behaviour and safety 67
Bloom, B. 31, *171*
body awareness 47, 89, *90*, *91*
brain development 31
Bronfenbrenner, U. 30
Brown, G.A. 169, 170

Bunker, D. 93, *94*, 116–17
Buschner, C. 47

Capel, S. 10–11
Casbon, C. 148, 185, 190, 191
CCPR 14
child development 29–41; early development
    32–3; importance of experiences 31–2; middle
    childhood 33–5, 37; milestones *36*; motor skills
    37, *38*, 39; questions for reflection 39
children's comments 9
Chorley example 69–70
Clancy, M.E. 71
closed-loop theory 52
cognitive development 34–5
communication 166–8
communication/collaboration *135*
continuity of learning 74–8
creative thinking 71, *72*, 73
critical reflection 202
critical thinking 70–1, *72*, 73
curriculum 74–6, *77–8*
curriculum map 143
cyclical process (AfL) *190*

dance: activities *174–5*; body awareness *174*;
    components of movement *112*; effort *174–5*;
    Key Stage 1 88, *89–92*; Key Stage 2 110–11,
    112–14, 115; levels statements *194*; movement
    concepts and skills *113*, 172–3, *174–5*;
    relationships *175*; space awareness *174*; teaching
    tips 89, 91, 111, 112, 114, 115; themes *92*
Davies, A. 110
DCMS 62
demonstrations 168–9

development, child *see* child development
developmental milestones *36*
DfE 17, 74
DfEE 16
DfES 62, *63–4*, 65
differentiation 120, *160*
direct and indirect teaching 175–6, *177*
documentation, planning 142–4
DoH 79–80
Douglas, M. 89, 110
dynamic systems theory 52

Early Years Foundation Stage (EYFS) 17, 74–6,
    77–8
early years PE 79
education, changes in 1
effort 48, *174–5*
emotional development 33, 35, *36*, 37
enquiry skills 73
evaluation skills 73
explanations and instructions, giving 166–8
extrinsic feedback 171–2

Fairclough, S. 81–2
feedback: assessment 192–6, *193*; giving 171–2;
    questioning 191–2
fitness and health 107, 136–7
Fitts, P.M. 51–2
forward roll: observation 168–9
foundation stage PE *78*
Fullan, M. 202

Gallahue, D. 30, 53, 54, *55–6*
games: beanbag ball bash *97*; classification of *93*;
    developing skills *95*; framework for
    introduction *94*; Key Stage 1 92, *93–7*; Key
    Stage 2 115–16, *117–18*; kicking rounders
    97; levels statements *195*; net/wall games *94*;
    skills of *93*; striking and fielding *94*, *118*; tag
    games *96*; target games *96*; travelling activities
    117
Gilbert Report, The (DfES) 65
Government influences 68
Graham, G. 47
Green, K. 9
gymnastics: balance 98, *99*, *100*; Key Stage 1
    98, *99–102*, 103; Key Stage 2 *119–24*;
    levels statements *194*; PACE continuum *119*;
    progress examples *120*; rotation 98, *99*, *101*;
    shape 98, *99*; short lessons *120*; skills *99*;
    teaching tips *98*, 100, 101, 103, 121; units
    of work 150–1

Hardy, C. 124–5
Hattie, J. 65–6

health and fitness 78–83, 107, 136–7
health and physical activity: children and
    young people 80; early years 79
Health and Self-Care 75
Healthy schools, healthy children? (Ofsted)
    81–2
height 33–4
higher-order questioning 170, *171*
Hopper, B. 45

IDEA 170
information-processing skills 72
instructions and explanations, giving 166–8
intellectual development 35, *36*
invasion games *93*
issues in PE 61–8; continuity of learning 74–8;
    critical thinking 70–3; health 78–83; high-
    quality PE 62, *63–4*, 65–7; questions for
    reflection 83; school sport 67–70; tasks 67,
    76

Jefferies, S. 187
Jess, M. 7, 14, 54
jumping 129, 130

Key Stage 1 87–108; dance 88, *89–92*; fitness
    and health 107; games 92, *93–7*; gymnastics 98,
    99–102, 103, *122*; National Curriculum 74,
    87–8; questions for reflection 108; swimming
    103–7; tasks 89
Key Stage 2 109–37; athletics 127, *128*, 129–30,
    131, 132; dance 110–11, *112–14*, 115; features
    of games *118*; fitness and health 136–7; games
    115–16, *117–18*; gymnastics *119–24*; outdoor
    activities 132, *133–5*; PE national curriculum
    109–10; questions for reflection 136; swimming
    124–5, *126–7*; task cards 123, *124*
kicking rounders *97*, *118*
Klesius, S.E. 23
knowledge, acquiring 71, *72*

Laban, R. 15, 47–8, *49*
Laker, A. 15, 202
language development 35, *36*
Lavin, J. 76, *77–8*
learning 64–7
learning activities 144
learning conversation 191
learning objectives (LOs) 144
Leeson, C. 202
Leitch, R. 189–90, 193
lesson example (Martin) 165
lesson plan 143
lesson planning *see* planning and preparation
lesson structure *153*, *158–9*, 160

levels statements *193–7*; athletics *195–6*; dance *194*; games activities *195*; gymnastics *194*; outdoor and adventurous activities *195*

locomotion skills 54, *55*

long term planning 144, 145

McMillan, J.H. 183, 198

McMorris, T. 49–50

Mail Online 67

manipulation skills 54, *55*

Martin, B. 132

Martin (lesson example) 165

maturation 30, 31

Maude, P. 21, 37, 51, 75, 186

Mawer, M. 146, 163, 167, 175, 176

medium term planning 144–5, *154–5*

metacognition 71, *72*

milestones of development *36*

Miliband, D. 65

Mosston, M. 175, *177*

motor learning theories 51–2

motor skills 37, *38*, 39

movement 42–58; approach 47–8, *49*; children learning 50–6; children's capabilities 42–3; concepts 47–8, *49*; dance 112, *113*, *174–5*; development of 49–50; education about 43–5; education in 46; education through 45; expressive ways of *90–1*, *92*; qualitative framework *49*; skills 50, 53–4, *55*, 56; tasks 53, 55

'movement alphabet' 47, 53

movement concepts and skills 172–3, *174–5*

Moving and Handling 75

National Association for Sport and Physical Education (NASPE) 22–3

National Curriculum *147*; EYFS 74–6, 77–8; Key Stage 1 74, 87–8; Key Stage 2 109–10; teaching and learning 78

National Curriculum Physical Education (NCPE) 15–18

net/wall games 93, *94*, 97, *118*

NHS 79

obesity 79, 81

observation 167–8, 187, *188*, 189

Observing Children Moving (Tacklesport/PEAUK) *188*

Ofsted 1, 15; assessment 183–5; PE issues 66, 69, 81; planning and preparation 142, 149

Olympic Games legacy 67–8

O'Neill, J. 128

orientation *134*

'Outcomes Project' (NASPE) 22–3

outdoor and adventurous activities 132; communication/collaboration *133*, *135*; Key Stage 2 *133–5*; levels statements *195*; orientation *133*; play 77–8; problem solving *133*; units of work *156–7*

outdoor play 75–6, *77–8*

PACE continuum *119*

PE 7–28, 201–4; aims of 14–18; assessment 183–5, *186*, 187; children's comments 9; defining 10–14; future of 201–4; high-quality 62, *63–4*, 65–7; history of 14–15; issues in; *see* issues in PE; learners of 20–3; perceptions of 7–10; policy 143; principals of 18; questions for reflection 24; tasks 10, 18, 21; teachers comments 7–8, 9; trainee teachers comments 8

PE planning web *152*

PEA UK 13, *188*

Penney, D. 1, 13, 14, 16

perceptual-motor development 33, 34

performance task card *131*

Perrott, E. 167

PESS (PE and school sport) 12

Peter (physical activity example) 80–1

phases of lesson *153*

physical activity guidelines 79–83

physical development 32–4, *36*, 74–5

physical literacy 19–20, *21*

Pickup, I. 9, 16, 34, 51

Piotrowski, S. 183, 185, 187

planning and preparation 141–62; differentiation *160*; initiating the process 144–6; lexicon of planning 143–4; pupil's learning 148–9, *150*, 151; questions for reflection 161; structuring 153, *158–9*, 160; swimming *158–9*; tasks 148, 151, 161; thinking about 146, *147*, 148; writing the plan 151, *152*, 153, *154–7*

planning documentation 142–4

planning gap, the 148

planning web *152*

play 75–6, *77–8*

policy 143

Posner, M.I. 51–2

Price, I. 9, 16, 34, 51

Prime Areas of learning 74–5

progress, profiling pupils' *197*

progression, athletics *128*

'propositional knowledge' 44

pupils: learning 148–9, *150*, 151; voice of 193, *197*

Qualifications and Curriculum Authority (QCA) 13, 17, 183, 184

quality teaching 66–7, 163–4

quantitative assessment data *186*

questioning 169–70, *171*, 191–2, 193
questions for reflection: assessment 199; issues in PE 83; Key Stage 1 108; Key Stage 2 136; PE 24; planning and preparation 161; teaching a lesson 178

Raymond, C. 142, 187
reasoning skills 72–3
recording systems 193, *194–196*
reports for parents 197–8
Reynolds, T. 98
Robertson, E. 111, *124–5*
role model, being a 165–6
running 129, *130*

safety and behaviour 67
schema theory 52
scheme of work 143
Schmidt, R.A. 50, 52
School PE Policy 143
school sport 67–70
School Sport Partnerships. A survey of good practice (Ofsted) 69
School Sport Partnerships (SSPs) 69–70
sensory development 32
shape *101*
short term planning 145–6
skills 49–50, *93*
Smith, B. 98, *99*
social development 33, 35, *36*, 37
space awareness 48
Spackman, L. 148, 185, 190, 191
Spectrum of Teaching Styles (Mosston) 175–6, *177*
sport 12, 16
stability skills 53, *55*
staircase of tasks *150*
STEP (space, task, equipment, people) 88, *89*, *96*, *97*, *160*
Stoll, L. 1
Stratton, G. 80, 82
striking and fielding *93*, *94*, *118*
striking, throwing and catching *118*
Sugden, D. 13, 30
swimming and water based activities: floating practices 105; games 106–7; Key Stage 1 103–7; Key Stage 2 124–5, *126–7*; lesson planning *158–9*; propulsion 106; teaching tips 104, 125, 127; walking practices 104–5

Tacklesport *188*
tag games 94, *96*
Talbot, M. 8–9, 11–12, 13
target games 94

target learning tasks 149, *150*, 151
task cards 123, *124*
tasks: assessment, recording and reporting 189, 192; issues in PE 67, 76; Key Stage 1 89; PE 18, 21; planning and preparation 148, 151, 161; teaching a lesson 164, 168
teachers, characteristics of effective *164*
teachers comments: PE 7–8, 9
teaching a lesson 163–80; direct and indirect approaches 175–6, *177*; movement concepts and skills 172–3, 174–5; quality teaching 163–4; questions for reflection 178; strategies 165–70, *171*, 172; tasks 164, 168, 176
teaching and learning in PE *78*
Teaching Games for Understanding (TGfU) 116–17
Teaching Physical Education: A Guide for Mentors and Students (Williams) 168
teaching points 144
teaching quality 66–7
teaching strategies 165–70, *171*, 172
teaching styles 175–6
teaching tips: athletics 129, 130, 132; dance 89, 91, 111, 112, 114, 115; fitness and health 107; gymnastics *98*, 100, 101, 103, 121, 123; swimming 104, 125, 127
thinking, pupils' *147*
thinking skills 72
Thorpe, R. 116–17
three stage model 51–2
throwing 130, *131*
trails and courses 77–*8*
trainee teachers comments 8

units of work 143; athletics *154–5*; gymnastics 150–1; medium term planning *154–5*; outdoor activities *156–7*

Visible Learning (Hattie) 65–6

wall games *97*
warming up 136
water-based activities *see* swimming and water based activities
weight problems 33–4, 79
Welford, A.T. 51
Whitehead, M. 12, 19, 20
Williams, A. 68, 152, 168, 176
word wall 111, *113*
Working towards 2012 and beyond (Ofsted) 184–5
Wragg, E.C. 170, 186
Wright, H. 30

Yeats, W. B. 1